World's Best Cakes

World's Best Cakes

250 Great Cakes from Raspberry Genoise to Chocolate Kugelhopf

jacqui small

Roger Pizey
Foreword by Marco Pierre White

Photography by Šárka Babická

Dedication: For my family, especially Penny, Alfie, Nell and my mother, Iris.

First published in 2013 by
Jacqui Small LLP
An imprint of Aurum Press
74–77 White Lion Street
London N1 9PF

Publisher: Jacqui Small
Associate Publisher: Joanna Copestick
Managing Editor: Lydia Halliday
Project Manager and Editor: Nikki Sims
Art Direction & Design: Sarah Rock
Photographer: Šárka Babická
Proofreader: Claire Wedderburn-Maxwell
Indexer: Vanessa Bird
Production: Peter Colley

ISBN: 978 1 906417 97 0

A catalogue record for this book is available from the British Library.

2015 2014 2013
10 9 8 7 6 5 4 3 2 1

Printed in China

Contents

Foreword

Let's go back to the late 1980s, when I was a year or so into my first restaurant. It was called Harvey's and sat beside Wandsworth Common, in south-west London. The great critic Egon Ronay came to eat, and loved it so much he wrote about it. From that moment Bentleys and Rollers crossed the Thames and lined Bellevue Road. It became a sort of Michelin-starred canteen for actors, models, aristocrats and artists.

But not all the guests were ridiculously rich and sun-tanned. Anaemic, exhausted, overworked chefs saved up to come, too. One of them was Roger Pizey.

At the time he was a young man employed in the kitchens of Le Gavroche (where I had trained a few years earlier). At some point after service, I emerged from the kitchen, shook Roger's hand for the first time, and we had a chat. I liked him.

A few weeks passed and I found the time to escape my own crazy kitchen to go for dinner at Le Gavroche. The feast ended with a Tarte Tatin that was so extraordinarily memorable I can still taste it to this day.

Its creator was Roger Pizey.

Successful careers are a succession of smart moves, and one of mine was to offer Roger a job. He joined the brigade of Harvey's on 23rd January 1990, the same day that the restaurant received its second Michelin star.

Later, he came with me to The Restaurant at the Hyde Park Hotel, where we would win three stars.

Swing doors, kitchens and dining rooms are a blur. But Roger was at my side at Mirabelle and at the Criterion, where he was head chef.

We have cooked and cooked and cooked together.

We have fished together and shot together.

We have travelled together, not only through the English countryside but also in Singapore, Sweden and Ireland.

Remember, throughout his career Roger has made thousands upon thousands of people extremely happy – let's face it, dessert is the course that always wins and woos.

I write with utmost sincerity when I say that this man is not only passionate about his craft, but also gifted beyond belief. Quite simply, Roger Pizey is one of the finest pastry chefs Britain has ever known. What a privilege to be asked to write this brief introduction to his beautifully enriching book.

Marco Pierre White, March 2013

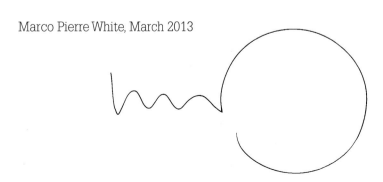

Introduction

I was just like any other child whose mother baked when they were young. My sister and I would always fight over which whisk had the most cake mix on and spend ages licking them until they were sparkling clean. Then we would fight about who got the bowl! My mother baked simple buns in little paper cups and we would wait expectantly by the oven for them to be ready. Cakes can be as simple or as complicated as you like. And this book covers the whole range from a simple Victoria Sponge (see page 16) through to a more complicated multi-layered Dobos Cake (see page 48), which involves many steps. Whichever cake you choose to bake, you will know that the philosophy behind its inclusion is the same – the joy of a freshly baked cake.

When I was a teenager I used to deliver milk to the local bakery shop and we would arrive just as a tray of Winberry Tarts or Hot Cross Buns came out of the oven. I can still remember the delicious smell of baking early in the morning. Sometimes we would deliberately run late so that we could stay to eat the freshly baked bread or a warm flapjack crammed with golden syrup and oats. Eating something freshly baked is one of life's great pleasures.

A home filled with the smell of baking is like no other. The wonderful thing about baking a cake is its welcoming nature. Arriving at someone's home to find they have baked a cake for your visit immediately makes you feel welcome. It doesn't matter if it is a cake you have eaten many times before or a cake that you have never tried – the fact that someone has gone to the effort of looking out a recipe, getting together the ingredients and baking is enough. This is the same the world over.

BAKING – AN AGE-OLD TRADITION

Cake has been making people feel welcome since ancient times. The Ancient Egyptians were the first to discover the wonder of baking using hot stones to bake their cakes and breads on. In Ancient Rome, cake was similar to small bread and honey would be used as a sweetener. Cakes today are generally round because they are descended from these first breads baked on round stones. As trade routes opened up, baking developed to include some of the more exotic ingredients from other countries – nuts, flower waters, citrus fruits, dates and figs from the Middle East and sugar cane from the Orient. Up until the Middle Ages in Europe these ingredients were only available to the wealthy and religious communities, and so began the tradition of important and luxurious cakes, rich with symbolism, being baked for religious festivals and special occasions.

Times of celebration and significant religious festivals have always been marked with a cake and this continues today. This book has a large selection of celebration cakes from all corners of the world, including Mooncakes from China (see page 268) to celebrate mid-Autumn through to the wonderfully moist Spanish Tarta de Santiago (see page 274) in celebration of St James and the German marzipan and fruit-laden Stollen (see page 278), often seen beautifully gift wrapped at Christmas time. There are so many celebration cakes that I haven't been able to include, but I have tried to choose a selection of signature cakes that cover many cultures.

DISCOVERING MY PASSION

The joy and wonder of baking aromas has stayed with me since those early mornings delivering milk. When I worked as a pastry chef at Le Gavroche Restaurant in London, the section was manned 24 hours a day and I would start work at midnight and bake saffron bread, olive bread, lemon tarts, pithiviers, clafoutis and brioche for the next day's service. This was my epiphany and my passion for pastry began, I was well and truly hooked. The smell of baking brioche is like no other and I have included a favourite recipe in this book – just make sure you have friends and children around when you make it to appreciate the unforgettable aroma.

I was lucky enough to be sent by Albert Roux to a Viennoiserie course at le Notre Cookery School in Paris and while there, learning how to make Tarte Tatin, Danish pastries and croissants, my love of classic French dishes was cemented. I have included some of these recipes, such as Tarte Tatin (see page 244) and Tarte aux Pommes (see page 249), in this book and they are all perfectly achievable in a home kitchen. There may be some baking techniques that are unfamiliar to you but if you love baking, as I do, then I would urge you to try them.

Over the many years I have worked with Marco Pierre White I have been lucky enough to be able to indulge my love of baking and constantly try and test new recipes; believe me when I say that they have not always worked out first time round. If at first the cake doesn't turn out the way you hope, try try again, because practice really does make perfect; and even if they don't look like you think they should they'll still taste delicious. I like to use a variety of cake tins but don't worry if you don't have the exact size or shape of tin I mention – you may just need to halve the recipe or make a different shaped cake instead.

SHARING THE PASSION

The tradition of baking is truly global and in the last few hundred years at least, cookery books have played a major part in spreading the influence of different cultures' baking traditions; now information is freely exchanged across the world online, allowing cake traditions to continue to evolve. For instance, you no longer need to travel to Macau to enjoy their custard tarts (see page 218) or fly to Greece to taste Baklava. I have tried to reflect some of the scope of these global recipes in the choices I've included in my book.

During my career I have been lucky enough to meet some amazing chefs. Some I have worked with and some I have met and become friends with through eating at their restaurants. Many now live and work in far flung corners of the world and as you browse through this book you will see cake contributions from some of these friends as I invited them to share a favourite recipe. There are Lamingtons from Australia, Cassava Cake from the Philippines and Olive Oil Cake from Los Angeles among others.

You will also find many of the book's cakes in the cities' bakeries that are listed in the 'Where to eat cake' pages. One of the joys of travelling to different countries for me is to visit local bakeries and pâtisseries. I have spent many a happy hour browsing the goodies in bakery windows in cities from Singapore to Sydney and I wanted to share these with you. From tasting Kasutera in Tokyo to enjoying Macarons in Paris, you can find the destination bakeries that have become part of the must-do tourist trails.

There are so many wonderful cakes in this book it would be impossible to choose a favourite. I have enjoyed baking each and every one of them. It has been an inspiring and enjoyable experience to visit the countries through their cuisine. I was intrigued, for example, to make the Bolo Polana (see page 109) and was gratified at the delicious results. The Middle Eastern cakes were also a pleasure to discover and an assault on the senses with their delicate perfumes of orange-flower and rosewater, their wonderful almond texture and the vibrant green pistachios.

Whether you feel like making a small cake, a sponge cake or a show-stopping cake I have included examples of them all. When choosing what to bake, work out how much time you have. If you're pushed for time, then opt for something simple, such as the Churros (see page 178) – quick and easy to make these bite-sized lovelies make everyone smile.

Most of all remember making cakes should always be fun and never a chore. A cake made with a smile is definitely the best kind of cake.

Roger Pizey, April 2013

Basic Techniques

Sometimes it's the small things you pick up when working in a kitchen every day that can make all the difference, so here I want to pass on some of my tips for basic techniques to help you on your way to become a skilful baker.

When it comes to **rubbing in** (that means rubbing fat into flour), the secret to a good crumb is making sure your ingredients are quite cold. Add the cubed butter to the flour mixture and then, using thumb and fingers, bring your hands slowly up through the mixture while continuously rubbing the butter through the flour. Use only a light touch, so as not to stress the flour and to persuade the butter to give in to the flour and then you are left with a light crumb. Think happy thoughts so you are only left with a happy cake, tart or crumble.

Once you have made your cake mixture make sure your tin is lined properly before starting to **pour** it in. I spray the tin with a natural butter compound, but greasing lightly with softened butter is just as good, and line the bottom with baking parchment. Try to cut the baking parchment as neatly as possible to fit the base of your tin. Slowly pour your mixture in.

For loaf tins I prefer to use non-stick tins, so I just cut the baking parchment to cover the length and ends of the tin. As long as the baking tin is slightly greased you will then be able to lift the cake easily out of the tin once cooled.

If you use a fan oven don't have too much paper coming over the edges of the tin as the fan will blow the paper onto your cake mixture and it won't cook evenly.

RUBBING IN

POURING

FOLDING IN

Once your mixture is poured into the tin, tap the tin gently a couple of times on the surface to remove any large air bubbles and then smooth out the surface evenly with a palette knife.

When you've spent time building air into a cake mixture (through separating eggs and whisking separately, for instance), you need to master how to **fold in** the remaining ingredients of the cake without losing that magical lightness. Once your egg mixture has doubled or trebled in size according to your recipe, start pouring in the flour mixture in two or three batches. Using a spatula gently start to fold in the mixture moving from bottom to top in a gentle movement, bringing the spatula over and through the flour mix while turning the bowl until slowly the dry mixture is fully incorporated into a smooth mixture. The secret

is not to over-fold, so as to trap as much air as you can in the mixture to make it as light as possible.

I like to **whisk by hand** and I always choose the right size whisk for the job. Small amounts of mixture require a small whisk, with larger amounts needing a large whisk. If you are using a machine or electric whisk to whisk err on the cautious side as overwhipped cream is useless. Give hand whisking a try – it's a good workout for certain muscles, I can tell you – and try to whisk in a figure-of-eight motion as this traps more air in the liquid. If you are whisking cream to a ribbon, your whisk should leave a trail of cream on the surface as you remove the whisk.

When whisking egg whites, soft peaks refers to the stage when a whisk drawn through the mixture forms a peak that

WHISKING

1
2
3
4

ROLLING

1
2
3
4

DECORATING

1
2
3
4

folds over on itself. If you whisk a little more then you'll get stiff peaks, which means that the mixture keeps its stiff form.

When **rolling out** pastry, always try to have your work surface cold as rolling on a warm surface not only softens the pastry too much but can also release butter – you'll end up with greasy pastry. If your kitchen is very hot or it is a very hot day cool down your work surface before you start by putting a large roasting dish with some ice in on the surface for a few minutes.

Always roll on an even surface if possible, marble being the the cook's choice as it keeps cool for longer.

Everyone has a stronger arm, so it is very important to rotate the pastry as you roll. Start off with a few rolls then turn a quarter turn to your left and continue rolling and turning until you have rolled enough to line or cover your dish. As a guide run your forefinger and thumb along the pastry you have rolled on either side to feel the thickness and you will be able to gauge the thicker and thinner parts of the pastry and can compensate to make it even.

You've made the cake, assembled it and now it's **time to decorate**. Before adding the frosting, gently brush away any excess crumbs. Put a couple of tablespoons of frosting in a separate bowl and use this to spread as a base over your cake. This base will pick up any excess crumbs without spoiling your finished frosting. Using a palette knife, smear the rest of the frosting on the cake until fully covered. If the frosting becomes too soft, simply pop it in the fridge for a few minutes until it becomes more manageable and start where you left off.

Happy baking!

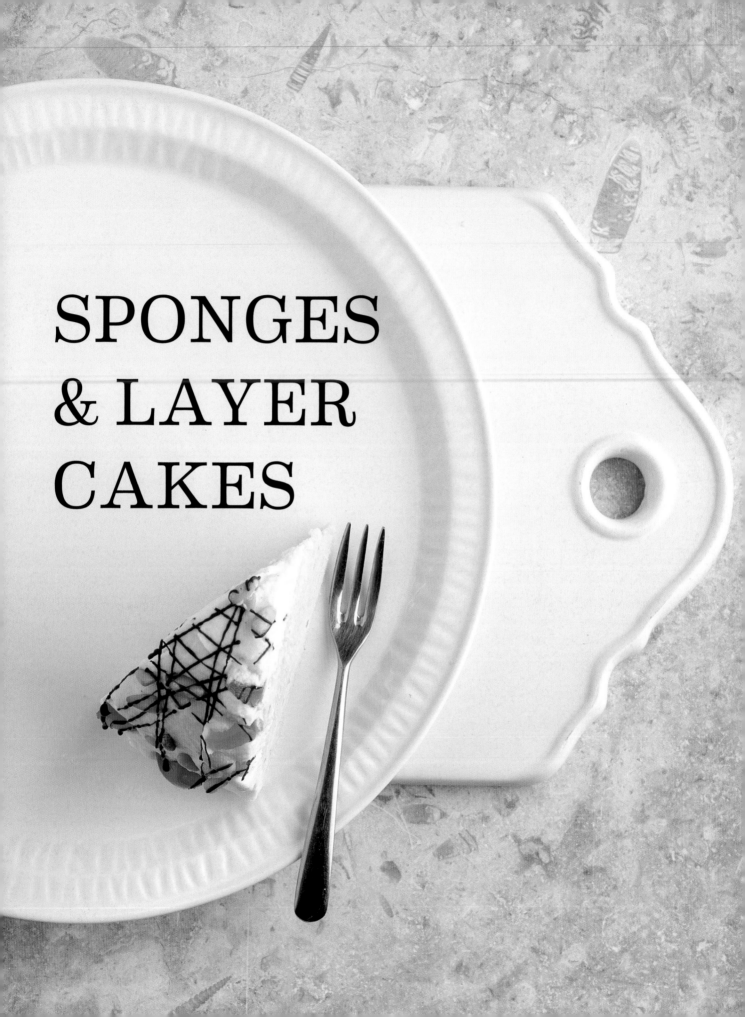

SPONGES
& LAYER
CAKES

Victoria Sponge

Serves 12

225g (8oz) butter, softened
225g (8oz) caster sugar
4 eggs
225g (8oz) self-raising flour, sifted
2 tsp baking powder
1 tsp vanilla extract
1 dsp full-fat milk

For the filling:

200ml (7fl oz) Crème Chantilly (see page 296)
200g (7oz) good-quality strawberry jam
icing sugar, for dusting

This buttery sponge cake was named after Great Britain's Queen Victoria who is said to have enjoyed a slice with her afternoon cup of tea. By 1885, the Victoria Sponge (also known as the Victoria Sandwich) took centre stage at tea parties, including those hosted by the Queen herself. There are endless versions of this ubiquitous British sponge but I like the traditional take on this cakey sandwich with jam and cream.

1 Preheat the oven to 180°C/350°F/gas mark 4 and grease two 21cm (8in) loose-bottomed tins.
2 Cream together the butter and the sugar until light and fluffy.
3 Add the eggs one at a time, scraping down the bowl after each addition, and mix until well combined.
4 Beat in the sifted flour and baking powder and combine well.
5 Finally, add in the vanilla extract and milk and mix together.
6 Spoon into the prepared tins and bake in a preheated oven for 15–20 minutes, or until a cocktail stick inserted into the centre comes out clean.

7 Remove from the oven, allow to cool for 10 minutes in the tin and then turn out onto a wire rack.
8 Meanwhile, make the crème Chantilly as instructed on page 296.
9 Reserve the best sponge for the top layer and neaten off the bottom layer, as necessary.
10 Carefully centre the bottom layer on a cake stand or plate. Spread the jam on the sponge, followed by the crème Chantilly to create the classic sandwich.
11 Top with the second sponge and dust liberally with icing sugar.
12 Serve with tea.

VARIATION

FAIRY CAKES If you like your sponges in the diminutive form, then you can use the same sponge recipe but spoon into paper cases to make butterfly fairy cakes. The quantity above should make about 16 fairy cakes. Slice off the top of each cake, cut each 'cap' in half and create butterfly wings after adding a generous helping of Classic Buttercream (see page 298).

Citrus Chiffon Cake

Serves 8

1 tsp baking powder
130g (4½oz) plain flour
¼ tsp salt
170g (6oz) caster sugar
finely grated zest and juice of
    3 oranges
finely grated zest of 3 lemons
30ml (1fl oz) vegetable oil
1 tsp vanilla extract
2 egg yolks
6 egg whites
½ tsp cream of tartar

For those who have never tried one before a Chiffon Cake is a delicate surprise. Similar to Angel Cake (below) but not as sweet, it was invented in the USA in 1927 by Harry Baker, an insurance salesman who loved to bake. The secret of his recipe was later discovered to be using oil instead of butter.

1 Preheat the oven to 170°C/325°F/gas mark 3, and you'll need an ungreased 18cm (7in) Angel Cake tin (it has a funnel up the middle and a removable bottom).
2 Sift together the baking powder, flour and salt in a bowl. Add in 130g (4½oz) of sugar and combine well.
3 In a separate bowl, mix together the orange juice, lemon and orange zests, oil, vanilla extract and egg yolks until well combined, and then add this mixture to the flour mixture.
4 Place the egg whites in a bowl and whisk until soft peaks form. Add the cream of tartar and the remaining sugar and whisk until stiff peaks form. Fold one-quarter of the egg white mixture into the floury mix and then fold in the remaining egg white mixture.
5 Spoon the mixture into the cake tin and break any air bubbles by cutting the mixture twice with a knife.
6 Bake in a preheated oven for 45 minutes or until the cake springs back to the touch. Remove from the oven, allow to cool for 10 minutes in the tin and then turn out onto a wire rack.
7 Serve with fruit tea.

Raspberry Angel Cake

Serves 8–10

160g (5¾oz) plain flour
¼ tsp salt
12 large egg whites
1 tsp cream of tartar
250g (9oz) caster sugar
½ tsp food colouring powder
1 tsp raspberry essence (or
    whatever flavour you like)
1 tsp vanilla extract
1½ tsp icing sugar

VARIATION
For a chocolatey version, simply replace 30g (1¼oz) of plain flour with 30g (1¼oz) of cocoa powder.

In North America Angel Cake is often called Angel Food Cake – some say it is because this cake is so light and airy it must be 'food for the angels'. There are no egg yolks or raising agents in this cake, so it relies solely on the beaten egg whites to give the cake its airiness. I have made a raspberry angel cake but you can add any flavour you like, or none at all if you prefer. And I find adding extra colour is always a crowd pleaser for a children's party.

1 Preheat the oven to 170°C/325°F/gas mark 3, and you'll need an ungreased 18cm (7in) Angel Cake tin (it has a funnel up the middle and a removable bottom).
2 Sift the flour and the salt together in a bowl and set aside.
3 Beat the egg whites until they become foamy. Add the cream of tartar and beat again until soft peaks form. Continue to beat while gradually adding the sugar, the colouring and the flavouring until stiff peaks form. Finally, add the vanilla and beat until well combined.
4 Transfer the mixture to large bowl and, in small batches, add the flour and salt mixture, using a spatula to carefully fold in the flour.
5 Spoon the mixture carefully into the cake tin and release air bubbles by cutting a knife through the mixture twice.
6 Bake in a preheated oven until golden (about 35–40 minutes). Remove from the oven and allow the cake to cool in the tin and then turn out onto a wire rack.
7 Dust with icing sugar and serve with lemonade at a party.

CITRUS CHIFFON CAKE

RASPBERRY ANGEL CAKE

Sponges & Layer Cakes **19**

Vanilla and Blood Orange Cake

Serves 8

2 blood oranges, plus extra
  to serve
300g (10½oz) caster sugar
200g (7oz) butter
1 vanilla pod, split and
  scraped
3 eggs, beaten
150g (5½oz) plain flour, sifted

Citrus fruits and vanilla are a classic combination and this wondrous pairing is used widely in the baking of the Mediterranean and the Middle East. This is my take on a caramelised cake using blood oranges, and it makes a great centrepiece for any gathering of friends and family.

1 Preheat the oven to 170°C/325°F/gas mark 3. You will need a 21cm (8in) round non-stick tin.
2 Cut one orange into thin slices and remove the pips. Finely grate the zest of the other orange and squeeze out the juice. Set aside.
3 Put 120g (4oz) sugar into a pan on a medium heat and, once the sugar begins to melt, stir with a wooden spoon until completely melted to a caramel. Then pour into the base of the tin.
4 The caramel is incredibly hot at this point so take extra care. Lay the orange slices evenly over the caramel on the bottom of the tin, start at the edges and work towards the centre.
5 Melt the butter in a small pan over a low heat then set aside to cool slightly.
6 Put the vanilla seeds, eggs and the rest of the sugar into a food mixer and cream together

until light and fluffy and doubled in volume (about 5 minutes).
7 Fold in the melted butter, orange zest and juice, followed by the sifted flour in two or three batches, mixing well after each addition. Once all the ingredients are fully combined, carefully pour the mixture into the tin over the orange slices.
8 Bake in a preheated oven for 30 minutes or until the cake has risen and a cocktail stick inserted into the centre comes out clean.
9 Remove from the oven and place a serving dish over the top of the tin, and flip over. Remove the tin to reveal the oranges, now on top of the cake.
10 Allow to cool and serve with a large dollop of crème fraîche and segments of blood orange.

Kasutera

Serves 10

13 egg yolks
290g (10¼oz) caster sugar
5 egg whites
40g (1½oz) honey
30g (1¼oz) rice syrup
30ml (1fl oz) water
30ml (1fl oz) sweetened
   condensed milk
130g (4½oz) plain flour, sifted
10g (¼oz) demerara sugar
mirin (rice wine), for brushing
baking parchment for
   turning out

VARIATION

MATCHA POWDER KASUTERA

Add in 3 tablespoons
of Matcha powder with
the sifted flour.

This is possibly the most popular cake in Japan. Kasutera – also known as 'Castella' – was introduced to Japan in the 16th century by the Portuguese, who valued it for its long-lasting ability to keep them going during long sea voyages. It is an ultra-light cake with hardly any crumb and is traditionally served with a cup of Japanese green tea. This cake has a fairly complicated baking process but, as you'll see, it is well worth the effort.

1 Preheat the oven to 170°C/325°F/gas mark 3, and prepare one deep 18cm (7in) square tin. You'll also need another 18cm (7in) square loose-bottomed tin and a water sprayer.
2 First, line your tin with two 40cm x 18cm (16in x 7in) strips of newspaper placed crossways to each other to insulate the bottom of the cake. Use sticky tape to secure the newspaper edges to the outsides of the tin. Layer with two sheets of baking parchment and use sticky tape to secure.
3 Beat the egg yolks with half of the sugar until pale and creamy.
4 In a separate bowl, whisk the egg whites until small bubbles appear, add a little of the remaining sugar and whisk until small peaks form. Slowly add the rest of the sugar and whisk until stiff peaks form.
5 In a pan, heat the honey, rice syrup and water until slightly warmed and then fold in to the egg yolk mixture. Mix well and then pour in the condensed milk and mix again.

6 Mix the egg yolk mixture into the egg white mixture and combine well.
7 Then, add in the sifted flour and mix.
8 Pour the mixture (from a height to release any air) into the prepared tin and sprinkle on the demerara sugar. Then begin the process of 'Awa Kiri', which means to eliminate the bubbles. Place the cake in a preheated oven and after about 3 minutes a thin film will appear on the surface of the mixture. Remove from the oven and spray with water to eliminate the film and then mix with a wooden spatula from the bottom to the top as if drawing circles vertically.
9 Return the cake to the oven and repeat this process four times every 3 minutes, which allows the cake to bake evenly.
10 Leave for a further 6 minutes and then place another cake tin (without its loose bottom) on top of the one in the oven and bake for a further 5 minutes.
11 Then add the loose bottom to the top of both tins and bake for a further 8 minutes.
12 Remove the loose-bottom 'lid' to release the steam, then replace it and cook for a further 8 minutes. Repeat, allow the steam to disperse, replace the lid and cook for a further 5 minutes.
13 You are now ready to remove the Kasutera from the oven.
14 Spread a double layer of parchment onto a work surface then brush all over with mirin.
15 Turn the cake upside down onto the parchment. Release the edges of the parchment from the side of the tin and remove the tin.
16 Leave to cool for 10 minutes then turn the right way up and peel off the parchment.
17 Square off the edges, as necessary, and cut into equal-size rectangles. Serve with green tea.

Where to Eat Cake…
TOKYO

There are an impressive number of bakeries in Tokyo and they are famous for their 'oyatsupan' – sweet or savoury snack breads. As well as traditional Japanese treats more and more bakeries now serve European cakes and bakes as well. A tour of a depachika, an epicurean gourmet food hall, is a must during your visit to marvel at its confectionery.

CONFECTIONERY WEST
7-3-6 Ginza, Chuo-ku, Tokyo
www.ginza-west.co.jp
This original tea parlour has been in business since 1947 and prides itself on using no artificial colours or flavours. Its interior offers a wonderful haven for tea and cake, but to enjoy fully make sure you have time for a leisurely visit.

CHOCOLATIER ERICA
4-6-43 Shirokanedai, Minato-ku, Tokyo
www.erica.co.jp
Not strictly a cake shop, it's impossible to pass by this wonderfully stylish chocolatier. Give into temptation and step inside.

JOHANN BAKERY SHOP
1-18-15, Kamimeguro, Meguro-ku, Tokyo
www.johann-cheesecake.com
You must try the Johann cheesecake! Established for over 30 years, this bakery creates legendary cheesecakes – not fluffy cheesecakes but something quite solid, reminiscent of a New York cheesecake.

PÂTISSERIE SATSUKI AT THE HOTEL NEW OTANI TOKYO
4-1, Kioi-cho, Chiyoda-ku, Tokyo
www.newotani.co.jp
This is the place to come if you want to try some of the most expensive pastries using the best ingredients. Chef Nakajima creates superb cakes that no other shop can offer, using organic ingredients no matter what the cost. While away some time here if money is of no concern; not for those on a budget.

TOSHI YOROIZUKA
9-7-2 Akaska, Minato-ku, Tokyo
www.grand-patissier.info/ ToshiYoroizuka
The layout of this pâtisserie enables you to watch as the chefs conjure up elaborate and extravagant creations. Toshi Yoroizuka trained for several years in Europe – so he knows more than a thing or two about wonderful pastry – before returning home to open this delightful bakery.

DELI BAKING & CO
1F, 2-29-2 Kitazawa, Setagaya-ku, Tokyo
No website
Discover one of Tokyo's longest dessert menus in the midst of the Shimokitazwa neighbourhood. With a stylish white wooden interior, you can relax here and enjoy the calm ambience before sampling one, two or more of the amazing confections.

PÂTISSERIE SATSUKI FUNABASHIYA
3-2-14 Kameido, Koto-ku, Tokyo
www.funabashiya.co.jp
You'll find a host of traditional Japanese deliciously sweet cakes at this confectionery. If you're in a hurry then you can buy something from the shop or, if you have time to linger, pop up to the first floor where there is a café. The must-order item to sample while you're here is the Kudzu Mochi, a sweet of steamed wheat flour dipped in molasses and dusted with soybean flour.

FUKUSAYA CASTELLA CAKE SHOP
3-1 Funadaiku-machi, Nagasaki
www.castella.co.jp
Outside of Tokyo but had to be mentioned is this historical cake shop famous for its Castella – the simple Japanese sponge cake (aka Kasutera, see opposite). This light moist cake has been baked at Fukusaya since 1624. It's a must-visit if you're in Japan.

CHIFFERS
B2F Ginza Mitsukoshi,, 4-6-16 Ginza, Chuo-ku, Tokyo
www.facebook.com/CHIFFERS. tokyo
Housed in the basement food hall of Ginza's Mitsukoshi department store, Chiffers offers a fabulous range of all things British, overseen by the pastry chef from the Savoy Hotel, London. The scones are what everyone comes to sample.

UME 1913
Sendagi 5-38-6, Bunkyo-ku, Tokyo
No website
This wonderful but tiny little café – it's truly tiny because it seats only six people! – only opens at weekends, so plan your trip with that in mind. Its beautiful cakes are all made by hand and so it's worth making the effort to squeeze in a weekend visit while you're in the city.

VARIATIONS

PASTEL BORRACHO (DRUNKEN CAKE)
To make a Pastel Borracho, simply add 2 tablespoons of rum into the 'three milk' mix before soaking the cake.

CHOCOLATE TRES LECHE
For a chocolatey edge to the cake, replace 50g (1¾oz) of the flour with 40g (1½oz) of cocoa powder. Sift the cocoa and add at the same time as the flour.

Tres Leche Cake

Serves 9

For the sponge:
225g (8oz) caster sugar
5 eggs, separated
100ml (3½fl oz) full-fat milk
225g (8oz) plain flour, sifted
1 tsp baking powder
½ tsp vanilla extract

For the 'three milk' sauce:
400g (14oz) can sweetened condensed milk
400g (14oz) can evaporated milk
200ml (7fl oz) double cream

Strawberries, raspberries, blackberries and blueberries, to serve

This cake is popular in most parts of Latin America and is a wonderfully light cake soaked with a caramel moistness. 'Leche' means milk in Spanish and the three milks of this cake are condensed, evaporated and full-fat. Here I have replaced the full-fat milk with double cream for extra richness. This cake is best when left overnight before serving to ensure all the milk and cream have been absorbed.

1 Preheat the oven to 170°C/325°F/gas mark 3, and grease and line a 22cm (8½in) square cake tin with baking parchment.
2 Add two-thirds of the sugar to the egg yolks and whisk until white and almost doubled in volume. Slowly add half of the milk and then the sifted flour and baking powder until well mixed. Add the rest of the milk and vanilla extract.
3 In another bowl, beat the egg whites until stiff peaks form and then gradually fold in the remaining sugar. Fold this mixture into the egg yolk mixture, combine well and pour into the prepared cake tin.
4 Bake in a preheated oven for 30–40 minutes.

5 Meanwhile, make the sauce by whisking together the milks and cream.
6 As soon as you take the cake out of the oven, leaving the cake in the tin, prick the top of the cake all over with a skewer and slowly (take your time – pour over a little every few minutes to allow for maximum absorption) pour over three-quarters of the 'three milk' sauce.
7 Chill overnight to allow the cake to soak up the sauce. When ready to serve, remove the cake from the fridge, take out of the tin and remove the baking parchment. Cover with the mixed red fruits, pour over the rest of the sauce and slice for your guests.

275g (9¾oz) caster sugar
4 eggs, plus 3 egg yolks
200g (7oz) plain flour
30g (1¼oz) desiccated
    coconut
1½ tsp baking powder
½ tsp salt
25g (1oz) creamed coconut
    (add into the melted
    butter)
375g (13oz) butter, melted

For the frosting:
50g (1¾oz) cream cheese
60g (2oz) creamed coconut
1 tbsp white rum
½ vanilla pod, split and
    scraped
75g (2¾oz) icing sugar, sifted
2–3 tbsp double cream
50g (1¾oz) coconut chips,
    to decorate

Caribbean Coconut Cake with Rum

Anything with coconut and rum flavours always conjures up images of sunshine and makes me smile. I hope that this cake, using two of the greatest flavours from the tropics, will do the same for you.

1 Preheat the oven to 170°C/325°F/gas mark 3, and grease and line a 23cm (9in) round cake tin with baking parchment.
2 Beat the sugar with the eggs till light and fluffy then fold in the dry ingredients. Add the creamed coconut to the melted butter, mix, then add to butter mixture to the eggs and sugar and mix well.
3 Place the mixture into the prepared tin and bake in a preheated oven for 40 minutes.
4 Remove from the oven, allow to cool for 10 minutes in the tin and then turn out onto a wire rack. When the cake is cold, remove the baking parchment.

5 Now, make the frosting. Blend the cream cheese, creamed coconut, rum and vanilla pod with the sifted icing sugar. Slowly add the double cream until the mixture falls in ribbons – a perfect pipeable consistency.
6 Next, turn the cake upside down on a serving plate. Toast half the coconut chips until lightly golden. Place the frosting in a piping bag with the smallest nozzle, and pipe criss-cross lines over the cake.
7 Finally, sprinkle the golden coconut chips onto the cake and layer up with the non-toasted coconut chips.

Genoise with Raspberries and Cream

Serves 12

6 eggs
200g (7oz) caster sugar
160g (5¾oz) plain flour
25g (1oz) cornflour
30g (1¼oz) butter, melted
500ml (18fl oz) Crème
    Chantilly (see page 296)
100ml (3½fl oz) stock syrup
    (see page 299)
625g (1lb 6oz) fresh
    raspberries

As you might guess from its name, this light and airy sponge cake hails from the Italian city of Genoa. Created at a time when chemical raising agents weren't yet invented, the airiness in a Genoise sponge comes just from the ultra-whipped eggs. Used across Europe, and especially in France, the Genoise is the sponge most favoured by pastry chefs – and that includes me. I use it for everything from the base of my champagne mousse and the Boston Cream Pie (see page 36) to a simple jam sponge or Stack Cakes (see page 40). I like to add a little melted butter to my Genoise for added richness.

1 Preheat the oven to 170°C/325°F/gas mark 3, and grease and line one 21cm (8in) round cake tin with baking parchment.
2 In a large bowl, whisk the eggs until white and foamy. Slowly add the sugar and beat until trebled in size.
3 Sift together in a bowl the flour and cornflour and fold in carefully to the egg mixture and lastly fold in the melted butter.
4 Pour the mixture into the prepared cake tin and bake in a preheated oven for 35 minutes or until a cocktail stick comes out clean.
5 Meanwhile, make the crème Chantilly as on page 296 and stock syrup as on page 299.

6 Remove from the oven, allow to cool for 10 minutes in the tin and then turn out onto a wire rack and remove the parchment.
7 Once cool, assemble the cake. Square off the top of the cake with a knife and then slice the cake horizontally using a serrated knife and turning the cake while cutting in order to achieve neat halves. Brush any excess crumbs from the cake and turn the cake upside down.
8 Dot the tops of both halves of the newly cut cake and the bottom of the top half with stock syrup and then spread a layer of the crème Chantilly on the bottom layer before carefully arranging the fresh raspberries in concentric circles on top.
9 Cover the raspberries with another layer of cream and then place the top layer on the raspberries. Spread a layer of cream and then place the raspberries carefully on top, again in concentric circles.
10 Serve with a raspberry coulis (see below).

RASPBERRY COULIS
Makes 500ml (18fl oz)

200g (7oz) caster sugar
500g (1lb 2oz) fresh or frozen raspberries
1 Place all ingredients in a blender.
2 Blitz with the pulse button then pass through a sieve.

Japanese Strawberry Shortcake

Serves 6

4 eggs, separated
120g (4oz) caster sugar
3 tbsp full-fat milk
½ tsp vanilla extract
120g (4oz) plain flour, sifted
25g (1oz) butter, melted

For the jellied crème Chantilly:

1 bronzed leaf of gelatin
    (or 1 tsp powdered gelatin)
2 tbsp water
240ml (8fl oz) double cream
25g (1oz) icing sugar
½ tsp vanilla extract

For the syrup:

50g (1¾oz) granulated sugar
65ml (2½fl oz) water
½ tsp vanilla extract

strip of 10cm (4in) deep
    acetate paper
200ml (7fl oz) raspberry coulis
    (see page 26), for dipping
    strawberries
500g (1lb 2oz) fresh
    strawberries, to sandwich
    and to decorate
icing sugar, to dust

The Japanese Strawberry Shortcake differs to the well-known American Strawberry Shortcake because it is a sponge layer cake filled with whipped cream, rather than a biscuit. It has become more and more popular in Japan and has replaced some of the more traditional Japanese cakes as a favourite cake.

1 Preheat the oven to 170°C/325°F/gas mark 3, and grease and line an 18cm (7in) loose-bottomed cake tin with baking parchment.
2 Beat together the egg whites and sugar until they are stiff and glossy. Add in the egg yolks and whisk again.
3 Add the milk, vanilla extract and the sifted flour and fold into the mixture. Then, fold in the melted butter.
4 Pour the mixture into the prepared tin and bake in a preheated oven for 25 minutes. A cocktail stick will come out clean when inserted into the centre when the cake is done.
5 Remove from the oven, allow to cool for 10 minutes in the tin and then turn out onto a wire rack and remove the baking parchment.
6 Chill the cake while preparing the other ingredients for assembly.
7 Make the jellied crème Chantilly. Soften the gelatin in iced water, which removes any residue gelatin flavour; discard this water. Heat up the water in a pan and dissolve the leaf in the hot water. Allow to cool for 10 minutes before adding to the mixture.
8 Meanwhile, in a bowl slowly whisk the cream, sugar and vanilla. Gradually add the gelatin and continue to whisk slowly until the cream reaches a ribbon. Then transfer to a piping bag with a No. 5 nozzle.
9 To make the syrup, place the ingredients in a pan and bring to the boil.

10 Using a serrated knife, slice the cake horizontally in half while turning the cake to get a level cut, and then brush away any excess crumbs.
11 Reserve five to six strawberries for decorating the cake. Slice the remaining strawberries into thin slices (about four slices per strawberry).
12 Line the inside of your tin with the acetate paper and cut to fit.
13 Place the bottom sponge layer back in the tin and dot the surface with the syrup.
14 Pipe a thin layer of cream over the sponge and arrange the slices of strawberry standing vertically against the acetate paper.
15 Fill with sliced strawberries and cream.
16 Dot the cut side of the top layer with the syrup until the cake is well covered and then carefully position it on top of the strawberries and cream.
17 Set in the fridge for 1 hour.
18 Meanwhile, make the coulis as instructed on page 26.
19 Dip the whole strawberries in the coulis and set aside.
20 Remove from the tin and then carefully remove the acetate paper. Decorate with icing sugar and the dipped strawberries.
21 Serve with green tea.

Bolo de Fuba

Serves 8

200g (7oz) fine cornmeal
15g (½oz) plain flour
200ml (7fl oz) full-fat milk
juice of ¼ lemon
1 egg yolk
10g (¼oz) butter, melted
10g (¼oz) lard or vegetable
    shortening, melted
100g (3½oz) caster sugar
2 egg whites
1 tsp baking powder
½ tsp ground star anise
icing sugar, to dust

This Brazilian corn cake is an afternoon cake – often taken with coffee – that uses cornmeal to give it a fabulous texture, similar to cakes using polenta. Cornmeal is a common ingredient in the cuisine of South America and this old Brazilian recipe has been handed down through many generations.

1 Preheat the oven to 190°C/375°F/gas mark 5, and grease a 21cm (8in) round cake tin.
2 Sift the cornmeal and flour into a bowl.
3 Heat the milk in a pan over a medium heat and add the lemon juice, which will separate the milk. When it boils take it off the heat.
4 Make a well in the centre of the flour and pour the milk in little by little, stirring continuously.
5 Add the egg yolk, the melted butter and lard (melt them together first) and 75g (2¾oz) of the sugar and beat well.
6 In a separate bowl, beat the egg whites to soft peaks with the rest of the sugar.

7 To the main cake mixture, add the baking powder and the star anise and gently fold in the beaten egg whites.
8 Pour into the prepared tin and bake in a preheated oven for 40 minutes.
9 Remove from the oven, allow to cool for 10 minutes in the tin and then turn out onto a wire rack.
10 Dust with icing sugar and serve, as the Brazilians do, with a cup of coffee.

Bee Sting Cake

Serves 10–12

340g (11¾oz) plain flour
3 tsp baking powder
a pinch of salt
120g (4oz) butter, softened
120g (4oz) caster sugar
1 tsp vanilla extract
2 eggs
100ml (3½fl oz) full-fat milk

For the topping:
60g (2oz) butter
40g (1½oz) caster sugar
40g (1½oz) honey
100g (3½oz) flaked almonds
1 tbsp full-fat milk

For the filling:
250ml (8½fl oz) Crème Légère
(see page 297)

This wonderfully named cake is possibly German in origin, although these days it is very popular in South Africa. According to legend, it is named for a baker who made the cake with a honey topping, which attracted a bee that stung him.

1 Preheat the oven to 160°C/310°F/gas mark 2½, and grease and line a 21cm (8in) loose-bottomed cake tin with baking parchment.
2 Sift the flour, baking powder and salt into a largish bowl.
3 In a separate bowl, cream the butter and sugar together until light and fluffy, then add the vanilla.
4 Add the eggs one at a time, scraping down the sides of the bowl after each addition.
5 Add the sifted dry ingredients, alternating with the milk, until everything is well combined.
6 Spread the mixture in the prepared tin, and prepare the topping before the cake goes into the oven.
7 To make the topping, combine all the ingredients in a pan, stir and heat until the sugar has dissolved. Then boil for 2 minutes. Pour over the cake mixture and spread evenly.

8 Bake in a preheated oven for 35–45 minutes, or until a cocktail stick inserted into the centre comes out clean.
9 While the cake is baking, make the crème légère according to the instructions on page 297 and set aside in the fridge.
10 Remove the cake from the oven, allow to cool for 10 minutes in the tin and then turn out onto a wire rack. Then, remove the baking parchment.
11 When the cake is cool, slice horizontally into three layers brushing away any excess crumbs.
12 Fill a piping bag with a No. 4 nozzle with the crème légère and pipe in spirals between the layers and sandwich together.
13 The texture of the nuts on the top and the creaminess of the filling means the cake needs no accompaniment. Enjoy simply as it is.

Red Velvet Cake

Serves 8–10

150g (5½oz) butter, softened at room temperature
320g (11¼oz) caster sugar
3 eggs
300g (10½oz) plain flour, sifted
220ml (7½fl oz) buttermilk
½ tsp salt
1 tsp vanilla extract
20g (¾oz) cocoa powder, sifted
2 tbsp red food colouring
1 tbsp white wine vinegar
1 tsp bicarbonate of soda

For the frosting:

250g (9oz) butter, softened at room temperature
200g (7oz) icing sugar, sifted
500g (1lb 2oz) cream cheese
1 tsp vanilla extract

This fabulous cake will be familiar to many people, particularly those in the south of the USA, and always seems to be on the favourites list as it works really well as a cupcake too. It's a stunner of a centrepiece for an afternoon tea party or dinner party dessert. The secret is to get the deep red colour just right. Some food historians think the red colour originated from times when sugar was scarce and beetroot was used as a sweet substitute.

1 Preheat the oven to 170°C/325°F/gas mark 3, and grease and line the bottom of two 21cm (8in) round non-stick cake tins with baking parchment.
2 Cream the butter and sugar together until light and fluffy.
3 Whisk the eggs, then slowly add half of the eggs into the creamed mix, mixing all the time.
4 Then add a tablespoon of the sifted flour (to prevent the mixture splitting) followed by the rest of the eggs.
5 Add half the buttermilk, followed by the rest of the sifted flour and then the remaining buttermilk.
6 Next, add the salt, vanilla and sifted cocoa powder, followed by the food colouring. Mix the vinegar and bicarbonate of soda then add to the cake mixture and mix well.

7 Divide the mixture between the prepared cake tins, and bake in a preheated oven for 25 minutes or until a cocktail stick comes out clean when inserted into the centre.
8 Remove from the oven, allow to cool for 10 minutes in the tin and then turn out onto a wire rack. Remove the baking parchment when the cake has cooled.
9 To make the frosting, place the softened butter in a mixing bowl and add the sifted icing sugar slowly and mix until smooth. Then add the cream cheese and vanilla and, again, beat until smooth.
10 Use a third of the buttercream to sandwich the cakes together then use the rest to cover the top and sides of the cake, using a palette knife to smooth it out.
11 Refrigerate for at least 30 minutes before serving at teatime.

Hummingbird Cake

Serves 12

360g (12½oz) plain flour
1 tsp bicarbonate of soda
1 tsp salt
1 tsp ground cinnamon
400g (14oz) caster sugar
3 large eggs, beaten
250ml (8½fl oz) vegetable oil
1½ tsp vanilla extract
225g (8oz) fresh pineapple,
    blitzed
150g (5½oz) pecans,
    chopped
2 bananas, chopped

For the frosting:
Cream Cheese Frosting (see
    page 298)
finely grated zest of 1 orange
chopped pecans, to decorate

This cake has long been a favourite at family gatherings and social occasions all over the Southern States of the USA. No-one really knows how the cake got its name but it has become the most requested recipe by readers of the famous *Southern Living Magazine* since it was first published in 1978. It is an incredibly rich cake and a small slice is all you need.

1. Preheat the oven to 170°C/325°F/gas mark 3, and grease three 21cm (8in) round cake tins and dust with flour.

2 In a bowl, sift the flour, bicarbonate of soda, salt and cinnamon together with the sugar.

3 Then add in the beaten eggs and the oil and stir carefully until everything is incorporated but do not beat. Stir in the vanilla, pineapple, the pecans and the bananas.

4 Pour the mixture into the prepared tins and bake in a preheated oven for 25–30 minutes or until a cocktail stick inserted into the centre comes out clean.

5 Remove from the oven, cool for 10 minutes in the tin and then turn out onto a wire rack.

6 Make the frosting, as instructed on page 298, add the orange zest and combine well.

7 Once cool, reserve the best sponge for the top layer, and neaten off the other two sponges with a knife then brush away any excess crumbs.

8 Spread the frosting on top of two sponges and layer them up. Then spread the remaining frosting on the top and sides of the cake, covering the whole sponge. Decorate with chopped pecans on the top of the cake.

9 Chill the cake for at least 1 hour before slicing and serving.

VARIATION

MANGO AND WALNUT HUMMINGBIRD Replace the pineapple with blitzed mango and the pecans with whole walnuts.

Where to Eat Cake...
SAN FRANCISCO

With its wonderful views and vibrant energy, the City on the Bay has a fantastic culture of bakeries and an enormous array of wonderful cakes and bakes to choose from.

LA BOULANGE DE COLE
1000 Cole St (Parnassus St),
San Francisco, CA 94117
www.laboulangebakery.com
This hugely popular local bakery has tables spilling onto the sidewalk. It has a delectable selection of French pastries, such as madeleines, canneles and all manner of tarts.

PINKIE'S BAKERY
1196 Folsom St (between Rogers and 8th St), San Francisco, CA 94103
www.pinkiesbakerysf.com
This award-winning modern bakery's most popular items are cream cheese-based, such as a gingersnap cookie sandwich stuck together with a wondrously thick layer of frosting. Don't limit yourself to the pastries, the cakes are to die for.

LA FARINE
6323 College Ave, Oakland, CA 94618
www.lafarine.com
French-style bakery with great tarts and cakes, such as the hazelnut chocolate torte. Known for their wedding cakes.

MIETTE
449 Octavia St (Hayes St),
San Francisco, CA 94102
www.miette.com
In French, 'miette' means crumb, though you'll be hard pushed to see any crumbs left on plates at this charming bakery, offering all manner of pastries, cakes and tarts. Owner Megan Ray has a minimalist approach to cakes and you can see at a glance why this bakery has soared into the élite.

SANDBOX BAKERY
833 Cortland Ave (at Gates St),
San Francisco, CA 94110
www.sandboxbakerysf.com
This phenomenal bakery is slightly off the beaten track and you have to get there before lunchtime as they have usually sold out of their freshly baked goods by then. The pastry chef here is Japanese but has extensive French training; the pastries are legendary as are the Japanese cakes.

BAKER AND BANKER
1701 Octavia St, San Francisco, CA 94109
www.bakerandbanker.com
This husband-and-wife team run neighbourhood restaurant also has its own bakery. Swing by to marvel at its wonderful array of morning-baked goods – muffins, scones, brioche and amazing breads.

BATTER BAKERY
2127 Polk St, San Francisco, CA 94109
www.batterbakery.com
Baked in small batches, their simple treats (think cupcake heaven and scones galore) will satisfy everything from an afternoon sweet tooth to an elegant event.

KNEAD PÂTISSERIE
3111 24th Street (between Folsom St and Shotwell St), San Francisco, CA 94110
www.kneadpatisserie.com
This bakery specialises in puff pastries with sweet and savoury fillings – so you can come and sample whatever your mood.

BAKESALE BETTY
5098 Telegraph Ave (51st St),
Oakland, CA 94609
www.bakesalebetty.com
Cakes and desserts with an Australian bent, sample the Lamingtons San Francisco style.

CRIXA CAKES
2748 Adeline St (Stuart St),
Berkeley, CA 94703
www.crixacakes.com
This Berkeley-based bakery serves up a truly international theme with its old-school Eastern European cakes sitting alongside Boston Cream Pies and Jamaican chocolate-rum cakes.

TARTINE BAKERY
600 Guerrero St (18th St),
San Francisco, CA 94110
www.tartinebakery.com
This destination bakery is perfect for people watching (it's on a corner), with a massive menu of all things lovely.

Boston Cream Pie

Serves 8–10

For the Genoise sponge:
6 eggs
200g (7oz) caster sugar
160g (5¾oz) plain flour
25g (1oz) cornflour
30g (1¼oz) butter, melted

For the filling:
500ml (18fl oz) Crème Légère
(see page 297)

For the topping:
300ml (10fl oz) Chocolate
Glaçage (see page 297)

In the mid-1850s in the Parker House Hotel of Boston, the chef – Monsieur Sanzian – tinkered with the hotel's long-standing Pudding-Cake Pie to create the Parker House Chocolate Pie, and this is what's known today as Boston Cream Pie. Although cream pie in name, its nature is more custardy cake: the cake (I use a Genoise sponge) has a glorious sandwich of custardy filling, which is traditionally custard or crème pâtissière. I have used crème légère in my pie as it is lighter than custard or crème pâtissière. This indulgent wonder of a cake has become the official cake of Massachusetts.

1 Preheat the oven to 170°C/325°F/gas mark 3, and grease and line one 21cm (8in) round cake tin with baking parchment.
2 In a large bowl, whisk the eggs until white and foamy. Slowly add the sugar and beat until trebled in size.
3 Sift together in a bowl the flour and cornflour and fold in carefully to the egg mixture and lastly fold in the melted butter.
4 Pour the mixture into the prepared cake tin and bake in a preheated oven for 35 minutes or until a cocktail stick inserted into the centre comes out clean.
5 Remove the cake from the oven, allow to cool for 10 minutes in the tin and then turn out onto a wire rack and remove the parchment.
6 Chill the sponge; it is important to leave the sponge to firm in the fridge for at least 1 hour before creating your pie.

7 Meanwhile, make the crème légère and chocolate glaçage as instructed on page 297, and chill until needed.
8 To assemble the cake, cut the Genoise horizontally in half and brush off any excess crumbs. Using a palette knife, spread all of the filling evenly over the bottom sponge, place on the top half and press down slightly.
9 Pour the glaçage over the top and tip the sponge up and around so that it spills randomly over the sides. Allow to set and slice for awaiting guests.
10 Serve with coffee.

Donovan Cooke's Filipino Cassava Cake

Serves 12

For the base:
1kg (2¼lb) cassava, peeled and grated
600ml (1 pint) coconut milk
225g (8oz) caster sugar
40g (1½oz) butter
50g (1¾oz) Cheddar cheese, grated

For the topping:
75g (2¾oz) plain flour
200ml (7fl oz) water
400ml (13½fl oz) coconut milk
200ml (7fl oz) condensed milk

This recipe has been sent to me by my great friend Donovan Cooke who I worked with for many years when he was Head Chef of Marco Pierre White's Harvey's. Yorkshire-born Donovan has also worked at The Savoy and the Waterside Inn in the UK, as well as La Côte St Jacques in France. Donovan moved to Australia in 1996 where he was co-creator of the influential Est Est Est. In 2005, while working in Hong Kong, Donovan was recognised as Honorary Commander by La Commanderie des Cordons Bleu des France for outstanding culinary achievement. Donovan is currently Executive Chef and partner at The Atlantic Restaurant in Melbourne.

This Cassava Cake is a favourite recipe of Donovan and his Filipino wife, Tanie. Cassava is a woody tuberous root commonly grown in the tropics but is available from certain ethnic markets.

1 Preheat the oven to 180°C/350°F/gas mark 4, and grease a 23cm (9in) loose-bottomed cake tin.
2 Mix all the base ingredients together in a bowl.
3 Spoon into the prepared tin and bake in a preheated oven for 1 hour.
4 Meanwhile, make the topping. Mix together the flour and the water well until smooth, then add in the coconut milk and condensed milk and mix well.
5 Briefly remove the cake from the oven and pour over the topping. Cook for a further hour or until brown.
6 Remove from the oven and allow to cool for 1 hour in the tin to room temperature before removing from the tin and serving.
7 Serve with some freshly sliced mango or papaya on the side and a cup of coffee.

Pineapple Stack Cakes

Serves 12

For the white Genoise sponge:
3 eggs
100g (3½oz) caster sugar
85g (3oz) plain flour, sifted
10g (¼oz) cornflour, sifted

For the chocolate Genoise sponge:
4 eggs
120g (4oz) caster sugar
85g (3oz) plain flour, sifted
30g (1¼oz) cocoa powder, sifted

For the filling:
2 fresh pineapples, peeled, cored and sliced into half rings
500ml (18fl oz) Stock Syrup (see page 299)

For the Grenadine syrup:
400ml (13½fl oz) Grenadine
200ml (7fl oz) water
180g (6½oz) caster sugar

300ml (10fl oz) runny Crème Chantilly (see page 296)

VARIATIONS

You can choose any poached fruit (pears/apricots/peaches) to use in place of the pineapple. Or, if you prefer, you could use fresh fruit, such as raspberries, blueberries or strawberries.

You could also make the whole stack just plain or just chocolate sponge.

Although these cakes are now popular across America during holiday season they originated in the Appalachian area of the country as a wedding cake. When the guests arrived, they would each bring a sponge layer and each layer would be added to the stack with filling between – the higher the stack, the more popular the wedding couple. There are no prizes for the highest tower but the just desserts of making this cake are its super-tasty flavours.

1 Preheat the oven to 170°C/325°F/gas mark 3, and grease and line a baking tray with baking parchment. You will also need a 16cm (6¼in) diameter cake ring.

2 On a sheet of baking parchment, draw six circles using the cake ring as a size guide. Turn the parchment over before spooning on the sponge mixture, so the pen or pencil marks do not bleed into the sponge mixture. Use a dot of mixture to stick the parchment down.

3 Make the white Genoise. In a large bowl, whisk the eggs until pale and doubled in volume. Mix in the sugar, and then fold the sifted flour and cornflour gently into the eggs, being careful not to remove any of the bubbles.

4 Now, repeat the same process with the chocolate Genoise sponge ingredients.

5 Spoon 2–3 tablespoons of the white Genoise mixture into each of three circles. Then do the same with the chocolate version. Smooth the mixture into the circle with a palette knife.

6 Bake in a preheated oven for about 7 minutes. Remove from the oven and allow to cool then remove the baking parchment.

7 Make the grenadine syrup by putting all the ingredients in a pan and boiling until syrupy.

8 Poach half the pineapple in stock syrup and half in the grenadine syrup until it's cooked through (5 minutes). Drain and set aside.

9 To assemble the cake, alternate layers of the chocolate and the white sponge with the pink and the white poached pineapple, topping each layer of pineapple with a generous layer of crème Chantilly.

Danish Layer Cake

Serves 6

110g (3¾oz) butter, softened
200g (7oz) caster sugar
5 eggs
1 tsp vanilla extract
330g (11½oz) plain flour,
    sifted
1 tsp baking powder

For the filling:
400g (14oz) raspberry jam
500ml (18fl oz) double cream,
    whipped
icing sugar, to dust

This is a traditional celebration cake in Denmark and you can ring the changes with your own favourite fillings. This recipe is a beautifully rich creamy cake that feels lovely and summery.

1 Preheat the oven to 180°C/350°F/gas mark 4, and you will need three large baking trays and baking parchment.

2 Draw six circles of 21cm (8in) diameter on three sheets of baking parchment (two on each sheet). Turn the paper over so the ink doesn't bleed into the cakes, and place the parchment on the baking trays.

3 Cream the butter and sugar together until light and fluffy.

4 Add in the eggs, one at a time, beating well after each addition, then add the vanilla extract.

5 Beat in the sifted flour and baking powder until all the ingredients are well combined.

6 Divide the mixture (about 130g (4½oz) per circle) onto the baking parchment and, using a palette knife, carefully spread the mixture out

to fill the circles. Use a small dot of the mixture to 'glue' the parchment to the baking tray, so it doesn't flap about once in the oven.

7 Bake in a preheated oven for about 15 minutes or until golden.

8 Remove the cakes from the oven and cool on a wire rack. Then remove the baking parchment.

9 Now, put the cake together. Spread a layer of raspberry jam on each sponge except the one chosen to be the top layer, followed by a layer of whipped cream and stack until complete.

10 Dust liberally with icing sugar and serve with a glass of cold champagne.

Coconut Layer Cake

Serves 12

225g (8oz) butter, softened
410g (14½oz) caster sugar
5 eggs
425g (15oz) plain flour, sifted
1 tsp bicarbonate of soda
1 tsp salt
20g (¾oz) desiccated
    coconut
240ml (8fl oz) buttermilk
15ml (1tbsp) vanilla extract

For the topping:

350g (12oz) Italian meringue
    frosting (see page 298)
120ml (4fl oz) coconut water
150g (5½oz) desiccated
    coconut

Though massively popular in the New World, multi-layered cakes have their roots firmly in the Old World of mainland Europe. From the age-old Dobos cake (see page 48), bakers have been creating concoctions of light sponge layers with a wondrous filling. As settlers moved from Europe to America, they took their cake traditions with them, including their penchant for layered cakes. My Coconut Layer Cake is slightly more modest (by American standards) but this sweet moist cake is worthy of any special occasion.

1 Preheat the oven to 180°C/350°F/gas mark 4, and grease and line two 21cm (8in) cake tins with baking parchment.
2 Cream the butter and sugar together until light and fluffy.
3 Add the eggs, one at a time, scraping down after each addition until well combined.
4 Add the sifted flour, bicarbonate of soda, salt and desiccated coconut in two batches, alternating with the buttermilk and vanilla extract and mix well until smooth.
5 Split the mixture between the prepared tins and bake in a preheated oven for 35 minutes or until a cocktail stick inserted into the centre comes out clean.

6 Remove from the oven, cool for 10 minutes in the tin and then turn out onto a wire rack.
7 Once cooled, reserve the sponge with the roundest top for the top and square off the top of the other sponge. Cut each cake horizontally in half and brush away any excess crumbs.
8 Meanwhile, make the frosting (see page 298).
9 Place one layer on a cake stand or serving plate, liberally brush with coconut water and spread with frosting. Sprinkle with the coconut and then continue with the next two layers.
10 Add the top layer, cover the rest of the cake with the remaining frosting, liberally sprinkle with desiccated coconut and refrigerate for 1 hour. Serve straight from the fridge.

Cassata alla Siciliana

Serves 10

For the cake:
6 eggs, separated
110g (3¾oz) caster sugar
juice of 1 lemon
finely grated zest of
 1½ oranges
2 tablespoons sherry
2 drops almond extract
150g (5½oz) plain flour
a pinch of salt

For the filling:
65ml (2½fl oz) Stock Syrup
 (see page 299)
120ml (4fl oz) dark rum
60g (2oz) icing sugar, sifted
575g (1lb 4oz) ricotta
30g (1¼oz) dark chocolate
 (minimum 55% cocoa
 solids), grated
40g (1½oz) glacé cherries,
 chopped
½ tsp ground cinnamon
50g (1¾oz) toasted almonds,
 chopped

For the decoration:
60g (2oz) butter, softened
160g (5¾oz) cream cheese
500g (1lb 2oz) icing sugar,
 sifted
500g (1lb 2oz) marzipan
1 tsp green food colouring
150g (5½oz) assorted glacé
 fruits

Originating in Palermo, the island's capital, Cassata is the iconic cake of Sicily. This layered alcohol-soaked sponge has a sweet ricotta filling, topped with marzipan and fruit. What began as an Easter tradition today sees Cassata spanning every season, including Christmas.

1 Preheat the oven to 170°C/325°F/gas mark 3, and grease and line a 23cm (9in) springform cake tin with baking parchment.

2 Whisk the egg yolks until thick and creamy. Add in the sugar, lemon juice, orange zest, sherry and almond extract, and beat until foamy.

3 Sift the flour into the egg yolk mix and fold in.

4 In a separate bowl, whisk the egg whites until soft peaks form and add the salt. Fold into the yolk-flour mixture and mix well.

5 Pour into the prepared tin and bake for 50 minutes or until a cocktail stick inserted into the centre comes out clean.

6 Remove from the oven, cool for 10 minutes in the tin and then turn out onto a wire rack. When totally cool, remove the baking parchment and slice the cake into three layers.

7 Make the sugar syrup as on page 299. When cool, add in half the rum to make a rum syrup.

8 In a bowl, add the sifted icing sugar to the ricotta and beat until smooth.

9 Mix in the remaining rum and then fold in the chocolate, cherries, cinnamon and almonds.

10 Place the first layer of cake on a board and brush the sponge with the rum syrup. Spread half of the ricotta mixture over the first layer and repeat with the second layer. Add the third sponge layer and rest in the fridge for 1 hour.

11 Meanwhile, in a bowl make the frosting by beating the softened butter with the cream cheese. Slowly add the sifted icing sugar. Leave in the fridge for 30 minutes before using.

12 Cover the sides and the top of the cake evenly with the frosting. Refrigerate again.

13 Soften the marzipan in your hands and place in a bowl with the food colouring and mix thoroughly with your hands until the required colour is achieved.

14 Flatten the marzipan on a surface dusted with icing sugar. Roll into a circle large enough to cover your cake.

15 Carefully lay the marzipan over the cake, smoothing and flattening down the top and sides with your hands. Trim any excess.

16 Decorate with assorted glacé fruit and serve with a sweet wine, such as Marsala.

Serves 12–14

For the cake:
85g (3oz) cocoa powder
120ml (4fl oz) boiling water
200ml (7fl oz) full-fat milk
300g (10½oz) butter, softened
475g (1lb 1oz) caster sugar
1 tbsp vanilla extract
4 eggs, beaten
475g (1lb 1oz) plain flour
1 tsp bicarbonate of soda
½ tsp salt

For the frosting:
6 egg yolks
200g (7oz) caster sugar
100ml (3½fl oz) water
450g (1lb) butter, cubed
20g (¾oz) dark chocolate
    (minimum 70% cocoa
    solids), melted

85g (3oz) dark chocolate
    shavings

Devil's Food Cake

Chocoholics rejoice! The Devil's Food Cake is the ultimate chocolate indulgence and will elicit many oohs and aahs from friends and family waiting for you to cut and hand out slices. Rumour has it that this cake got its name either because of the hedonistic amount of chocolate frosting or because it's the absolute opposite of another American favourite, the Angel Cake (see page 18).

1 Preheat the oven to 170°C/325°F/gas mark 3. Grease, line with baking parchment and dust with cocoa three 21cm (8in) round cake tins.
2 Sift the cocoa and add to the boiling water and mix. When cooled slightly add in the milk.
3 Cream the butter and sugar together until light and fluffy. Add in the vanilla extract and beat in the eggs a little at a time, scraping down every so often.
4 Sift the flour, bicarbonate of soda and salt into a bowl and add to the egg mixture, alternating with the cocoa mixture and combine well.
5 Divide the mixture evenly into the prepared cake tins and bake in a preheated oven for

35 minutes or until a cocktail stick inserted into the centre comes out clean.
6 Remove from the oven, allow to cool for 10 minutes in the tin and then turn out onto a wire rack.
7 Now, make the frosting. Put the egg yolks in a large bowl. Bring the sugar and water to the boil until the temperature reaches 118°C/244°F. Then start whisking the egg yolks. When the sugar reaches 120°C/248°F, remove from the heat and let the bubbles subside. Add to the yolks in three batches, turning off the mixer between additions. Add in the cubed butter and slowly fold in the melted chocolate and combine well.
8 Now, you're ready to assemble the cake. Remove the baking parchment and place one cake layer onto a serving plate and spread frosting over the top. Add a second layer and repeat with more frosting. Add the final layer and then cover the entire cake with the remaining frosting. Sprinkle with chocolate shavings if you like, as I do; create them using a peeler or knife. Serve with coffee.

VARIATION

COFFEE DEVIL'S FOOD CAKE
For an even richer cake, add a paste-like mixture of 3 tablespoons of instant coffee granules with a little water and add it after the flour mixture in the recipe above.

Willie Harcourt-Cooze's Cloud Forest Chocolate Cake

Serves 12

180g (6½oz) 100% cacao, finely grated
225g (8oz) butter
6 eggs
50g (1¾oz) light muscovado sugar
120g (4oz) caster sugar
100g (3½oz) ground almonds

For the icing:
250ml (8½fl oz) double cream
75g (2¾oz) golden caster sugar
85g (3oz) 100% cacao, finely grated

Known as 'The Chocolate Man', Willie Harcourt-Cooze is a British-based chocolate maker who has inspired people from all over the world to change the way they enjoy chocolate with his range of world-class cacao.

His passion for chocolate was born of a love of adventure. That spirit took him to Venezuela, led him to buy a hacienda in the cloud forest and made his early forays in harvesting cacao a perfect point of purpose and excitement. His quest for flavour continues to take him around the world.

He says of this cake: 'This was the first cake born out of the cacao from my farm in Venezuela. One day, while walking down from the cloud forest, I stopped in San Pablo, a sugar plantation, and chatted to Santiago Blanco who gifted me some raw sugar cane. And with only almonds and eggs this emperor of a cake came alive.'

1 Preheat the oven to 170°C/325°F/gas mark 3, and grease and line a 25cm (10in) springform cake tin with baking parchment.
2 Melt the cacao and butter together in a heatproof bowl set over a pan of gently simmering water, making sure the bottom of the bowl is not in contact with the water. Remove from the heat and set aside.

3 Beat the eggs with the sugars in a large bowl until pale and doubled in volume.
4 Stir in the melted cacao and butter mixture, then carefully fold in the ground almonds until evenly mixed through.
5 Tip the mixture into the prepared cake tin and bake in a preheated oven for 35 minutes, or until slightly risen and a cocktail stick inserted into the centre comes out clean.
6 Remove from the oven and leave in the tin on a wire rack to cool.
7 Meanwhile, make the icing. Put the cream and sugar in a pan over a low heat and bring just to the point of boiling. Remove from the heat and stir in the grated cacao until melted and evenly mixed through. Set aside to cool.
8 When the cake is completely cold, remove the baking parchment, place on a serving plate or cake board and spread the cooled icing evenly over the top and sides.
9 Keep at room temperature until ready to serve. Don't store in the fridge as the cake and icing can become too hard.

Dobos Cake

Serves 12

For the sponge:
40g (1½oz) butter
50g (1¾oz) icing sugar
6 eggs
100g (3½oz) plain flour, sifted

For the chocolate buttercream:
4 eggs
200g (7oz) icing sugar
270g (9½oz) butter
20g (¾oz) caster sugar
40g (1½oz) 100% cacao, melted
200g (7oz) dark chocolate (minimum 70% cocoa solids), melted

For the caramel:
250g (9oz) caster sugar

This multi-layered cake with chocolate buttercream and a super-crisp caramel layer on top is named after its creator Jozsef Dobos, a famous restaurateur and confectioner from the Austro-Hungarian Empire. Its popularity in Hungary as a showstopping cake has not diminished since.

1 Preheat the oven to 170°C/325°F/gas mark 3, and line three large baking trays with baking parchment. You'll also need to line a 21cm (8in) springform cake tin with baking parchment.
2 Draw six circles (of 21cm (8in)) on the three sheets of parchment and turn over to prevent any bleeding of the pencil or pen into the cake.
3 Cream the butter and sugar together until light and fluffy.
4 Add in the eggs, one at a time, scraping down the bowl each time and combine well.
5 Add the sifted flour and mix well.
6 Divide the mixture into six and pour the mixture onto each circle and spread evenly with a palette knife.
7 Bake in a preheated oven for 6–8 minutes or until light golden. Remove from the oven, cool on a wire rack, then remove the parchment.
8 Make the buttercream. Heat the eggs and the icing sugar in a heatproof bowl over a pan of simmering water until it becomes thick and pale. Then, transfer to a bowl and whisk till cool.

9 In another bowl, beat the butter and caster sugar until light and fluffy. Add in the melted cacao and chocolate, then fold in the cooled egg mixture.
10 In the prepared tin, place the first sponge on the bottom and spread one-sixth of the buttercream (that's about 150g (5½oz)) evenly over and repeat with four more sponges and buttercream, reserving the top layer.
11 Next, make the caramel. Heat the sugar in a pan until it becomes a light caramel (about 170°C/338°F on a thermometer).
12 Place the top sponge layer on a lightly greased work surface and, working quickly, using a greased palette knife, pour the caramel over the sponge and spread it out.
13 Before it sets, using a greased knife, cut this sponge into 12 equal sections. Allow to cool.
14 Remove the cake from the tin and spread the remainder of the buttercream around the edges of the cake. Then place the caramel sections on the top. Slice and serve with coffee.

Pastel de Chocolate Mexicano

Serves 8

75g (2¾oz) dark chocolate
(minimum 75% cocoa
solids), chopped
65ml (2½fl oz) full-fat milk,
plus 2 tbsp
½ tsp chipotle chilli flakes
120g (4oz) plain flour
½ tsp baking powder
a pinch of salt
60g (2oz) demerara sugar
65ml (2½fl oz) groundnut oil
1 egg

For the decoration:
cocoa powder, for dusting
chillies, for decoration

This wonderfully warming chocolate cake hails from Mexico. It is super-easy to make, intensely chocolatey and very sultry – as here I've used the chipotle chilli rather than regular chilli. It'll last well too, up to three days, but I can't imagine it'll be around that long.

1 Preheat the oven to 170°C/325°F/gas mark 3, and grease and line a 15cm (6in) round cake tin with baking parchment.
2 Melt the chocolate in a heatproof bowl over a pan of simmering water and, when melted, add 1 tablespoon of the milk. Mix until smooth. Remove from the heat then add the chipotle chilli and set aside to cool slightly.
3 In a large bowl, mix the flour, baking powder and salt. Set aside for later.
4 Pour the remaining milk into the chocolate and mix well. Then, add the sugar and oil and again mix well.

5 Next whisk in the egg until light and frothy.
6 Add the dry ingredients to the chocolate mixture and fold in well.
7 Pour the mix into the prepared tin and bake in a preheated oven for 30 minutes.
8 Remove from the oven, allow to cool for 10 minutes in the tin and then turn out onto a wire rack and strip off the parchment.
9 Keep the decoration simple with just a light dusting of cocoa or icing sugar, if you prefer. Top with red chillies and serve to friends.

Thierry Busset's Ten Layer Coffee Chocolate Cake

Serves 10–12

For the chocolate Genoise:
120g (4oz) plain flour
25g (1oz) cornflour
20g (¾oz) cocoa powder
5 eggs
170g (6oz) caster sugar
12g (⅓oz) butter, melted

For the coffee chocolate mousse:
600ml (1 pint) whipping cream
250g (9oz) caster sugar
175ml (6fl oz) espresso or
    strong filter coffee
8 egg yolks
300g (10½oz) dark chocolate
    (minimum 70% cocoa
    solids)

For the coffee syrup:
50g (1¾oz) caster sugar
50ml (2fl oz) water
500ml (18fl oz) filter or
    cafetière coffee
100ml (3½fl oz) Kahlua

For the chocolate glaçage:
175g (6¼oz) dark chocolate
    (minimum 50% cocoa
    solids)
175g (6¼oz) dark chocolate
    (minimum 80% cocoa
    solids)
500ml (18fl oz) whipping
    cream
100g (3½oz) liquid glucose

Thierry Busset is an award-winning French pastry chef who, via a 10-year stint in London that included The Restaurant, Marco Pierre White where I worked with him, now runs a hugely successful high-end chocolaterie and pâtisserie in downtown Vancouver, Canada.

He says of this cake: 'I started to make this cake at L'Auberge du Père Bise in the Haute Savoie, France, with my friend and the pastry chef at the time, Christophe Marquant. I love it because it reminds me of a French version of tiramisu. In Canada, this cake is incredibly popular. Canadians love their coffee, and the combination of flavours is unbeatable.'

1 Preheat the oven to 180°C/350°F/gas mark 4, and grease and line a 25cm (10in) cake tin with baking parchment.
2 Sift the flour, cornflour, and cocoa powder together, and set aside.
3 Whisk the eggs and sugar together in a bowl over a pan of boiling water until doubled in volume and hot to the touch.
4 Cool down in a mixer on high speed until lukewarm and fluffy.
5 Fold in the butter, followed by the dry ingredients.
6 Bake in a preheated oven for 25 minutes, or until a cocktail stick inserted into the centre comes out clean.
7 Remove from the oven, cool for 10 minutes in the tin and then turn out onto a wire rack. When cool, strip off the baking parchment.
8 Now, make the mousse. Whip the cream to a soft peak and set aside.
9 Bring the sugar and coffee to the boil and pour over the egg yolks. Whisk continuously in a bowl over a pan of simmering water until 83°C/181°F. As before, cool in a mixer on high speed until lukewarm and doubled in volume.
10 Melt the chocolate in a bowl over a pan of simmering water.
11 By hand, whisk the melted chocolate into the egg mixture followed by the cream.
12 Fill a piping bag with the coffee chocolate mousse and refrigerate until needed.
13 Next, make the syrup. Dissolve the sugar in the water and coffee and boil until it becomes syrupy, then add in the Kahlua.
14 You're now ready to assemble the cake. Slice the chocolate Genoise horizontally into five thin layers.
15 Carefully centre the first layer on a cake board or stand.
16 Soak the sponge generously with the coffee-infused syrup.
17 Remove the piping bag from the fridge and pipe a thin layer (about the same thickness as the Genoise) on to the first cake layer.
18 Repeat this process with all the layers of sponge, finishing with the last layer of Genoise.
19 Transfer to the fridge to set for 1 to 2 hours.
20 Meanwhile, make the glaçage. Break the chocolate into pieces in a bowl. Bring the cream to a boil and pour over the chocolate. Mix with a spoon until emulsified. Leave to cool until warm, then stir in the glucose.
21 When the cake is set, remove from the fridge and pour the glaçage over, completely covering the cake.
22 Enjoy with coffee or a glass of champagne.

Chocolate Layer Cake

Serves 8

50ml (2fl oz) water
25g (1oz) cocoa powder
½ vanilla pod, split and
    scraped
110g (3¾oz) butter
110g (3¾oz) caster sugar
3 eggs, separated
85g (3oz) hazelnut powder,
    toasted and cooled
½ tsp cream of tartar

For the decoration:
75g (2¾oz) hazelnut flakes

For the ganache:
110g (3¾oz) dark chocolate
    (minimum 70% cocoa
    solids)
120ml (4fl oz) double cream
40g (1½oz) butter, cubed

This super-rich cake is typical of many confections found on the European continent and is pure melt-in-the-mouth indulgence. Using hazelnut powder instead of flour gives the sponge its richness; but if you can't find hazelnut powder, then roast whole hazelnuts in the oven, leave them to cool then blitz in a blender. If you prefer, this heavenly chocolate cake would also work well as a dessert – the choice is yours.

1 Preheat the oven to 170°C/325°F/gas mark 3 and line the bottom of a 25cm x 8cm x 8cm (10in x 3¼in x 3¼in) loaf tin with parchment.
2 Bring the water to the boil in a pan, add the cocoa powder and stir to form a paste. Stir in the vanilla seeds, remove from the heat and leave to cool.
3 In a bowl, soften the butter with a spatula then cream with one-third of the sugar.
4 Add the yolks, beat, then fold in the hazelnut powder followed by the cooled cocoa paste.
5 Whisk the egg whites, adding the rest of the sugar slowly once the whites start to form peaks, followed by the cream of tartar. Continue to whisk until they are stiff.
6 Fold the egg white mixture into the yolk mixture and pour into the prepared loaf tin.
7 Bake in a preheated oven for about 45 minutes. Remove from the oven, allow to cool for 20 minutes in the tin and then turn out onto a wire rack and remove the parchment very carefully as the sponge is quite fragile.
8 Next, toast the hazelnut flakes on a baking tray in the oven for about 10 minutes then remove and leave to cool.
9 Now make the ganache. Melt the chocolate in a bowl over simmering water. In a separate pan, bring the cream to the boil, then pour onto the melted chocolate and start to stir. Slowly add the butter and bring together until the chocolate starts to thicken. Remove from the heat.
10 When the cake's cold, square off all the sides of the sponge with a sharp knife and cut in half lengthways. Place one sponge on a cake board or serving plate and use a palette knife to spread one-third of the ganache over the top. Place the second sponge on top of the first and spread a second layer of ganache over the top of that. Use the remaining ganache to cover the sides of the cake and smooth all the surfaces.
11 Sprinkle the golden toasted hazelnut flakes over the top and press gently to ensure they stick. Slice the cake thinly – it is incredibly rich – and serve with a stiff coffee.

VARIATION
For an extra-rich cake, mix 2 tablespoons of instant coffee with a little water and add this paste after the egg whites.

Where to Eat Cake...
BERLIN

Kaffee und küchen (translating from the German as coffee and cake) is a national pastime in Germany, and the capital is packed with choice when it comes to finding the perfect place for coffee and cake. With cafés on every street corner and more between, you'll find this city's café culture a totally relaxing one, especially if you're visiting in the summer months as tables and chairs spill out onto the pavements and into the parks.

OLIV CAFÉ
Münzstrasse 8 – Ecke Almstadtstrasse, 10178 Berlin
www.oliv-cafe.de
Come to this modern café for a true slice of German cake (be it cheesecake, streusel or a rich chocolate and nut torte, see opposite). You'll be spoilt for choice and the coffee's pretty spot on too.

KONDITOREI BUCHWALD
Bartningallee 29, 10557 Berlin
www.konditorei-buchwald.de
If you fancy tasting some baumkuchen before making your own (see Sakotis on page 292) then wander over to this old-fashioned café, overlooking the River Spree, where they serve this classic layered German cake. In fact, the Buchwald family has been making baumkuchen for more than 150 years.

LES ENFANTS GÂTÉS
Falckensteinstrasse 33, 10997 Berlin
www.qype.com/place/814877-Les-Enfants-Gates-Berlin
This pâtisserie is a little bit of France in Berlin and is renowned for serving the best – and most intense – hot chocolate in the city, made from a staggeringly high 99% cocoa. Sip a cup while sampling any of the exquisite pâtisserie creations on offer that day.

FASSBENDER & RAUSCH
Charlottenstrasse 60, 10117 Berlin
www.fassbender-rausch.com
See if you can pass the chocolate marvels in the window without finding yourself opening the door and heading inside.

CAFÉ EINSTEIN
Café Einstein Stammhaus, Kurfürstenstrasse 58, 10785 Berlin
www.cafeeinstein.com
For the most authentic Apfelstrudel in the city, head on over to this café that describes itself as 'a European coffee house'. Though if you prefer your strudel with something stronger, cocktails are not too far away.

PASAM BAKLAVA
Goebenstrasse 12a, 10783 Berlin
www.pasam-baklava.de
This family-run bakery sells only baklava but using a variety of pastries and with numerous fillings – all of which has to be said are delicious.

KORIAT CAKE MAKER
Pannierstrasse 29, 12047 Berlin
www.koriat.de
Israeli baker Aviv Koriat's small but handmade selection of bakes are so popular that his pastries are even bought by some other bakeries to sell.

WEICHARDT BROT
Mehlitzstrasse 7, 10715 Berlin
www.weichardt.de
Sublime Schokosahne Torte (melt-in-the-mouth chocolate and bitter cream), sells out by noon every day – but you can also buy pastries, sweet breads and marzipan confections.

CAFÉ ANNA BLUME
Kollwitzstrasse 83, 10405 Berlin
www.cafe-anna-blume.de
Flowers and excellent cakes in one place – will feel like spring whatever the season – but get here early as fills up fast.

WOHNZIMMER
Lettestrasse 6, 10437 Berlin
www.wohnzimmer-bar.de
In German, 'wohnzimmer' means 'living room' and this café is really like a home from home; although your home might not have such good views. The great-value coffee and cake will have you coming back for more.

Black Forest Gâteau

Serves 14

For the sponge:
6 eggs
180g (6½oz) caster sugar
130g (4½oz) plain flour
50g (1¾oz) cocoa powder

For the sugar syrup:
100g (3½oz) caster sugar
100ml (3½fl oz) water
20ml (⅔fl oz) Kirsch

For the filling:
100ml (3½fl oz) Crème
    Chantilly (see page 296)

For the decoration:
60g (2oz) griottine cherries,
    roughly chopped, plus
    10–15 cherry halves, for
    decoration
50g (1¾oz) white chocolate
500g (1lb 2oz) dark chocolate
    (minimum 70% cocoa
    solids)
strip of 10cm (4in) deep
    acetate paper (long enough
    to encircle the cake)

This dessert-style cake became a classic in the 1970s when it was served in every restaurant and sold in every bakery. Originating from the Black Forest area of Germany it is still a magnificent-looking and incredibly indulgent combination of cherry, cream and chocolate. Take a trip down memory lane and try a slice of this wonderfully rich cake.

1 Preheat the oven to 170°C/325°F/gas mark 3, and grease and line a 23cm (9in) round cake tin with baking parchment.

2 Whisk the eggs until they peak and go pale.

3 Slowly add the sugar until the mixture doubles in size.

4 Sift the flour and cocoa together and then fold into the egg mixture, being careful not to take the air out of the eggs.

5 Place the mixture in the prepared tin and bake in a preheated oven for 25–30 minutes or until a cocktail stick inserted into the centre comes out clean.

6 Remove from the oven and allow to cool in the tin for 10 minutes before turning out onto a wire rack. Once cooled, strip off the baking parchment, wrap the sponge with clingfilm and refrigerate overnight to firm it up.

7 To make the sugar syrup, bring the sugar and water to the boil in a pan and then remove from the heat. Pass through a sieve, add the kirsch and leave to cool.

8 Next, make the crème Chantilly as instructed on page 296 and set aside in the fridge.

9 Take the sponge out of the fridge and, using a sharp knife, slice the top off to square it off and discard the top (or keep to have with a cup of coffee). Slice again into three horizontal slices. Remove excess crumbs from the cakes.

10 Now, place the bottom layer onto a cake board and, using a pastry brush, dab the kirsch syrup all over the top of the sponge.

11 Spread one-third of the crème Chantilly over the sponge and smooth with a palette knife. Spread one-third of the roughly chopped cherries on top of the cream. Repeat with the second layer.

12 Add the top layer. Now, pipe the remaining crème Chantilly with a spiral nozzle, making mounds and add the remaining cherries.

13 To make the chocolate marbling, first melt the white chocolate in a bowl over simmering water and smear randomly onto your acetate (which should be long enough and deep enough to be placed all round the outside of the cake). Place in the fridge to set.

14 Meanwhile put some ice in a baking tray and place the tray on the work surface where you will be using the melted dark chocolate. This is to cool the area and enable you to work at speed with the melted chocolate. Remove the cake from the fridge and set next to the ice.

15 Meanwhile melt 400g (14oz) of the dark chocolate, again in a bowl over simmering water. Once melted, remove the ice and wipe the work surface to remove any water.

16 Take the acetate out of the fridge and place it on the chilled area. Pour the chocolate evenly over the acetate and, using a palette knife, quickly smooth the chocolate. Once the chocolate turns from glossy to matt (that is, beginning to set) carefully pick up the acetate and place around your gâteau and secure. Put back in the fridge to set.

17 Now, make some chocolate curls. Melt the remaining dark chocolate and pour onto a clean baking tray. Smooth with a palette knife and put in a cool area for about 20–30 minutes until nearly set. Using a round pastry cutter (size 8cm (3¼in)) scrape over the chocolate pulling towards you until a curl forms. If the chocolate pulls straight up and doesn't curl the chocolate is not set enough; conversely, if it's too brittle the chocolate will snap. Add the curls to the top of the cake along with the cherry halves.

18 Before serving, remove the acetate to reveal a beautifully marbled chocolate pattern around your gorgeous gâteau.

Flourless Chocolate Torte

Serves 6

225g (8oz) butter, cubed
225g (8oz) dark chocolate
(minimum 55% cocoa
solids), broken into pieces
5 eggs, separated
120g (4oz) caster sugar
icing sugar, for dusting

Cakes come in all shapes and sizes but what they share is some form of raising agent – egg yolk, baking powder, self-raising flour – to make them rise. Elsewhere in the book, you'll see my take on Angel Cake (see Raspberry Angel Cake (page 18)) or a meringue-based cake, such as Hazelnut Dacquoise (see page 121), and there are plenty of cakes that use ground nuts instead of flour (see Chocolate Layer Cake, page 52). But this cake simply relies on the richness of chocolate and super-whisked egg whites for its cakeyness (and not flour), making it a perfect treat for anyone with a gluten allergy. Don't worry when the cake collapses – it's supposed to!

1 Preheat the oven to 160°C/310°F/gas mark 2½, and grease and line a 21cm (8in) loose-bottomed cake tin with baking parchment.
2 Melt the butter and the chocolate together in a bowl over a pan of barely simmering water, stirring occasionally.
3 In a bowl, whisk the egg yolks with half the sugar until light and creamy.

4 In a separate bowl, whisk the egg whites until stiff peaks form and then slowly whisk in the second half of the sugar.
5 Fold the melted chocolate and butter into the egg yolk mixture and then carefully, with a metal spoon, fold in the egg white mixture.
6 Spoon the mixture into the prepared tin and bake in a preheated oven for 1 hour or until a cocktail stick inserted into the centre comes out clean.
7 Remove from the oven, allow to cool for 10 minutes in the tin and then turn out onto a wire rack and strip off the parchment.
8 Dust with icing sugar and serve with raspberries and crème fraîche.

VARIATION

HAZELNUT AND RASPBERRY TORTE Fold in 30g (1¼oz) flaked hazelnuts and 120g (4oz) fresh raspberries carefully before adding in the meringue (in the recipe above) for a rich, tangy torte.

Sacher Torte

Serves 8–10

For the cake:

175g (6¼oz) dark chocolate (minimum 70% cocoa solids), chopped into small pieces
120g (4oz) butter, at room temperature, cubed
150g (5½oz) caster sugar
5 eggs, separated, plus 1 extra egg white
150g (5½oz) plain flour, sifted
½ tsp baking powder
50ml (2fl oz) Apricot Glaze (see page 299)

For the chocolate icing:

175ml (6fl oz) double cream
2 tbsp golden syrup
225g (8oz) dark chocolate (minimum 70% cocoa solids), chopped into small pieces

Austria has a rich tradition of amazing cakes and pastries and one of the most famous is Sacher Torte. This intense chocolate cake was invented by Franz Sacher in 1832, when he was just 16 and worked in the kitchens of the Austrian Prince. The grand Hotel Sacher in Vienna was opened by his son in 1876 and still stands today where the Sacher Torte is a sought-after dessert.

1 Preheat the oven to 170°C/325°F/gas mark 3, and grease and line a 23–25cm (9–10in) springform cake tin with baking parchment.
2 Put the chopped chocolate in a bowl over a pan of simmering water on a low heat. Melt until smooth but do not allow the water to boil as this will burn the chocolate. Once melted remove from the heat and set aside.
3 Meanwhile, add the butter to a large bowl and cream until soft before adding half the sugar. Cream until pale and fluffy then add the egg yolks one at a time, beating thoroughly to incorporate after each addition.
4 Now add the cooled chocolate and mix well until fully combined.
5 Add the flour and baking powder into the cake mix and fold in with a metal spoon.
6 In a large clean bowl, whisk the egg whites to soft peaks, adding the remaining sugar 1 tablespoon at a time, whisking well between each tablespoon of sugar.
7 Gently fold the egg whites into the chocolate mixture then turn into the prepared cake tin.
8 Ensure the surface is level, then bake in a preheated oven for 1 hour or until a cocktail stick inserted into the centre comes out clean.

9 Remove from the oven, allow to stand in the tin for 10 minutes then turn out onto a wire rack and remove the baking parchment.
10 Meanwhile, make the glaze as instructed on page 299. Set aside, and brush all over the cold cake to coat fully.
11 Next, make the chocolate icing. Bring the cream and golden syrup to the simmer for 30 seconds.
12 Put the chopped chocolate in a bowl and pour on the hot liquid mixture. Mix well with a spatula rather than a whisk as you don't want to incorporate air into the icing.
13 Place the cake on a wire rack with a sheet of baking parchment beneath to catch any dripping icing. Pour the icing over the cake on the top and sides. Use a warmed palette knife to help coat the sides, if needed.
14 Allow to stand in a cool place until set but do not refrigerate as this will cause condensation to form on the cake's surface.
15 Decorate with a piped 'S' or the word 'Sacher' in milk chocolate or with decoration of your choice.
16 Store in an airtight container and eat within a week.

Paul A. Young's Torta Gianduja

Serves 12

160g (5¾oz) butter, at room temperature
180g (6½oz) dark chocolate (minimum 70% cocoa solids; I use Valrhona Guanaja)
65ml (2½fl oz) hot water
60g (2oz) cocoa powder, plus extra for dusting
1 tsp vanilla extract
1 tbsp Frangelico or Amaretto liqueur
260g (9¼oz) light muscovado sugar
4 eggs, separated
150g (5½oz) ground hazelnuts, plus 1 tbsp to decorate
a pinch of well-crushed Maldon sea salt

For the sweet mascarpone:

30g (1¼oz) icing sugar, sifted
200g (7oz) mascarpone

Paul A. Young is a groundbreaking and inspirational chocolatier, based in London, UK, who is at the forefront of the British chocolate scene. Paul's passion for his craft and his cutting-edge creativity have led to him being ranked among the world's best chocolatiers. Paul and I worked together at The Criterion Restaurant in the mid-1990s. We have remained friends ever since and I am thrilled to be including one of his recipes in this book.

The Torta Gianduja is a flourless chocolate and hazelnut cake from Piedmont, Italy. Of this cake, Paul says 'I have few words to say how intensely enjoyable this cake is. It's something of a noble cake; it delivers texture, intensity, indulgence and refinement. You'll work up a sweat if making entirely by hand, as I still do, but your reward is that there will be none left over.'

1 Preheat the oven to 160°C/310°F/gas mark 2½, and line a 21cm (8in) round cake tin with baking parchment.
2 Melt the butter with the chocolate in a bowl over a pan of simmering water on a low heat stirring constantly.
3 Pour the hot water into a bowl with the cocoa powder and whisk until there are no lumps. Then add the vanilla and the liqueur.
4 Add the cocoa mixture to the chocolate and butter mixture off the heat and stir well to form a smooth paste or batter.

5 In a separate bowl, whisk the sugar with the egg yolks until thick and light in colour then pour in the chocolate mixture, add the ground hazelnuts and fold well until fully mixed.
6 In a clean, dry bowl, beat the egg whites with a pinch of salt until you have soft peaks. Take care not to over-whisk.
7 Gently fold the egg whites through the chocolate mixture using a large metal spoon.
8 Pour the batter into the prepared cake tin and bake for 40–45 minutes, or until the edges are firm and the surface is slightly cracked and feels soft in the middle. It should 'shimmer' slightly and have a delicate wobble.
9 Remove from the oven and allow to cool completely in the tin. This cake sinks and cracks slightly when cool to form a rich buttery melting centre. Strip off the baking parchment.
10 Mix the icing sugar into the mascarpone and set aside in a bowl.
11 Dust the top of the torta with some cocoa powder (over two-thirds) and with 1 tablespoon of ground hazelnuts (one-third).
12 Serve with a large dollop of the sweet mascarpone on the side.

LOAVES
& POUND
CAKES

Marble Bundt Cake

Serves 6

85g (3oz) butter, softened
60g (2oz) caster sugar
3 eggs
130g (4½oz) plain flour
1 tsp baking powder
20ml (⅔fl oz) full-fat milk
10g (¼oz) cocoa powder
a few drops vanilla extract
icing sugar, to dust

I first learnt to make this Marble Cake when I worked at the restaurant Le Gavroche, in London, in the late 1980s for Albert Roux. I have been using this recipe ever since and it never fails to delight. I like to use a Bundt tin to give it a distinctive shape.

1 Preheat the oven to 170°C/325°F/gas mark 3, and grease a 17cm x 9cm (6½in x 3½in) Bundt tin well.
2 Cream the butter and sugar together until light and fluffy, and add the eggs one at a time.
3 Sift the flour and baking powder and fold into the creamed mixture. Divide the mixture in half.
4 Make a paste with the milk and cocoa powder and add to one half of the mix. Add the vanilla extract to the other mix.
5 Fill two piping bags with the different mixtures and pipe alternating layers into the prepared Bundt tin.
6 Bake in a preheated oven for 45 minutes or until a cocktail stick inserted into the centre comes out clean.
7 Remove from the oven, allow to cool for 10 minutes in the tin and then turn out onto a wire rack.
8 Dust with icing sugar and serve.

Espresso Marble Cake

Serves 6–8

345ml (11⅔fl oz) double
    cream
80ml (3fl oz) full-fat milk
2 tsp instant coffee
425g (15oz) plain flour
1 tsp bicarbonate of soda
120g (4oz) butter, softened
360g (12½oz) icing sugar
5 eggs
25g (1oz) cocoa powder
50g (1¾oz) dark brown sugar

For the espresso glaze:
100g (3½oz) chocolate chips
50ml (2fl oz) sweet wine, such
    as Muscat
10g (¼oz) instant coffee
    granules

I've given this delightful variation of a marble cake an extra twist to give a rich and luxurious flavour.

1 Preheat the oven to 170°C/325°F/gas mark 3, and grease and line a 21cm x 12cm x 8cm (8in x 4½in x 3¼in) loaf tin with baking parchment.
2 Pour the cream, milk and coffee into a bowl.
3 Sift the flour and bicarbonate of soda into a separate bowl.
4 Cream the butter and sugar together until light and fluffy, and add the eggs one at a time.
5 Add one-third of the liquid and one-third of the dry ingredients to the egg mixture gradually until well mixed. Continue to add in two more batches until all the mixture is used.
6 Mix one-third of the cake mixture with the cocoa and brown sugar and fill a piping bag. Put the rest of the mixture in another piping bag with a No. 6 nozzle.
7 Starting with the light-coloured mixture, pipe layers alternately into the prepared loaf tin.
8 Bake in the preheated oven for 50–55 minutes or until a cocktail stick inserted into the centre comes out clean.
9 Remove from the oven, allow to cool for 10 minutes in the tin and then turn out onto a wire rack and strip off the baking parchment.
10 Meanwhile, make the glaze. Place the chocolate chips and sweet wine in a pan and melt over a low heat, then add the coffee granules. Stir until everything is dissolved and then trickle over the cooled cake before serving with a glass of dessert wine.

MARBLE BUNDT CAKE

MARBLE BUNDT CAKE

MARBLE BUNDT CAKE

ESPRESSO MARBLE CAKE

VARIATIONS

BLUEBERRY SOUR CREAM CAKE Add 50g (1¾oz) of blueberries at the last stage and gently mix in. If using frozen blueberries roll them in a little flour first, which prevents the colour from bleeding into the cake.

COFFEE SOUR CREAM CAKE Mix 10g (¼oz) of instant coffee granules with just enough hot water to become liquid and stir in to the batter at the final stage before turning into the tin.

APPLE SOUR CREAM CAKE Add uncooked 3 medium-sized apples, cubed quite small, to the batter at the final stage before turning into the tin.

American Sour Cream Cake

Serves 6–8

160g (5¾oz) butter, softened
225g (8oz) caster sugar
4 large egg yolks
160g (5¾oz) soured cream
1 tsp vanilla extract
225g (8oz) plain flour, sifted
½ tsp salt
½ tsp baking powder
¼ tsp bicarbonate of soda
icing sugar, to dust

This popular cake is oh-so easy to make and as the soured cream replaces some of the traditional butter content the texture is super-light and fluffy. You'll mostly find what we commonly call sour cream with the label 'soured cream' in supermarkets and groceries. Distinct from crème fraîche, this cream gives a rich tanginess that other creams fail to give.

1 Preheat the oven to 170°C/325°F/gas mark 3, and grease and line a 18cm x 8cm x 8cm (7in x 3¼in x 3¼in) loaf tin with baking parchment.
2 Cream the butter and sugar together until light and fluffy, and add the egg yolks one at a time. Mix in well.
3 Add one-third of the soured cream along with the vanilla extract and half of the sifted flour. Mix well before adding the rest of the soured cream, the remaining flour, along with the salt, baking powder and bicarbonate of soda. Mix again, scraping down the sides before turning into the prepared loaf tin.

4 Bake for approximately 1 hour or until a cocktail stick inserted into the centre comes out clean.
5 Remove from the oven, allow to cool for 10 minutes in the tin and then turn out onto a wire rack. Strip off the baking parchment.
6 Dust with icing sugar and serve this cake any time of day with a cup of coffee or tea.

Banana Loaf

Serves 8

2 really ripe bananas
150g (5½oz) butter
225g (8oz) caster sugar
50g (1¾oz) ground hazelnuts
2 eggs
175g (6¼oz) plain flour
1 tsp salt
1 tsp bicarbonate of soda
1 tsp baking powder
130g (4½oz) soured cream
100ml (3½fl oz) Apricot Glaze,
    see page 298

Back in the mid-1800s, bananas from the Caribbean were seen as a rare and exotic fruit, coming all the way to the UK and Europe across the Atlantic Ocean in what came to be known as 'banana boats'. In the 20th century, though (with brief respites for the World Wars), bananas became a weekly feature of everyone's food bowls and they started appearing in all sorts of baking recipes. For the tastiest banana loaf – some call it banana bread – use the ripest bananas you have; the skins should be really freckly or even black.

1 Preheat the oven to 170°C/325°F/gas mark 3, and grease and line a 18cm x 8cm x 8cm (7in x 3¼in x 3¼in) loaf tin with baking parchment.
2 Purée (or mash until smooth) one banana.
3 In a mixing bowl, cream the butter and sugar together until light and fluffy. Add the ground hazelnuts, followed by the eggs.
4 Sift the flour, salt, bicarbonate of soda and baking powder into the mixture and mix together well. Mix in the soured cream, followed by the banana purée.
5 Pour the mixture into the prepared tin and bake for 10 minutes before removing from the oven and adding the remaining banana, sliced lengthways, in a line along the length of the loaf (this prevents the banana from sinking).
6 Return to the oven for 45–50 minutes or until a cocktail stick inserted into the centre comes out clean.
7 Remove from the oven, allow to cool for 20 minutes in the tin and then turn out onto a wire rack and strip off the baking parchment.
8 Make the glaze as on page 299 and brush all over the cooled cake. Enjoy a slice with tea.

VARIATION
I like to add 3 tablespoons of Malibu to the finished mixture for a wonderful flavour kick.

Mark Hix's Oyster Ale Cake

Serves 8–10

60g (2oz) sultanas
450g (1lb) self-raising flour, sifted
a good pinch of salt
a good pinch of freshly grated nutmeg
a good pinch of mixed spice
a good pinch of ground cinnamon
225g (8oz) molasses sugar
225g (8oz) butter, cold, cubed
finely grated zest of 2 oranges
finely grated zest of 1 lemon
1 large egg, beaten
200ml (7fl oz) Hix Oyster Ale (or a stout or porter ale)
icing sugar, to dust

Celebrated chef, restaurateur and food writer Mark Hix is known for his original take on British gastronomy. He opened his first restaurant in 2008 – the distinguished Hix Oyster & Chop House in Smithfield, London – and has since opened a further five establishments including Hix Oyster & Fish House in Lyme Regis, Dorset, the award-winning Mark's bar and the latest Tramshed all to great critical acclaim. I have known Mark for many years and have always respected and admired his commitment to British cooking.

Of this cake, Mark says 'This is a nice rich teatime cake but you could also serve it as a dessert. If you can't find my dark Oyster Ale you could use a stout or a porter ale instead'.

1 Put the sultanas in a large bowl, pour on enough boiling water to cover and leave to soak overnight.
2 The next day when you're ready to bake, preheat the oven to 160°C/310°F/gas mark 2½, and grease and line a 21cm x 10cm (8in x 4in) loaf tin with baking parchment.
3 Drain the sultanas. Sift the flour, salt and spices together into a bowl and stir in the sugar, then rub in the butter with your fingertips until the mixture resembles breadcrumbs.

4 Stir in the orange and lemon zests, then gently mix in the egg, sultanas and ale.
5 Transfer the mixture to the prepared tin, spreading it out evenly.
6 Bake in a preheated oven for 1½–1¾ hours or until golden and firm to the touch. To test, insert the point of a cocktail stick in the centre; it should come out clean.
7 Remove from the oven, allow to cool for 5 minutes or so in the tin and then turn out onto a wire rack. Leave to cool, strip off the baking parchment and dust with icing sugar before serving.

Pandan Kaya

Serves 8–10

For the sponge:
6 eggs
150g (5½oz) caster sugar
2 tsp yellow food colouring
120g (4oz) plain flour, sifted
25g (1oz) cornflour
60g (2oz) butter
65ml (2½fl oz) coconut milk

For the topping:
100ml (3½fl oz) Pandan juice
 (see step 8)
400ml (13½fl oz) coconut milk
½ tsp green food colouring
 (optional, add if you aren't
 using Pandan juice)
120ml (4fl oz) water
110g (3¾oz) caster sugar
a pinch of salt
110g (3¾oz) butter
100ml (3½fl oz) evaporated
 milk
½ tsp agar agar powder
 (available from health food
 shops)
12g (⅓oz) cornflour
2 eggs

In every Chinatown throughout the world you will find bakeries with windows full of baked goods made with Pandan leaf extract – easily spotted by their exuberant green colour. The Pandan tree is a tropical plant and its leaves are used throughout Southeast Asia to add a sweet taste and aroma to dishes. This cake, popular in Singapore, tastes great and its vibrant green colour is from Pandan juice. If you can't get the juice, just use food colouring.

1 Preheat the oven to 170°C/325°F/gas mark 3, and line three 21cm (8in) round cake tins with baking parchment.
2 To make the sponge, beat the eggs and the sugar together until light and fluffy.
3 Add in the food colouring until desired golden yellow colour is reached.
4 Fold in the sifted flour and cornflour.
5 Melt the butter and coconut milk together and add and mix until well combined.
6 Divide into the prepared tins and bake in a preheated oven for 15 minutes or until it springs back when lightly pressed with fingers.
7 Remove from the oven, cool for 10 minutes in the tin and then turn out onto a wire rack.
8 Meanwhile, make the topping. To make 100ml (3½fl oz) of Pandan juice, blitz eight chopped Pandan leaves with 120ml (4fl oz) water and sieve. Then, in a large pan, put the Pandan juice, coconut milk, food colouring (if needed), water, sugar, salt, butter and half of

the evaporated milk and bring to the boil.
9 Sift the agar agar and cornflour together and make it into a paste with the remainder of the evaporated milk. Add this paste to the eggs and whisk well.
10 Pour the boiling milk mixture onto the eggs and whisk again. Put the mixture back in the pan and heat until it thickens. Take off the heat and allow to cool slightly.
11 To assemble, use scissors to trim the edges of the sponges and neaten the tops of the sponges.
12 Strip off the parchment and lay one sponge in the bottom of a 21cm (8in) loose-bottomed cake tin and pour one-third of the topping mixture onto the sponge. Leave for 2 minutes then repeat with the other sponges, layering them up. The topping will fill the sides of the tin and cover the top of the cake.
13 Place in the fridge to set for about 2 hours.
14 Remove from the tin before serving with fresh tropical fruit.

Where to Eat Cake...
SINGAPORE

With so many different cultures coming together in one of the world's great trading centres, the choices for indulging in cake are endless. With everything from Chinese pastries to French fancies to Japanese shortcake on offer, you will need an extended trip to sample them all.

TIONG BAHRU BAKERY
56 Eng Hoon St (and branches), #01-70, Singapore 160056
www.tiongbahrubakery.com
Opened in collaboration with celebrity baker, Gontran Cherrier, offering a huge range of bread, pastries and desserts.

CARPENTER AND COOK
19 Lorong Kilat #01-06, Singapore 598120
www.carpenterandcook.com
A vintage café with fab tarts and cakes – dessert-lovers will be spoilt for choice.

CANELÉ PÂTISSERIE
350 Orchard Road, Shaw House #05-21 (and other branches), Singapore 238868
www.canele.com.sg
One of the best places in Singapore to eat cake – the Matcha cake is a must-try for lovers of green tea.

MARMALADE PANTRY
2 Orchard Turn, #03-22, Singapore 238801
www.themarmaladepantry.com.sg
Come for a fantastic afternoon tea.

ANTOINETTE
30 Penhas Road (off Lavender Street) Singapore 208188
www.antoinette.com.sg
With interiors reminiscent of a Parisian boudoir, this pâtisserie and salon du thé serves the best French vienoisserie.

BAKER & COOK
77 Hillcrest Road, 288951 Singapore
www.bakerandcook.biz
Here, you'll encounter a wide selection of breads, cakes and pastries influenced by many cultures from all across the globe.

B BAKERY
15 Bussorah St, Singapore 199436
A charming little bakery with an eclectic selection of savoury dishes as well as cakes, in the heart of the Arab street area.

FLOR PÂTISSERIE
2 Duxton Hill #01-01, Singapore 089588
www.cakeflor.com.sg
This Japanese-styled pâtisserie serves authentic Japanese-inspired French pastries; dine in or take away.

PLAIN VANILLA BAKERY
34A Lorong Mambong, Singapore 277691
www.plainvanillabakery.com
The best cupcakes in Singapore; favourites include Red Velvet, Cookies and Cream and Early Grey Lavender. Which to try?

PÂTISSERIE GLACÉ
12 Gopeng Street, #01-33/34 Icon Village, Singapore 078877
www.cakeglace.com
Offers a taste of Japan – from strawberry shortcake to mont blanc and chiffon cake.

OBOLO PÂTISSERIE
112 East Coast Road #B1-11/29 112 KATONG, Singapore 428802
www.obolo.com.sg
These artisans of cakes and pastries bake their award-winning cheesecakes and macarons on a daily basis.

LOOLA'S BY AWFULLY CHOCOLATE
8 Raffles Avenue #02-14, Singapore 039802
www.loolas.sg
If you're in the mood for chocolate, then Loola's fits the bill. Wonderful chocolate mille crêpe, hazel crumble, brownie, cupcake, chocolate tart and churros.

PIQUE NIQUE
391A Orchard Road #B1-01/02, Takashimaya Shopping Centre, Ngee Ann City Tower A, Singapore 238873
www.piquenique.com.sg
Fancy a Whoopie Pie? Head to this café; then try making your own (see page 186).

TAMPOPO DELI
177 River Valley Road, #B1-16 Liang Court, Singapore 179030
No website
Come for the best cream puff in Singapore. This Japanese bakery also bakes a very good chiffon cake, which is available in cheese, matcha and coffee flavours.

Ginger Cake

Serves 10

200g (7oz) butter
180g (6½oz) dark brown sugar
2 tbsp golden syrup
2 eggs
150ml (5fl oz) full-fat milk
300g (10½oz) self-raising flour
2 tsp ground ginger
½ tsp salt
75g (2¾oz) crystallised
    ginger, roughly chopped

For the syrup:

150ml (5fl oz) ginger wine
50g (1¾oz) caster sugar

If you like your ginger cakes super-charged, then this is the recipe for you. This classic ginger cake has a big hit of ginger with the addition of a gingery wine syrup. So, prepare your taste buds.

1 Preheat the oven to 170°C/325°F/gas mark 3, and grease and line a 18cm x 8cm x 8cm (7in x 3¼in x 3¼in) loaf tin with baking parchment.
2 Place the butter, sugar and golden syrup in a largish pan and heat until it is all melted.
3 Beat the eggs into the milk and then add this to the melted mixture.
4 Sift the flour, ginger and salt together in a bowl and then add the crystallised ginger before pouring this into the egg and milk mixture and combining gently.

5 Pour into the prepared tin and bake in a preheated oven for 1 hour.
6 Remove from the oven, cool for 10 minutes in the tin and then turn out onto a wire rack. Remove the baking parchment.
7 Make the ginger wine syrup. Bring the alcohol and sugar to the boil and continue boiling until a syrup forms. Pass the liquid through a sieve. Remove from the heat and leave to cool.
8 While the cake's still warm, glaze with the ginger wine syrup for an extra whack of gingeryness.
9 Serve with a big dollop of crème fraîche alongside and enjoy!

Pain d'Epices

Serves 6–8

200g (7oz) honey
120ml (4fl oz) full-fat milk
50g (1¾oz) caster sugar
3 eggs
finely grated zest of ½ orange
finely grated zest of ½ lemon
2 tsp vanilla extract
100g (3½oz) rye flour
100g (3½oz) plain flour
2 tsp baking powder
2 tsp mixed ground spice
2 tsp ground ginger

This classic French spiced bread has a beautifully delicate taste and is great to serve all year round, not just at Christmas. Many different areas in France – such as Reims, Dijon and Alsace – have their own subtly different recipes and historically this cake was left to ferment (the honey helped it do that), which made it rise, before baking; though these days we don't have to wait as we simply add a little baking powder.

1 Preheat the oven to 160°C/310°F/gas mark 2, and grease and line a 18cm x 8cm x 8cm (7in x 3¼in x 3¼in) loaf tin with baking parchment. Use a good-quality tin that is lined very well, as the mixture is very liquid and may leak!
2 Melt the honey in the milk in a pan.
3 In a bowl, cream the sugar and eggs together until light and fluffy, and add the zests and vanilla extract.

4 In another bowl, sift all the dry ingredients together.
5 Now, fold all three mixtures together, and pour into the loaf tin and bake in a preheated oven for 20 minutes. Then, turn down to 150°C/300°F/gas mark 2 for a further 45 minutes.
6 Allow to cool completely before removing from the tin. Strip off the baking parchment.
7 Serve with coffee.

Lemon Drizzle

Serves 8

3 eggs
225g (8oz) caster sugar
a pinch of salt
180g (6½oz) plain flour, sifted
1 tsp baking powder
75g (2¾oz) butter, melted
100ml (3½fl oz) double cream
finely grated zest of 3 lemons

For the lemon drizzle:
100ml (3½fl oz) water
75g (2¾oz) caster sugar
juice of 2 of the lemons used
    for their zest

VARIATIONS

ORANGE OR LIME
Replace the lemon with
the same quantity of
orange or lime for great
results but a slightly
different citrus tang.

This is my version of a French cake called a Gâteau Weekend – so named because it is eaten at the weekends and stays fresh all weekend. I was taught to bake this gem of a cake in Paris more than 20 years ago. Delicately fragranced with lemon zest, it has won many hearts along the way. It has also become Marco Pierre White's favourite teatime treat.

1 Preheat the oven to 160°C/310°F/gas mark 2½, and grease a 18cm x 8cm x 8cm (7in x 3¼in x 3¼in) loaf tin.
2 In a mixing bowl, beat the eggs and slowly add the sugar, salt, flour and baking powder. Add the melted butter to the mixture then pour in the cream and the lemon zest.
3 Pour the mixture into the prepared tin and bake in a preheated oven for about 45 minutes. To test the cake is cooked, gently insert a cocktail stick into the centre – it should come out clean.

4 While the cake is baking, make the lemon drizzle by boiling the water, sugar and lemon juice together for about 10 minutes, then remove from the heat and set aside.
5 Remove the cake from the oven and immediately brush plenty of the lemon drizzle on to the cake. As well as putting a nice shine on the cake, the drizzle is absorbed into the cake, keeping it lovely and moist.Leave the cake to cool in the tin for 15 minutes and then turn out onto a wire rack.
6 Serve as Marco does with a nice cuppa.

Sobaos Pasiegos

Makes 2 loaves/
Serves 12

300g (10½oz) butter, melted
300g (10½oz) caster sugar
a pinch of salt
3 tsp of dark rum
finely grated zest of 2 lemons
6 eggs, separated
360g (12½oz) plain flour, sifted
1½ tsp baking powder

These little traditional sponges come from the Pasiegos Valleys in the Cantabrian region of Spain and are typically eaten for breakfast or for a snack. The cakes themselves are rich and fluffy and are often baked and sold in individual rectangular paper moulds. I have used loaf tins here instead and they can be made as smaller versions in muffin cases as well. The inclusion of rum gives an extra hit of flavour.

1 Preheat the oven to 180°C/350°F/gas mark 4, and grease and line two 19cm x 9cm x 5cm (7½in x 3½in x 2in) loaf tins with baking parchment.
2 Beat together the butter, sugar, salt, rum and lemon zest until light and creamy.
3 Add the egg yolks and beat well.
4 In a separate bowl, beat the egg whites until stiff then mix half into the buttery mixture.
5 Fold in the sifted flour and baking powder, followed by the rest of the beaten egg whites

and mix until well combined.
6 Spoon the mixture into the loaf tins, filling three-quarters full only as the mixture rises quite a bit, and bake in a preheated oven for 15 minutes or until golden.
7 Remove from the oven, allow to cool for 10 minutes in the tin and then turn out onto a wire rack and strip off the baking parchment.
8 Serve as a midday snack with a café con leche (milky coffee).

SOBAOS PASIEGOS

SOBAOS PASIEGOS

Loaves & Pound Cakes **73**

Green Tea Pound Cake

Serves 10

375g (13oz) plain flour
1 tsp baking powder
2 tbsp Matcha (green tea powder)
275g (9¾oz) butter, softened
275g (9¾oz) caster sugar
4 eggs, beaten

In Japan, green tea is traditionally served with the dessert course, which used to be fruit, though in recent years the Japanese have certainly discovered cake and Western pastries in a big way. In this East meets West cake, the subtle flavour of the green tea infuses a Western pound cake – with fabulous and colourful results.

1 Preheat the oven to 170°C/325°F/gas mark 3, and grease and line a 25cm long x 8cm x 8cm (10in x 3¼in x 3¼in) deep loaf tin with baking parchment.
2 Sift the flour, baking powder and Matcha powder together into a bowl.
3 Cream the butter and sugar together until light and fluffy, and then slowly add the eggs, mixing in a little flour halfway through.

4 Add the rest of the flour mixture and mix together until fully combined.
5 Turn into the prepared tin and bake in the preheated oven for 30–35 minutes. Allow to cool for 10 minutes in the tin and then turn out onto a wire rack. Strip off the baking parchment.
6 Serve with green tea or any other delicately flavoured tea.

Greek Coconut Cake

Serves 12

250g (9oz) butter, softened
465g (1lb½oz) caster sugar
9 eggs, beaten
350g (12oz) desiccated
    coconut
320g (11¼oz) self-raising flour,
    sifted

For the syrup:
275g (9¾oz) caster sugar
300ml (10fl oz) water
juice and finely grated zest of
    ½ lemon

For the topping:
160g (5¾oz) soft brown sugar
240ml (8fl oz) double cream
160g (5¾oz) flaked or
    shredded coconut

Despite coconuts not being native to Greece, Coconut Cake is a traditional Greek sweet often known as Revani and usually contains semolina; it is similar to Turkish Basbousa (see page 130). This cake has a wonderful citrus syrup perfectly matched with the crunchy coconut topping.

1 Preheat the oven to 150°C/300°F/gas mark 2, and grease and line a 23cm (9in) round cake tin with baking parchment.

2 Cream the butter and sugar together until light and fluffy.

3 Add in the beaten eggs, coconut and sifted flour in several batches, taking care to scrape down the bowl after each addition to make sure the mixture doesn't curdle.

4 Spoon the mixture into the prepared cake tin and bake in a preheated oven for 1½–2 hours or until a cocktail stick inserted into the centre comes out clean.

5 Meanwhile, make the syrup. Put all the ingredients in a pan and bring to the boil ensuring all the sugar is dissolved. Allow to cool and set aside.

6 To make the coconut topping, put the brown sugar and cream in a pan and boil until the sugar has dissolved. Remove from the heat and stir in the coconut; but you'll need to use this while it's still warm.

7 Remove the cake from the oven, allow to cool for a good 30 minutes before pricking tiny holes in the top of it and pouring over the syrup.

8 Immediately spread the coconut topping evenly over the top.

9 Turn up the oven to 190°C/375°F/gas mark 5 and bake until the cake's topping is golden brown, about 5 minutes.

10 Remove from the oven, allow to cool for 10 minutes in the tin and then turn out onto a wire rack. Strip off the baking parchment.

11 Serve with a small, strong coffee.

Lucas Glanville's Sticky Date Cake with Caramel Sea Salt Sauce

Serves 6

180g (6½oz) stoned dates
250ml (8½fl oz) water
1 tsp bicarbonate of soda
180g (6½oz) caster sugar
180g (6½oz) self-raising flour
2 eggs
60g (2oz) butter
50ml (2fl oz) extra virgin olive
     oil
1 vanilla pod or ½ tsp
     vanilla extract

For the caramel sea salt sauce:

150g (5½oz) brown sugar
150ml (5fl oz) double cream
100g (3½oz) butter
10g (¼oz) Maldon sea salt
1 vanilla pod or ½ tsp
     vanilla extract

In 2011, I was fortunate enough to be invited to attend the World Gourmet Summit with Marco Pierre White in Singapore, and while there I met Lucas Glanville, the Executive Chef of The Grand Hyatt in Singapore. Lucas is an Australian national and, following training in England and a stint at Le Gavroche in London, he returned to Australia to run Browns Restaurant in Melbourne. In 2002 he moved to Asia and has since headed up restaurants in both Bangkok and Singapore.

When I told him I was writing a book on the best cakes from around the world, he kindly sent me his favourite one for inclusion. Here it is.

1 Preheat the oven to 180°C/350°F/gas mark 4, and grease a 21cm (8in) round cake tin (but not a loose-bottomed one as it needs to be watertight).
2 In a pan, cook the dates in the water until they are the consistency of jam. Add the bicarbonate of soda and mix well.
3 Then add all of the remaining ingredients and mix to the consistency of a batter.
4 Pour the mixture into the prepared tin and place in a water bath (I used a high-sided roasting tin, filled with boiling water until it's at least halfway up the sides of the tin) in the preheated oven for 25 minutes or until firm to touch in the middle.
5 Meanwhile, make the sauce. Place all the ingredients in a pan and gently bring to the boil for 5 minutes. Set aside.
6 Remove the cake from the oven and allow to cool in the tin then turn out onto a wire rack.
7 Serve the cake warm or at room temperature with the sauce poured over the top.

Pistachio and Lemon Cake

Serves 8

For the sugar syrup:
100g (3½oz) caster sugar
100ml (3½fl oz) water

For the cake:
1 lemon, sliced
1 lime, sliced
120g (4oz) butter, softened
175g (6¼oz)caster sugar
3 eggs, lightly beaten
120g (4oz) plain flour
a pinch of salt
½ tsp baking powder
120g (4oz) good-quality
 pistachios, chopped
juice and finely grated zest
 of 1 lemon
finely grated zest of 1 lime

Pistachios and lemons both grow plentifully in Turkey and the Middle East and it is a common combination in the cuisine of that region. I have created a recipe here to combine these two stunning flavours. The result is a delightfully tangy teatime treat with fantastic flavour.

1 Preheat the oven to 160°C/310°F/gas mark 2½, and grease and line a 16cm x 6cm deep (6¼in x 2½in) round cake tin with baking parchment.
2 Make the sugar syrup by heating the ingredients in a pan. Cook over a low heat until clear, stirring continuously, then boil for a minute or so. Pass the liquid through a sieve. Remove from the heat and leave to cool.
3 Place the lemon and lime slices and the sugar syrup in a pan and gently simmer for 10 minutes. Drain and leave to cool.
4 Cream the butter and sugar together until light and fluffy, and add the eggs one at a time.
5 Sift in the flour, salt and baking powder, then add two-thirds of the pistachios, the lemon and lime zests and the lemon juice. Mix well.
6 Pour the mixture into the prepared cake tin, place the fruit slices on top and sprinkle over the remaining pistachios. Bake in a preheated oven for 40 minutes or until a cocktail stick inserted into the centre comes out clean.
7 Remove from the oven, allow to cool for 15 minutes in the tin and then turn out onto a wire rack and strip off the parchment.
8 Serve with a glass of aromatic Turkish tea.

Plum Madeira

Serves 8

200g (7oz) plums
100g (3½oz) butter, softened
100g (3½oz) icing sugar
2 eggs, lightly beaten
120g (4oz) self-raising flour
½ tsp baking powder
50g (1¾oz) oatmeal
½ tbsp Madeira
finely grated zest of 1 orange
  and 4 tbsp of juice

The Madeira is a classic English sponge that is also a fantastic all-round loaf cake and is slightly denser than a Genoise (see page 26). When it was first baked in the 18th or 19th centuries, it was traditionally served with a glass of Madeira, hence its name. But as you'll see below, I like to include the Madeira in the cake, rather than with it, for added flavour. This cake works wonderfully well as a dessert, too, with a generous dollop of crème fraîche or custard.

1 Preheat the oven to 160°C/310°F/gas mark 2½, and grease and line a 16cm round x 6cm deep (6¼in x 2½in) cake tin with baking parchment.
2 Cut the plums into quarters, removing the stones.
3 Cream the butter and sugar together until light and fluffy, and add the eggs one at a time.
4 Sift the flour and baking powder together into a bowl, add the oatmeal, Madeira, orange zest and juice, and fold into the butter mix.

5 Pour the mixture into the prepared cake tin and stud with the plum quarters along the top.
6 Bake in a preheated oven for 40 minutes or until a cocktail stick inserted into the centre comes out clean.
7 Remove from the oven, allow to cool for 15 minutes in the tin and then turn out onto a wire rack and strip off the parchment.

VARIATIONS

PEACH MADEIRA Replace the plums with 200g (7oz) peaches.

APRICOT MADEIRA Replace the plums with 200g (7oz) apricots.

PLAIN MADEIRA Leave out the plums for a classic Madeira sponge.

Jewish Honey Cake

Serves 8

150g (5½oz) brown sugar
1 egg
280ml (9½fl oz) cold tea
(using 2 teabags)
150ml (5fl oz) vegetable oil
180g (6½oz) honey
330g (11½oz) self-raising
flour
½ tsp mixed spice
½ tsp ground ginger
½ tsp ground cinnamon
1 tsp bicarbonate of soda

This cake works best when it is made a few days before being served, as the sweet honey flavours develop over time. Traditionally this cake is served at Jewish New Year – Rosh Hashanah – a time to reflect on the past and look forward to the future. Honey has played a significant role in this celebration for a long time and symbolises hopes for a sweet year ahead.

1 Preheat the oven to 160°C/310°F/gas mark 2½, and grease and line a 21cm (8in) round cake tin with baking parchment.
2 Combine the sugar, egg, tea, oil and honey well in one bowl.
3 In a separate bowl, sift the dry ingredients and then mix everything together.
4 Pour the cake batter into the prepared cake tin and bake for 1 hour or until a cocktail stick inserted into the centre comes out clean.

5 Remove from the oven, allow to cool for 10 minutes in the tin and then turn out onto a wire rack. Strip off the baking parchment.
6 Enjoy this cake at teatime or after dinner as a tasty dessert.

Olive Oil Cake with Fresh Peaches

Serves 6

3 eggs
2 tbsp finely grated orange
  zest
275g (9¾oz) caster sugar
120ml (4fl oz) olive oil
80ml (3fl oz) full-fat milk
150g (5½oz) plain flour, sifted
150g (5½oz) self-raising flour,
  sifted
2 peaches, sliced
85g (3oz) apricot jam, warmed
  and strained

Olive oil has been used in cooking and baking for centuries in the countries bordering the Mediterranean Sea. Using oil rather than butter gives this cake a lovely light texture with a subtle flavour, as well as cutting back on its cholesterol content. It's positively healthy.

1 Preheat the oven to 180°C/350°F/gas mark 4, and grease a deep 18cm (7in) round springform cake tin well.
2 Beat together the eggs, orange zest and sugar really well.
3 Add in the oil and the milk, alternating these wet ingredients with the sifted flours until everything is well combined.
4 Spoon the mixture into the prepared tin and bake in a preheated oven for 10 minutes.
5 Carefully remove the cake from the oven and if a crust has formed make several cuts at even intervals on the surface of the cake and place the sliced peaches in the cuts.
6 Return the cake to the oven and bake for 40 minutes.
7 Remove from the oven, allow to cool for 10 minutes in the tin and then turn out onto a wire rack.
8 While the cake's still warm, brush liberally with the warmed jam for a glossy finish.
9 Serve a generous slice with a small glass of grappa or vin santo.

Where to Eat Cake...
STOCKHOLM & COPENHAGEN

As desserts are not typically served in Scandinavia, cakes and pastries have become everyday treats to be served up as an essential part of 'fika' or coffee breaks. This is reflected in the number of wonderful bakeries in these two cities.

STOCKHOLM

ROSENDALS TRÄDGÅRD CAFÉ
Rosendalsterrassen 12, Stockholm
www.rosendalstradgard.se
This café, housed in an old greenhouse in the elegant botanical gardens, serves up home-made heavenly cakes and pastries made from produce sourced organically and from its own gardens.

ELVERKET
Linnégatan 69, Stockholm
www.brasserieelverket.se
Slick and cosy, Elverket sits within an old electricity plant. Try out the Scandi staples, Asian extras and wickedly good chocolate brownies. Also does a lazy weekend brunch.

CAFÉ LILLAVI
Folkungagatan 73, Stockholm
No website
Quirky café, set in a sidewalk kiosk, this cute-as-a-button café is run by two chatty friends. Choose a table (there are two) and tackle the devilish chocolate cake.

CONDITORIET LA GLACE
Skoubogade 3, 1158 Copenhagen
www.laglace.dk
This is the Danish equivalent to the Parisian Ladurée (see page 160). The interiors transport you to a bygone age and the cakes are delicious.

CAFÉ SATURNUS
Eriksbergsgatan 6, Stockholm
www.cafesaturnus.se
Try out the biggest and the best cinnamon bun or kanelbulle (see page 200) the city has to offer. And Saturnus does a great line in 'proper' coffee, too, to sample alongside.

LUX DESSERT OCH CHOKLAD
Patentgatan 7, Stockholm
www.dessertochchokladstockholm.com
Run by the little brother to Lux Stockholm, this is the haute pâtisserie of the celebrated confectioner Ted Johansson. Renowned for 'semla' – a cardamom bun, hollowed out and filled with sweet almond paste, and topped with fresh whipped cream – served during Lent.

COPENHAGEN

STRANGAS DESSERT BOUTIQUE
Åboulevard 7, 1635 Copenhagen V
www.strangas.dk
Here, cakes are decorated individually as works of art. Although you can't eat in, enjoy taking away a box of Macarons in a rainbow of delicate pastel shades.

KONDITORI ANTOINETTE
Østergade 24 b2, 1100 Copenhagen
www.konditori-antoinette.dk
Enjoy the elegant 'Rococo' rooms and idyllic backyard while sampling the excellent pastries and cakes at Antoinette.

SANKT PEDERS BAGERI
Sankt Peders Stræde 29, 1454 Copenhagen
No website
Wednesday is the day to visit one of the city's oldest bakeries, famous for its 'onsdagssnegle' (Wednesday snails). It sells over 4000 every Wednesday.

SUMMERBIRD
Kronprinsensgade 11, Indre By, Copenhagen
www.summerbird.com
The cream buns, or 'flødeboller' are the reason for your visit here. That said, it's not a bun and there's no cream. This luxurious treat is a Danish biscuit topped with meringue and coated in chocolate.

A C PERCH TEAROOM
Kronprinsensgade 5, Indre By, 1114 Copenhagen
www.perchs.dk
It's not unusual to see huge queues form outside on a weekend. This is a reflection of both the quality of the tea and the selection of incredible cakes and desserts.

LA GALETTE
Larsbjørnsstraede 9, Copenhagen K 1454
www.lagalette.dk
Discover the best sweet pancakes in this courtyard café in the city's Latin quarter.

Sandkaka

Serves 10

25g (1oz) butter, softened
2 tbsp Panko breadcrumbs,
  slightly blended
225g (8oz) butter
225g (8oz) caster sugar
225g (8oz) self-raising flour,
  sifted
1 tsp baking powder
4 eggs, lightly beaten
2 tbsp brandy
icing sugar, to dust

This recipe is Swedish in origin although there is a similar Sandkake from Denmark but it usually doesn't include the brandy. The 'sand' in the title refers to the crunchy breadcrumb coating of the cake. I prefer to use the Japanese breadcrumbs (Panko) because they have a finer, lighter texture.

1 Preheat the oven to 180°C/350°F/gas mark 4.
2 Use the softened butter to grease a 21cm (8in) round cake tin well and sprinkle in the breadcrumbs. Turn the tin round until the breadcrumbs evenly coat the inner surface.
3 Cream the butter and sugar together until light and fluffy.
4 Gently fold in the sifted flour and baking powder, followed by the eggs and the brandy until all the ingredients are fully combined.

5 Spoon the mixture into the prepared cake tin and bake in a preheated oven for 40 minutes or until a cocktail stick inserted into the centre comes out clean.
6 Remove from the oven, allow to cool for 10 minutes in the tin and then turn out onto a wire rack.
7 Dust with icing sugar and serve Scandinavian style with a coffee.

Turkish Lemon Cake

Serves 8–10

170g (6oz) butter, softened
300g (10½oz) caster sugar
3 eggs
300g (10½oz) self-raising flour, sifted
1 tsp baking powder
½ tsp bicarbonate of soda
3 tsp finely grated lemon zest
80ml (3fl oz) orange juice

For the lemon syrup:
100ml (3½fl oz) water
75g (2¾oz) caster sugar
50ml (2fl oz) lemon juice

With lemons growing so abundantly in Greece and Turkey, a lemon cake is a perennial favourite tea-time treat for every family.

1 Preheat the oven to 170°C/325°F/gas mark 3, and grease and line a 25cm x 8cm x 8cm (10in x 3¼in x 3¼in) loaf tin with baking parchment.
2 Cream the butter and sugar together until light and fluffy.
3 Add the eggs one at a time, scraping down the bowl after each addition and mix until well combined.
4 Add in the sifted flour, baking powder and bicarbonate of soda and combine well followed by the lemon zest and orange juice. Mix well.
5 Pour into the prepared tin and bake in a preheated oven for 45 minutes, or until a cocktail stick inserted into the centre comes out clean.
6 Remove from the oven, allow to cool for 10 minutes in the tin and then turn out onto a wire rack and strip off the parchment.
7 Meanwhile, make the lemon syrup. Boil the water and sugar together to 140°C/284°F then add the lemon juice. Boil for 10 minutes, remove from the heat and allow to cool a little.
8 Slice when warm and serve drizzled with the lemon syrup.

Turkish Yogurt Cake

Serves 6

4 large eggs, separated
100g (3½oz) caster sugar
3 tbsp plain flour, sifted
400g (14oz) strained Greek yogurt
finely grated zest and juice of 1 lemon
icing sugar, to dust

In Turkey, where this recipe originates, yogurt is an important part of everyday cuisine. Yogurt frequently accompanies many main meat dishes as well as being used in soups, pastries and, of course, cakes. I like this cake because of its simplicity and lightness; it is a little like a cheesecake.

1 Preheat the oven to 180°C/350°F/gas mark 4, and grease a 23cm (9in) round cake tin.
2 Beat together the egg yolks and the sugar.
3 Add in the sifted flour, the yogurt, the zest and juice of the lemon and mix all the ingredients thoroughly together.
4 Whisk the egg whites until stiff and fold them into the yogurt mixture.
5 Pour the mixture into the prepared tin and bake in a preheated oven for 50–60 minutes until the top is brown. It will puff up like a soufflé and then subside.
6 When cool, dust with icing sugar.
7 I like to bake this in the summer months when I serve it warm or cold with slices of fresh stoned fruit, such as apricots or peaches, on the side.

TURKISH YOGURT CAKE

TURKISH YOGURT CAKE

TURKISH LEMON CAKE

TURKISH LEMON CAKE

Almond Honey
Spice Cake

Serves 6–8

120g (4oz) butter, softened
75g (2¾oz) caster sugar
2 tbsp honey
1 tsp ground ginger
1 tsp ground allspice
2 eggs
180g (6½oz) ground almonds
75g (2¾oz) semolina
1 tsp baking powder
65ml (2½fl oz) full-fat milk

For the spice syrup:
100g (3½oz) caster sugar
120ml (4fl oz) water
4 cardamom pods, crushed
1 cinnamon stick

For the lemon and honey glaze:
100g (3½oz) apricot jam
40ml (1½fl oz) lemon juice
40g (1½oz) honey

The almond tree goes back to biblical times and it grows in abundance in many areas of the Mediterranean and Middle East. In fact, now almond trees are grown all over the world – from California to eastern India. A combination of almonds and honey is a traditional marriage in the baking of many areas of the Mediterranean, particularly for gatherings to celebrate Christmas and other national holidays. In this recipe, I've used some delicious spices to give the almond and honey flavours extra depth.

1 Preheat the oven to 180°C/350°F/gas mark 4, and grease and line a deep 21cm (8in) springform round cake tin with baking parchment.
2 Cream the butter, sugar, honey and spices together until light and fluffy. Add the eggs, one at a time, scraping down the side of the bowl between each addition.
3 Fold in the ground almonds, semolina, baking powder and milk and combine well.
4 Spoon the mixture into the prepared tin and bake in a preheated oven for about 40 minutes or until a cocktail stick inserted into the centre comes out clean.
5 Meanwhile, make the syrup. Place all the ingredients together in a small pan over a medium heat. Bring to the boil, stirring until the sugar dissolves and becomes syrupy.
6 Remove from the oven and allow the cake to cool for 5 minutes then pour the hot syrup through a sieve (to strain the syrup) all over the cake while still in the tin.
7 Cool the cake to room temperature in the tin then turn out upside down onto a serving plate and strip off the baking parchment. Refrigerate overnight.
8 To make the glaze, place all the ingredients in a pan, bring to the boil and reduce by half.
9 Remove the cake from the fridge, turn it right way up and brush the warm glaze all over the top of the cake.
10 Slice and serve with coffee.

Rhubarb Crumble Cake

Serves 8

225g (8oz) Champagne
    rhubarb
175g (6¼oz) butter, softened
270g (9½oz) caster sugar
3 eggs
5 tsp orange juice
175g (6¼oz) self-raising flour
grated zest of 1 lemon
60g (2oz) ground almonds
4 tbsp full-fat milk

For the crumble topping:

60g (2oz) ground almonds
50g (1¾oz) caster sugar
85g (3oz) plain flour
50g (1¾oz) butter, cubed

A crumble is hard to resist – ask any Brit – and a fruit crumble of apple and blackberry or rhubarb is a typical weekend pudding for homes all over the UK. I wanted to create the comfort and textures of a crumble but in a crumble cake and use one of my all-time favourite fruits – rhubarb. I like the rhubarb to have a great tartness to it, and with the cake and sweet crunchy topping it's like heaven in a mouthful.

1 Preheat the oven to 170°C/325°F/gas mark 3, and grease and line a 17cm (6½in) round x 6cm (2½in) deep tin with baking parchment.
2 Wash and cut the rhubarb into 2.5cm (1in) lengths. (If the rhubarb is very green, peel before chopping.) Place in a roasting tin and sprinkle with 130g (4½oz) of the caster sugar and orange juice. Cover with foil and bake for 20 minutes. Remove from the oven and drain the juices; you could reserve the juices to use as a syrup on a summer dessert.
3 Meanwhile, cream the butter and remaining sugar together until light and fluffy, and add the eggs one at a time.

4 Sift the flour and fold in with the lemon zest, ground almonds and milk. Mix together then tip the mixture into the prepared cake tin.
5 To make the crumble topping, mix together the ground almonds, sugar and flour, then slowly rub in the butter using your fingertips until the mixture resembles breadcrumbs.
6 Spread the cooked rhubarb evenly over the cake mixture, followed by an even layer of the crumble topping. Bake in a preheated oven for 40 minutes.
7 Remove from the oven, allow to cool for 10 minutes in the tin and then turn out onto a wire rack and remove the baking parchment.

VARIATION

Use the same amount of fruit but instead use apples (quickly fried in a little butter) and blackberries – another English classic.

Sugee Cake

Serves 10–12

200g (7oz) semolina
5 eggs, beaten
finely grated zest and juice of
  1 orange
330g (11½oz) butter, softened
250g (9oz) caster sugar
5 egg yolks
130g (4½oz) plain flour, sifted
a pinch of salt
½ tsp baking powder

Semolina is used in baking all over the world and this aromatic semolina-based cake – popular throughout Asia and India – is one such cake, often served at festive occasions and celebrations. Sugee Cake has a high proportion of egg yolks to egg whites and the result is a super-rich cake. Try it out at your next celebration to share with friends and family.

1 Preheat the oven to 170°C/325°F/gas mark 3, and grease and line a 21cm (8in) round loose-bottomed cake tin with baking parchment.
2 In a bowl, soak the semolina with the beaten eggs, orange zest and juice for 1 hour.
3 In a separate bowl, cream the butter and sugar together until light and fluffy.
4 Beat in the egg yolks, one at a time, and then fold in the semolina mixture.
5 Add the sifted flour, salt and baking powder and mix until well combined.
6 Spoon into the prepared tin and bake in a preheated oven for about 45 minutes or until a cocktail stick comes out clean when inserted into the centre.
7 Remove from the oven, cool for 10 minutes in the tin, turn out onto a wire rack and remove the parchment. Serve with Jasmine tea.

Chocolate Rye Cake with Caramelised Bananas

Serves 10–12

10 eggs, separated
440g (15½oz) caster sugar
450g (1lb) dark chocolate,
  broken into pieces
50g (1¾oz) butter
50g (1¾oz) soft brown sugar
3 large bananas
70g (2½oz) ground almonds
40g (1½oz) plain flour
60g (2oz) rye flour
½ tsp salt

To decorate:

75g (2¾oz) white chocolate,
  melted
150g (5½oz) milk chocolate,
  melted

For many years rye flour was a staple of baking all over the world – especially in traditional breads in Germany, Switzerland, Russia and Scandinavia (to name a few) – but in recent history its popularity has lost out to wheat flour. Rye flour is still used extensively in Germany in both bread and cakes and is recognised as being highly nutritious as well as tasting great.

1 Preheat the oven to 160°C/310°F/gas mark 2½, and grease and line a 23cm (9in) loose-bottomed cake tin with baking parchment.
2 Beat the eggs yolks with half of the sugar until pale and creamy.
3 Melt the chocolate in a bowl over simmering water and then pour into the mixture.
4 Melt the butter in a frying pan, add the brown sugar until it melts and starts to form a caramel.
5 Meanwhile, slice the bananas into 3mm (⅛in) discs and add to the caramel. Turn over once coloured. Drain the pieces of banana in a sieve and leave to cool.
6 Fold the nuts and flours into the mixture.
7 Add the caramelised bananas to the chocolate mixture and fold in.
8 Beat the egg whites with the rest of the sugar and salt until soft peaks form.
9 Fold into the chocolate mixture, combine well. Spoon into the prepared tin and bake in a preheated oven for 1 hour.
10 Remove from the oven, cool for 10 minutes in the tin and then turn out onto a wire rack and strip off the baking parchment.
11 Once the cake is completely cool, melt the chocolate in separate bowls.
12 Transfer each of the melted chocolates into a piping bag with a fine nozzle (No. 2) and, working from the edges of the cake, swirl a pattern across. Serve with a hot chocolate.

SUGEE CAKE

CHOCOLATE RYE CAKE

SUGEE CAKE

CHOCOLATE RYE CAKE

Loaves & Pound Cakes **91**

FRUIT, NUT & SEED CAKES

Dundee Cake

Serves 8

150g (5½oz) butter, softened
150g (5½oz) caster sugar
3 eggs
225g (8oz) plain flour
1 tsp baking powder
175g (6¼oz) currants
175g (6¼oz) sultanas
50g (1¾oz) glacé cherries,
    quartered
2 tbsp ground almonds
finely grated zest of 1 lemon
finely grated zest of 1 orange
2 tbsp dry sherry or similar
    spirit (optional)

For the decoration:
30–40 whole blanched
    almonds
3 tbsp apricot jam, sieved and
    warmed

Bursting with fruit, moist and lightly spiced, this cake is spongier than a traditional fruit cake but has a great flavour and crumbly texture. It's traditionally eaten as a Christmas Cake in Scotland and is named after the city of Dundee where it was first made in the 19th century. Some rumours abound that Dundee Cake was, in fact, Mary Queen of Scots' favourite cake, but that her version omitted the cherries, which she didn't like. I like the cherries so it's fortunate I don't have to worry about her royal approval.

1 Preheat the oven to 160°C/310°F/gas mark 2½, and line a 16cm wide x 7cm deep (6¼in x 2¾in) round cake tin with baking parchment. You'll also need a baking tray.
2 Cream the butter and sugar together until light and fluffy, and add the eggs one at a time.
3 Sift together the flour and baking powder and add to the mixture.
4 Add in all the fruit, ground almonds, zest and sherry, if using. Mix together well and set aside.
5 Spread the blanched almonds on a baking tray and toast them in a preheated oven for 15 minutes until golden brown. Remove from the oven and set aside.

6 Fill the prepared tin with the mixture and stud the toasted almonds in two concentric circles on the top of the cake. Bake in a preheated oven for 1 hour.
7 Test the cake is cooked – when a cocktail stick inserted into the cake comes out clean. Remove from the oven, allow to cool for 5 minutes in the tin and then turn out onto a wire rack and strip off the baking parchment.
8 Brush the top with the warmed apricot jam and transfer to a serving plate.

Carrot and Walnut Cake

Serves 8

2 eggs
150g (5½oz) dark brown sugar
150ml (5fl oz) olive oil
1 generous tbsp honey
½ tsp vanilla extract
120g (4oz) wholemeal flour
40g (1½oz) plain flour
½ tsp baking powder
½ tsp bicarbonate of soda
½ tsp salt
120g (4oz) carrots, peeled and
    grated
50g (1¾oz) walnuts, chopped
50g (1¾oz) sultanas

For the topping:

30g (1¼oz) butter, softened
85g (3oz) full-fat cream
    cheese
250g (9oz) icing sugar, sifted
finely grated lime zest, to
    decorate

It's not clear when carrot cakes first started being baked and eaten but documents show that carrot puddings were made in Medieval times across Europe, where the sweetness of the carrots made up for the lack of pricey ingredients such as sugar or dried fruits. Recipes in the UK date as far back as the late 16th century and George Washington was said to be served carrot tea cake in lower Manhattan, New York, in 1783. Some people like their carrot cake without nuts, but I like to use chopped walnuts and dark brown sugar to give extra depth to this classic recipe.

1 Preheat the oven to 170°C/325°F/gas mark 3, and grease and line an 18cm x 8cm x 8cm (7in x 3¼in x 3¼in) loaf tin with baking parchment.
2 Combine the eggs with the sugar and olive oil. Add the honey and vanilla extract.
3 Sift over the two lots of flour, baking powder, bicarbonate of soda and salt. Add the carrots, walnuts and sultanas and mix well.
4 Pour the mixture into the prepared tin and bake in a preheated oven for 40 minutes, or until a cocktail stick inserted into the centre comes out clean.

5 Meanwhile, in a bowl, beat the butter and cream cheese together. Slowly add the icing sugar and continue beating until smooth. Then refrigerate for an hour before using.
6 Remove from the oven, allow to cool for 20 minutes in the tin and then turn out onto a wire rack and strip off the parchment.
7 Spread the frosting over the top of the cake and sprinkle over some finely grated lime zest as a finishing touch. Serve with a cup of tea.

Caribbean Black Cake

Serves 12

150g (5½oz) each of raisins, prunes, currants and glacé cherries, blitzed

60g (2oz) candied lemon peel, blitzed

60g (2oz) candied orange peel, blitzed

345ml (11⅖fl oz) white wine

345ml (11⅖fl oz) white rum

300g (10½oz) dark brown sugar

250g (9oz) plain flour

2 tsp baking powder

½ tsp grated nutmeg

½ tsp ground cinnamon

175g (6¼oz) butter, softened

4 eggs

½ tsp vanilla extract

75g (2¾oz) icing sugar

This smooth Caribbean fruit cake is unlike any fruit cake you will have ever tasted before, since the dried fruit is blitzed beforehand (in a food processor). And it is certainly not for the faint-hearted, since it's drenched (literally) in alcohol. As with many fruit cakes, this one is traditionally served at Christmas in Jamaica and neighbouring islands; but it also turns up as a wedding cake. I would recommend soaking the fruit for up to a week, if you can – your taste buds will thank you for it.

1 Mix the blitzed fruit and alcohol together and leave to soak for up to a week (at least 1 day).

2 Preheat the oven to 180°C/350°F/gas mark 4 and grease a 25cm x 9cm (10in x 3½in) Bundt tin really well.

3 In a large pan mix 120g (4oz) of the sugar and 3 tablespoons of water and bring to the boil. Boil until the mixture turns dark brown and caramelised, then cool and set aside.

4 Sift together the flour, baking powder and spices. Cream the butter and remaining sugar until light and fluffy. Add the eggs, one at a time.

5 Add the vanilla extract, the flour mix and the burnt caramel to the creamed mixture and beat until fully combined.

6 Finally add in the fruit, mix together and then divide between the prepared cake tins and bake in the preheated oven for 2 hours.

7 Remove from the oven, cool for 10 minutes in the tin and then turn out onto a wire rack.

8 Make the frosting. Sift the icing sugar into a bowl and gradually add water, stirring continuously, to make a smooth paste until just pourable. Pour over the cake and let it set.

Greek Fig Cake

Serves 6–8

3 eggs, separated
150g (5½oz) caster sugar
175g (6¼oz) plain flour, sifted
1 tsp ground cinnamon
3 tsp baking powder
4 tbsp full-fat milk
120g (4oz) walnuts, roughly
    chopped
120g (4oz) almonds, roasted
    and roughly chopped
150g (5½oz) sultanas
120g (4oz) fresh figs, finely
    chopped
Honey Glaze (see page 298),
    to decorate

Figs have been used in cakes in Greece for centuries; in fact, documents of original Greek recipes date back to 180CE. They passed on recipes via the Romans and now wherever figs grow, you'll find someone baking a fig cake. This recipe, which includes nuts as well as figs, is for a wonderful cake and was given to me by Greek friends who love the combination of flavours – it reminds them of long hot holidays under the vines. You can substitute dried figs for fresh, if necessary, but you'll be more than rewarded on the taste front for tracking down some fresh black figs during the summer months, rather than using the fresh green or dried figs.

1 Preheat the oven to 150°C/300°F/gas mark 2. Then, grease and line a 25cm x 8cm x 8cm (10in x 3¼in x 3¼in) loaf tin with baking parchment.
2 Beat the egg whites until soft peaks form and then gradually add the sugar and beating until stiff peaks form.
3 Add the egg yolks and beat well until smooth and glossy.
4 Fold in the sifted flour, cinnamon and baking powder in alternate batches with the milk and combine well.
5 Gently fold in the chopped walnuts, almonds, sultanas and fresh figs, being careful not to knock out the air.
6 Spoon the mixture into the prepared tin and bake in a preheated oven for 1 hour.
7 Remove from the oven, allow to cool for 10 minutes in the tin and then turn out onto a wire rack and strip off the parchment.
8 Meanwhile, make the Honey Glaze as instructed on page 298 and brush the top of the cake with it for a super-glossy finish.
9 Serve with an intensely strong coffee.

Apple and Cinnamon Damper

Serves 8

375g (13oz) self-raising flour
pinch of salt
60g (2oz) soft brown sugar
1 tsp ground cinnamon
75g (2¾oz) butter, chilled and cubed
2 apples, grated
175ml (6fl oz) full-fat milk
50ml (2fl oz) water

At its most basic, a damper was a bread made of just flour, salt and water and was cooked over a campfire (wrapped around a stick) or buried in among its coals by Australian settlers. In fact, the name 'damper' comes from the fact that the fire was damped down to allow the bread to be cooked in the hot coals. This 'bread' remains popular to this day but now comes in a multitude of flavours, both sweet and savoury. I like the classic combination of apple and cinnamon here.

1 Preheat the oven to 170°C/325°F/gas mark 3, and lightly grease a baking tray.
2 Sift the flour, salt and cinnamon together in a bowl and add in the sugar and cubed butter. Either use a paddle attachment of a food mixer or your fingers to rub in the butter until it resembles breadcrumbs.
3 Add the apple and combine well.
4 Add the milk and just enough of the water to form a dough.
5 Turn the dough out onto a lightly floured work surface and knead the dough lightly – so knead once, turn, knead again about six times.
6 Form the dough using your hands into a circle roughly the size of a side plate and place on the prepared tray.
7 Using a floured knife score eight wedges into the top of the damper.
8 Bake in a preheated oven for 1 hour.
9 Remove from the oven and leave to cool on a wire rack.
10 Serve sliced warm or cold with butter.

Vinegar Cake

Serves 10–12

225g (8oz) butter
450g (1lb) self-raising flour
225g (8oz) caster sugar
225g (8oz) raisins
225g (8oz) sultanas
175ml (6fl oz) full-fat milk,
   plus 1 tbsp
2 tbsp white wine vinegar
1 tsp bicarbonate of soda
100ml (3½fl oz) Apricot Glaze
   (see page 299)

This traditional English fruit cake contains no eggs – and was popular during the rationing era in the UK during and after the Second World War – so the vinegar and the bicarbonate of soda act as the raising agents instead. And once the cake is cooked you won't taste the vinegar at all! Go on, try it.

1 Preheat the oven to 180°C/350°F/gas mark 4, and grease and line a 21cm (8in) round springform or loose-bottomed cake tin with baking parchment.
2 Rub the butter into the flour until it resembles breadcrumbs, or use a food mixer. Next add the sugar and the dried fruit.
3 In a separate bowl, mix 1 tablespoon of the milk with the vinegar before adding the bicarbonate of soda. Then add this mixture to the rest of the milk. Pour this into the dry mix and stir until fully combined.

4 Pour the mixture into the prepared tin and bake in the preheated oven for 30 minutes. Then, reduce the heat to 160°C/310°F/gas mark 2½ and bake for another hour.
5 Remove from the oven and allow to cool for 10 minutes in the tin before turning out on the wire rack and removing the baking parchment.
6 Make the glaze as instructed on page 299 and brush over the cooled cake.
7 Then, slice and serve with a nice cup of tea.

Bara Brith

Serves 8

500g (1lb 2oz) mixed fruit
500ml (18fl oz) strong tea
1 heaped tsp black treacle
75g (2¾oz) orange
   marmalade
225g (8oz) dark brown sugar
2 eggs
525g (1lb 2½oz) self-raising
   flour, sifted
2 tsp ground mixed spice

I spend many holidays with my family on the island of Anglesey, North Wales, and this popular tea bread is baked all over Wales. Bara Brith in Welsh means 'speckled bread' – with the dried fruit being the speckles – and there are many versions of the recipe. Originally Bara Brith included yeast, but I prefer this yeast-free version that tastes better the day after you have made it. You can eat it any day of the year but why not bake it to celebrate St David's Day (the patron saint of Wales) on March 1st.

1 Preheat the oven to 160°C/310°F/gas mark 2½, and grease and line a 18cm x 8cm x 8cm (7in x 3¼in x 3¼in) loaf tin with baking parchment.
2 Put the mixed fruit in a large bowl, cover with the strong tea and leave to soak overnight.
3 Warm the treacle and marmalade in a small pan and add to the sugar in a bowl.
4 Beat in the eggs and then fold in the sifted flour, the mixed spice and the mixed fruit (along with any remaining liquid). Mix until fully combined.

5 Spoon the mixture into the prepared tin and bake in a preheated oven for 1 hour.
6 Remove from the oven, allow to cool for 10 minutes in the tin and then turn out onto a wire rack and strip off the baking parchment.
7 Slice and spread with salted Welsh butter for the ultimate teatime treat.

BARA BRITH

BARA BRITH

VINEGAR CAKE

Fruit, Nut & Seed Cakes 101

Danish Apple Cake

Serves 6–8

180g (6½oz) butter, softened
180g (6½oz) caster sugar
2 eggs
180g (6½oz) self-raising flour, sifted
30g (1¼oz) sultanas
2 apples (I use Braeburns)
50g (1¾oz) demerara sugar, to decorate

The Danish are famous for their cakes and pastries, and in Denmark there are bakeries on every street corner. Ask any Dane what their favourite cake is and the majority are sure to say 'Aeblekage' or 'Apple Cake', which is served up whatever the occasion.

1 Preheat the oven to 170°C/325°F/gas mark 3, and grease and line a 21cm (8in) springform cake tin with baking parchment.
2 Cream the butter and sugar together until light and fluffy. Add the eggs one at a time and beat until well combined.
3 Beat in the sifted flour and mix well. Fold in the sultanas and then spoon the mixture into the prepared cake tin.
4 Peel, core and cut the apples into 1cm (½in) wedges. Arrange neatly around the top of the cake, pushing them slightly into the mixture, and spread out evenly so that everyone gets some on their slice.
5 Sprinkle with demerara sugar and bake in a preheated oven for 35 minutes or until golden.
6 Remove from the oven, allow to cool for 10 minutes in the tin and then turn out onto a wire rack and strip off the parchment.
7 I think it's the most delicious when served warm from the oven with a scoop of ice cream.

'Jewish' Apple Cake

Serves 8

For the apples:
25g (1oz) caster sugar
1 tsp ground cinnamon
1 tsp vanilla extract
400g (14oz) apples (I use Braeburns), half thinly sliced, half cubed

For the cake:
225g (8oz) caster sugar
250g (9oz) plain flour, sifted
1 tsp baking powder
a pinch of salt
150ml (5fl oz) vegetable oil
1 tsp vanilla extract
40ml (1½fl oz) orange juice
2 eggs
100ml (3½fl oz) Apricot Glaze (see page 299)

This cake is dairy-free as it uses oil instead of butter, and so has probably become to be known as 'Jewish' because it can be eaten at a kosher meal. This hearty cake has a secret layer of cinnamon-flavoured apple and can hold its own as a dessert, if you so wish.

1 Preheat the oven to 180°C/350°F/gas mark 4, and grease and line a 17cm (6½in) round tin with baking parchment (only needs to be lined at the bottom but the sides must be greased).
2 In a bowl add half the sugar, half the cinnamon and half the vanilla to the sliced apples, coat and set aside. Do the same in another bowl with the cubed apples.
3 In a bowl, mix the sugar, sifted flour, baking powder and salt together.
4 In another bowl combine the oil, vanilla extract, orange juice and eggs and mix in a food mixer until smooth on a medium speed for 30 seconds to stretch the gluten.
5 Pour this wet mixture onto the dry ingredients and mix thoroughly.

6 Pour half the batter into your lined tin and lay the sliced apples on top of the batter, then pour over the rest of the batter. Smooth over and lay the cubed apples evenly on the surface. Cover with foil and pierce in several places.
7 Bake in the preheated oven for an hour.
8 Remove the foil and bake for another 20–30 minutes or until a cocktail stick inserted into the centre comes out clean.
9 Remove from the oven, allow to cool for 10 minutes in the tin and then turn out onto a wire rack and remove the baking parchment.
10 Make the glaze as instructed on page 299. When the cake's completely cool, brush the glaze over when you're ready to serve – it's delicious with cinnamon ice cream.

Richard Corrigan's More Stout Than Treacle Cake

Serves 8

150ml (5fl oz) stout
120g (4oz) plain flour
100g (3½oz) treacle
250g (9oz) golden syrup
100ml (3½fl oz) double cream
3 eggs, beaten
2 cooking apples, peeled and grated
200g (7oz) breadcrumbs

For the whiskey cream:
200ml (7fl oz) double cream
75g (2¾oz) caster sugar
80ml (3fl oz) Irish whiskey

icing sugar, to dust

Richard Corrigan has cooked all his life. He's opened numerous restaurants, gained a Michelin star, cooked for the Queen, appeared on television on countless occasions and recently toured America hosting *Chef Race USA vs UK*.

His passion for seasonal food is matched only by his enthusiasm for ingredients sourced in Britain and Ireland. Richard is a keen supporter of the Slow Food Movement, for which he is an ambassador. He is also a founding member of the Slow Food UK Chef Alliance and Chef Spokesperson for the project. Richard's also written his own book and *The Clatter of Forks and Spoons* is a personal history of growing up in Ireland and recipes inspired by his rural upbringing.

Richard, who I first met way back in 1989, sent me this recipe for one of his favourite cakes. He says of this cake 'Although I don't really have a sweet tooth – I love this cake. The stout adds depth of flavour and the acidity from the apples help to balance out the treacle.'

1 Preheat the oven to 160°C/310°F/gas mark 2½, and grease and line a 21cm (8in) springform cake tin.
2 Mix all the ingredients together in a bowl until well combined.
3 Pour the mixture into the prepared tin and bake in a preheated oven until almost set (about 1 hour).

4 Meanwhile, whisk together all the ingredients for the whiskey cream and chill until cold.
5 Remove the cake from the oven, allow to cool for 10 minutes in the tin and then turn out onto a wire rack. Strip off the baking parchment.
6 When cool, dust with icing sugar and serve with the luxurious whiskey cream on the side.

Mango Cake

Serves 8–10

75g (2¾oz) butter, at room
temperature
250g (9oz) caster sugar
3 eggs
330g (11½oz) plain flour, sifted
1 tsp bicarbonate of soda
1 tsp baking powder
1 tsp vanilla extract
170g (6oz) fresh mango,
puréed (I prefer Alphonso
mangoes)
icing sugar, to dust

Just the sunshine yellow skin and the wonderfully sweet taste of an
Alphonso mango are cause for celebration, so it seems unfair that their
growing season is so short – from late March to June. India is the largest
worldwide producer of mangoes and during mango season (which heralds
the start of summer) they are served up in all manner of savoury and sweet
dishes. Even if you can't get hold of the Alphonso mango, just be sure that
the mango you use is ripe and ready.

1 Preheat the oven to 170°C/325°F/gas mark
3, and grease and line a 21cm (8in) springform
cake tin with baking parchment.
2 Cream the butter and sugar together until
light and fluffy.
3 Add in the eggs one at a time, scraping down
after each addition and mix well.
4 Slowly fold in the sifted flour, bicarbonate
of soda and baking powder followed by the
vanilla extract.
5 Finally mix in the mango purée.

6 Pour into the prepared tin and bake in
a preheated oven for 30 minutes or until
a cocktail stick inserted into the centre
comes out clean.
7 Remove from the oven, allow to cool for
10 minutes in the tin and then turn out onto
a wire rack. Remove the baking parchment.
8 Dust with icing sugar and serve with slices
of fresh mango and crème fraîche or Greek-
style yogurt.

Mandarin, Polenta and Macadamia Cake

Serves 8–10

4 small mandarins, unpeeled
250g (9oz) butter, softened
225g (8oz) caster sugar
1 tsp vanilla extract
3 eggs
170g (6oz) polenta
1 tsp baking powder
275g (9¾oz) macadamia
    nuts, blitzed into a coarse
    meal
icing sugar, to dust

Polenta is traditionally an Italian savoury dish but if you have never used it in a cake it is well worth trying, and because it doesn't use any flour it's naturally gluten-free. The polenta grains give the cake a lovely soft crumbly texture and when combined with the super-buttery Australian macadamia nuts and the tangy citrus fruit the result is one delicious cake. This cake is a popular one in Australia and New Zealand since mandarins grow plentifully in tropical and subtropical climates.

1 Preheat the oven to 170°C/325°F/gas mark 3, and line a 22cm (8½in) round cake tin with baking parchment.
2 Pulp the mandarins by placing them whole in a pan and cover with cold water. Bring to the boil, drain and then repeat the process three times. Once cool halve the mandarins and discard any seeds then blend until pulpy.
3 Cream the butter and sugar together with the vanilla extract until light and fluffy. Add the eggs one at a time and beat well.
4 Stir in the polenta, baking powder, nut meal and mandarin pulp, and mix well until combined.
5 Spoon the mixture into the prepared tin and bake in a preheated oven for 1 hour.
6 Remove from the oven, allow to cool for 10 minutes in the tin and then turn out onto a wire rack. Strip off the baking parchment.
7 Serve dusted with icing sugar.

Caraway Seed Cake

Serves 6

120g (4oz) butter, softened
120g (4oz) caster sugar
3 large eggs
1½ tsp caraway seeds
180g (6½oz) self-raising flour
60g (2oz) ground almonds
2½ tbsp full-fat milk

This delicious loaf cake can be thrown together easily for impromptu afternoon guests. Cakes using the wonderful flavour of caraway seeds can be found as far back as the 1500s in the history of English cake making.

1 Preheat the oven to 160°C/310°F/gas mark 2½, and grease and line a 18cm x 8cm x 8cm (7in x 3¼in x 3¼in) loaf tin with baking parchment.
2 Cream the butter and sugar until light and fluffy. Beat in the eggs slowly one at a time.
3 Add the caraway seeds, flour and ground almonds followed by the milk.
4 Scrape down the sides of the bowl to ensure that all the ingredients are fully combined before turning into the prepared tin.
5 Bake in a preheated oven for about 45 minutes or until a cocktail stick inserted into the centre comes out clean.
6 Remove from the oven, allow to cool for 10 minutes in the tin, then turn out onto a wire rack and remove the baking parchment.
7 Serve with a lovely cup of tea.

Bolo Polana

Serves 10

250g (9oz) potatoes, peeled and quartered
375g (13oz) butter, softened
410g (14½oz) caster sugar
50g (1¾oz) plain flour
300g (10½oz) roasted unsalted cashews, finely chopped
2 tsp finely grated lemon zest
2 tsp finely grated orange zest
9 egg yolks
4 egg whites

This delicate potato and cashew cake hails from Mozambique, along the east coast of Africa. Mozambique was colonised by Portugal in the 16th century, after Vasco da Gama first reached its shores in 1498, and this cake has strong Portuguese overtones. However, the Mozambiquans have made it their own, adapting the original recipe to include the indigenous ingredient of cashews – one of the country's principal crops.

1 Preheat the oven to 180°C/350°F/gas mark 4, and grease a 21cm (8in) springform cake tin.
2 Boil the potatoes until they are soft enough to be easily mashed. Drain, mash and set aside.
3 Beat together the butter and the sugar until light and creamy.
4 Beat in the potatoes, flour, cashews and the lemon and orange zests.
5 Add the egg yolks, one at a time, scraping down after each addition until thoroughly combined.
6 In a separate bowl, whisk the egg whites until stiff then spoon into the potato mixture and fold in gently but thoroughly.

7 Pour the mixture into the prepared tin and bake in a preheated oven for 1 hour or until a cocktail stick inserted into the centre comes out clean.
8 Remove from the oven, allow to cool for 10 minutes in the tin and then turn out onto a wire rack.
9 Serve the Bolo Polana while it is still warm with coffee.

Nancy Silverton's Olive Oil Cake

Serves 12

3 whole oranges
140g (5oz) raisins
175ml (6fl oz) dark rum
4 eggs
270g (9½oz) caster sugar
10g (¼oz) bicarbonate of soda
10g (¼oz) baking powder
220ml (7½fl oz) extra virgin
   olive oil
540g (1lb 3oz) plain flour

For the decoration:
40g (1½oz) pine nuts, toasted,
fresh rosemary sprigs
4 tbsp granulated sugar

Nancy Silverton is an American chef and baker who has written several cookbooks and has been hugely influential in revitalising the popularity of sourdough and artisan breads in the United States. In 1989, she began the famous La Brea Bakery in Los Angeles and her breads are now available in over 17 countries around the world. In 1996, Nancy signed one of her books to me with the words 'Bake bread not cakes!' Thankfully, 16 years later, she still happily agreed to be in my cake book!

Nancy's recipe has the rosemary and pine nuts sprinkled on the top before baking, but as I used a Bundt tin I placed these in the bottom before pouring in the cake mixture.

1 Preheat the oven to 200°C/400°F/gas mark 6, and grease a large Bundt tin (2.4 litres (4 pints).
2 Chop the oranges with rinds into 5mm (¼in) slices and then cut into strips and squares.
3 Combine the raisins with the rum in a bowl and set aside.
4 Either in an electric mixer or in a bowl, whisk the eggs and the sugar together until light in colour (it'll take about 3–4 minutes), scraping down the sides of the bowl as needed.

5 Add the bicarbonate of soda and baking powder and mix to combine (about 1 minute if using a mixer on low).
6 With the mixer on a medium speed, drizzle the olive oil in a slow steady stream down the side of the bowl until it is emulsified.
7 Add the flour and rum-soaked raisins in three batches, alternating on low speed until combined, scraping down the sides of the bowl as needed. The cake batter should be thick with a nice olive oil tinge.
8 Remove the bowl from the mixer, if using. And with a rubber spatula, fold the chopped oranges into the mixture. Let the batter sit for 10 minutes.
9 Scatter the decorations of pine nuts, rosemary sprigs and sugar into the prepared Bundt tin and pour in the cake batter.
10 Bake in a preheated oven for 10 minutes, then turn down the temperature to 170°C/325°F/gas mark 3, turning the cake every 10–15 minutes until golden brown or until a cocktail stick inserted into the centre comes out clean (about 30–35 minutes).
11 Serve with a glass of Grand Marnier liqueur.

Scandinavian Cardamom Coffee Cake

Serves 10

110g (3¾oz) butter, softened
210g (7½oz) caster sugar
3 eggs
300g (10½oz) plain flour
1 tsp bicarbonate of soda
2 tsp ground cardamom
½ tsp ground cinnamon
120g (4oz) soured cream

For the decoration:
150ml (5fl oz) Chocolate
    Ganache (see page 297)

There isn't actually any coffee in this cake but it is so named because it is served with coffee at coffee time. Cardamom is a member of the ginger family and grows in India, but was taken back to Scandinavia by the Vikings and is more popular there than cinammon for spices used in baking. While this cake is baking, your home will be filled with tantalising aromas and you'll be glad the Vikings introduced this wonderful spice into the baking of Norway and Sweden.

1 Preheat the oven to 160°C/310°F/gas mark 2½, and grease a 23cm (9in) Bundt tin.
2 Cream the butter and sugar together until light and fluffy, and add the eggs one at a time, scraping down after each addition.
3 Sift the dry ingredients into a bowl and then fold in the soured cream. Mix in with the butter, sugar and eggs until well combined.
4 Spoon into the prepared tin and lightly bash the tin on a work surface, to even out the mixture. Bake in a preheated oven for 30 minutes or until a cocktail stick inserted into the centre comes out clean.
5 Meanwhile, make the Chocolate Ganache as instructed on page 297 and set aside.
6 Remove the cake from the oven, allow to cool for 10 minutes in the tin and then turn out onto a wire rack.
7 Decorate with the ganache and serve with coffee, of course!

Coffee and Walnut Cake

Serves 10

85g (3oz) walnut halves
175g (6¼oz) butter, softened
175g (6¼oz) caster sugar
3 eggs
2 tbsp instant coffee granules
    mixed to a paste with
    water
190g (6¾oz) self-raising flour,
    sifted
1½ tsp baking powder

For the filling and topping:

1 tbsp boiling water
1 tbsp instant coffee granules
250g (9oz) mascarpone
40g (1½oz) icing sugar, sifted
200ml (7fl oz) double cream

Every family has a recipe for this classic cake and who can blame them? Coffee and walnuts go so well together, and the creamy coffee icing is a match made in heaven – put them all together and you have an amazing crowd-pleasing confection. Here's my recipe for this rich and luscious cake to add to your family's repertoire – all that's left to do is to cut a large slice.

1 Preheat the oven to 170°C/325°F/gas mark 3, and grease and line a 21cm (8in) springform cake tin with baking parchment. You'll also need a baking tray.

2 Spread the walnuts on a baking tray and toast in the oven for 6 minutes.

3 Remove from the oven and allow to cool a little before rubbing in a tea towel to remove any skin. Reserve the nine most perfect halves (for the top of the cake) and crush the rest.

4 Cream together the butter and the sugar until light and fluffy. Add the eggs one at a time, scraping down after each addition until well combined. Then add in the coffee paste.

5 Mix in the sifted flour and baking powder, followed by the crushed walnuts and fold in.

6 Pour into the prepared tin and bake in a preheated oven for 30 minutes or until a cocktail stick inserted into the centre comes out clean.

7 Remove from the oven, cool for 10 minutes in the tin and then turn out onto a wire rack and strip off the baking parchment.

8 Meanwhile, make the filling. Make a paste with the boiling water and the instant coffee.

9 In a bowl, soften the mascarpone with the sifted icing sugar and then add the double cream followed by the coffee mixture.

10 When the cake is completely cool, cut it in half horizontally and brush away any excess crumbs.

11 Using a palette knife, spread a third of the filling on the bottom layer of the cake, position the top layer of sponge and spread the rest of the coffee filling on the top and all around the sides of the cake.

12 Carefully position the nine walnut halves around the top and chill to set the icing.

13 Serve chilled or at room temperature with more coffee.

Turkish Tahini Cake

Serves 12–14

250g (9oz) tahini
200g (7oz) caster sugar
1 tsp bicarbonate of soda, sifted
2 tbsp cognac
200g (7oz) plain flour
2 tsp ground cinnamon
150g (5½oz) walnuts, chopped
75g (2¾oz) glacé fruit, such as cherries and mixed peel
75g (2¾oz) sultanas
240ml (8fl oz) orange juice
sesame seeds, to decorate

Tahini is a sesame seed paste used in many traditional Turkish and Middle Eastern recipes. You may well have cooked with it in a savoury dish, but here I've used it in a traditional sweet cake. The tahini gives a delicious nutty flavour, a little like peanut butter.

1 Preheat the oven to 170°C/325°F/gas mark 3, and grease and line a 23cm (9in) round cake tin with baking parchment.
2 In a bowl, beat the tahini, gradually adding the sugar.
3 Mix together the sifted bicarbonate of soda with the cognac and add to the tahini mix.
4 In a separate bowl, sift the flour and cinnamon and mix in the walnuts, glacé fruits and raisins.

5 Add half of the flour mixture to the tahini and beat in well, followed by half the orange juice and beat again. Repeat with the remaining halves until everything is fully combined. The cake should be thicker than an average cake mixture, so add a little more flour, if necessary, to achieve this.
6 Pour the mixture into the prepared tin, sprinkle with sesame seeds and bake in a preheated oven until the cake is a deep brown nut colour (about 50 minutes).
7 Remove from the oven, allow to cool in the tin and then turn out onto a wire rack and remove the baking parchment.
8 Serve a slice with a small, intense coffee.

Serves 8

225g (8oz) self-raising flour
1 tsp baking powder
a pinch of salt
75g (2¾oz) ground almonds
100g (3½oz) caster sugar
2 eggs
50g (1¾oz) honey
250ml (8½fl oz) natural
    yogurt
150ml (5fl oz) sunflower oil
finely grated zest of 1 lime
40g (1½oz) chopped
    pistachios

For the syrup:
150ml (5fl oz) water
100g (3½oz) caster sugar
juice of 1 lime
1–2 tsp rosewater

rose petals, to decorate
    (optional)

Rachel Allen's Lime Yogurt Cake with Rosewater and Pistachios

Rachel Allen is a busy TV chef, author, journalist and mother, and still teaches at Ballymaloe Cookery School in Ireland. As well as writing four best-selling cookery books, she has appeared regularly on television in Ireland and in the UK. Rachel is columnist and contributor to a number of Irish publications, including *The Sunday Tribune* magazine.

She says of this cake 'The combination of the limes, rosewater and pistachio nuts in this cake result in a flavour that sings of the Middle East, and the yogurt ensures it stays deliciously moist. I adore a slice of this divine cake with a cup of coffee.'

1 Preheat the oven to 180°C/350°F/gas mark 4, and grease a 22cm (8½in) round springform tin.
2 Sift the flour, baking powder and salt into a large bowl. Add the ground almonds and caster sugar and mix together.
3 Mix the eggs, honey, yogurt, sunflower oil and lime zest together well in a largish bowl.

4 Make a well in the centre of the dry ingredients and slowly pour in the wet ingredients, bringing them together with a whisk until they are just combined.
5 Add some chopped pistachios to the mixture if you wish, or retain for decorating.
6 Pour this mixture into the prepared tin and bake in a preheated oven for 50 minutes or until a cocktail stick inserted into the centre comes out clean.
7 Remove from the oven, allow to cool for 20 minutes in the tin and then turn out onto a wire rack.
8 While the cake is cooling, make the syrup. In a small pan, boil the water and sugar for about 5 minutes until reduced by half. Add the lime juice and boil for a further 2 minutes, then cool and add the rosewater according to your taste.
9 With a fine skewer or cocktail stick, make holes in the top of the warm cake and spoon the syrup all over. Scatter the pistachios over, if you didn't use them in the cake, and leave to settle for 1 hour.
10 Decorate with rose petals, if using, and serve with cream, yogurt, sliced mangoes or some berries.

Lime and Poppy Seed Syrup Cake

Serves 16

40g (1½oz) poppy seeds
120ml (4fl oz) full-fat milk
250g (9oz) butter, softened
1 tbsp finely grated lime zest
275g (9¾oz) caster sugar
4 eggs
350g (12oz) self-raising flour, sifted
110g (3¾oz) plain flour, sifted
250g (9oz) soured cream

For the lime syrup:

120ml (4fl oz) lime juice
250ml (8½fl oz) water
225g (8oz) caster sugar

Poppy seeds are used in many recipes originating from Eastern Europe and Russia. Their sweet toasted flavour combines well with citrus flavours, whether it's lemon or lime as in this recipe. The lime syrup intensifies the citrus notes and leaves a lovely sugary crust on the top.

1 Preheat the oven to 180°C/350°F/gas mark 4, and grease a 2.4 litre (4 pint) Bundt tin well.
2 Soak the poppy seeds in the milk for at least 10 minutes.
3 Meanwhile cream the butter, lime zest and sugar together until light and fluffy.
4 Then, add the eggs one at a time, mixing well after each addition.
5 Add in the sifted flours and the soured cream.
6 Finally, mix in the poppy seed mixture and mix together until well combined.
7 Turn your mixture into the prepared tin and bake in a preheated oven for 1 hour.

8 While the cake's in the oven, make the lime syrup. Place all the ingredients in a pan and stir over a lowish heat until all the sugar has dissolved. Allow it to simmer until the liquid thickens and the mixture has reduced by half.
9 Remove the cake from the oven and pour the slightly cooled syrup over the cake while it is still warm to allow the flavours to infuse the cake. The syrup is very light and so soaks into the cake easily, without the need for any pricking of the cake.
10 When cool, serve this perfect teatime treat with some refreshing afternoon tea.

Nusskuchen

Serves 10

200g (7oz) butter, softened
250g (9oz) caster sugar
6 eggs, separated
200g (7oz) flaked hazelnuts
100g (3½oz) dark chocolate (minimum 70% cocoa solids), cut up into small pieces
a pinch of salt
130g (4½oz) plain flour, sifted
1½ tsp baking powder
½ tsp ground cinnamon
icing sugar, to dust

The name of this everyday – and popular – cake literally translates from the German as Nut Cake. It is a simple recipe for a lovely light but moist cake; some versions are baked in a round tin and made as a sandwich with a tart apple filling, but I like mine as a loaf with a nice strong coffee.

1 Preheat the oven to 180°C/350°F/gas mark 4 and grease and line a 25cm x 8cm x 8cm (10in x 3¼in x 3¼in) loaf tin with baking parchment.
2 Cream the butter and sugar together until white and fluffy, and then add the egg yolks one at a time, scraping down after each addition, until doubled in volume.
3 Add in the nuts and the chocolate pieces and mix together.
4 Whisk the egg whites with a pinch of salt until stiff peaks form.

5 Next, add the sifted flour, baking powder and cinnamon to the buttery mixture, alternating with the egg whites so the mixture doesn't become too stiff. Ensure everything is well combined but do not mix too much.
6 Spoon the mixture into a prepared tin and bake in a preheated oven for 1 hour.
7 Remove from the oven, cool for 10 minutes in the tin, turn out onto a wire rack and strip off the baking parchment.
8 Dust with icing sugar and serve with coffee.

LIME AND POPPY SEED SYRUP CAKE

LIME AND POPPY SEED SYRUP CAKE

NUSSKUCHEN

NUSSKUCHEN

Fruit, Nut & Seed Cakes **119**

Baked Chocolate and Nut Cake

Serves 16

For the meringue base:
7 egg whites
a pinch of salt
a few drops of lemon juice
140g (5oz) caster sugar
175g (6¼oz) chopped
   roasted walnuts
15g (½oz) ground almonds
finely grated zest of 1 lemon

For the chocolate sponge:
225g (8oz) dark chocolate
   (minimum 70% cocoa
   solids)
75g (2¾oz) butter
4 eggs
85g (3oz) caster sugar
½ tsp instant coffee, made to
   a paste with a little water
icing sugar, to dust

I have included this cake because it is a great combination of a crunchy meringue-based cake with a soft sponge layer of chocolate; such cakes are popular in Italy. Meringues have been a staple of cakes and desserts for many years, as they require only the simplest of ingredients – egg whites.

1 Preheat the oven to 170°C/325°F/gas mark 3, and grease a 23cm (9in) square cake tin.
2 Beat the egg whites with the salt until they begin to form soft peaks. Slowly add a few drops of lemon juice and half the sugar and beat until stiff peaks form.
3 Mix together the walnuts, the rest of the sugar, ground almonds and lemon zest until well combined and then fold into the meringue mixture.
4 Spoon into the prepared tin and bake in a preheated oven for 10 minutes then reduce the heat to 150°C/300°F/gas mark 2, and bake for a further 40 minutes.

5 Meanwhile, make the chocolate mixture. Melt the chocolate and butter in a heatproof bowl over a pan of simmering water.
6 Separately beat the eggs and the sugar until fluffy and add the instant coffee paste and mix together. Then fold into the chocolate mixture.
7 Remove the meringue from the oven and pour the chocolate mixture over it. Turn up the oven to 160°C/310°F/gas mark 2½ and bake for a further 20–25 minutes.
8 Remove from the oven, allow to cool for 20 minutes in the tin and then turn out onto a wire rack.
9 Dust liberally with icing sugar and serve.

Hazelnut Dacquoise

Serves 8

200g (7oz) Crème Pâtissière
(see page 296)
250g (9oz) Chocolate Crème
Pâtissière (see page 297)
100g (3½oz) ground
hazelnuts
100g (3½oz) ground almonds
180g (6½oz) icing sugar, plus
extra for dusting
7 egg whites
200g (7oz) caster sugar

cocoa powder, for dusting

Impress your friends and family by baking your own French dessert cake with an equally impressive name – Dacquoise. In the same family of dessert cakes as Marjolaines (which are rectangular and use chocolate fillings), this melt-in-the-mouth cake comprises layers of almond or hazelnut meringue, sandwiched together with a range of fillings from hazelnut mousse and crème pâtissière to humble buttercream.

1 Follow the instructions on pages 296 and 297 to make the crèmes pâtissières and set aside in the fridge until needed.
2 Preheat the oven to 150°C/300°F/gas mark 2, and line two large baking trays with baking parchment.
3 Draw three circles of 12cm (4½in) diameter on the baking parchment. Turn the parchment over so that the ink doesn't bleed into your cake and place on the large baking trays.
4 Sift the ground hazelnuts, ground almonds and icing sugar together.
5 Whisk the egg whites until they start to form soft peaks. Slowly add the sugar until glossy and then fold in all the dry ingredients.

6 Divide the mixture between the three circles and, using a palette knife, spread out evenly.
7 Bake in a preheated oven for about 1 hour.
8 Remove from the oven and leave to cool.
9 Put the first meringue layer on a cake stand or serving plate. Fill a piping bag with the crème pâtissière and, using a No. 10 nozzle, pipe it in concentric circles onto the meringue.
10 Pop on the second meringue layer and fill a piping bag, using a No. 10 nozzle, with the chocolate version and pipe in the same way.
11 Place the third meringue layer on top. Lay a palette knife down the middle and dust half with icing sugar and half with cocoa powder.
12 Serve chilled.

TRAY BAKES

Gingerbread

Serves 16

180g (6½oz) butter, softened
150g (5½oz) caster sugar
3 eggs
390g (13½oz) plain flour, sifted
1½ tsp bicarbonate of soda
½ tsp salt
1 tsp ground cinnamon
1½ tsp ground ginger
360ml (8fl oz) full-fat milk
3 tbsp golden syrup
3 tbsp black treacle
finely grated zest of 1½ lemons
200g (7oz) Royal Icing (see page 297)

Europeans have been eating gingerbreads since the first travellers came bearing its recipe in the first century AD. Originally baked and eaten for ginger's digestive powers, we now eat gingerbread whenever it takes our fancy. It's an easy-to-throw together cake but always makes a crowd-pleasing tray bake – with or without icing.

1 Preheat the oven to 170°C/325°F/gas mark 3, and grease and line a 23cm (9in) square cake tin with baking parchment.
2 Cream the butter and sugar together until light and fluffy, and add the eggs one at a time.
3 Add the sifted flour, bicarbonate of soda, salt and spices and mix until well combined.
4 Warm the milk slightly in a pan on a low heat and add in the syrup and treacle then pour into the mixture. Then stir in the lemon zest.
5 Pour the mixture into the prepared cake tin and bake in a preheated oven for 40 minutes or until a cocktail stick inserted into the centre comes out clean.

6 Remove from the oven, allow to cool for 10 minutes in the tin and then turn out onto a wire rack. Strip off the baking parchment.
7 Slice once cool and serve with tea.
8 If you prefer your gingerbread topped with icing, then make the Royal Icing as instructed on page 297. Complex decorations such as the one opposite take many hours of practice and I would suggest starting with simple patterns and using a parchment-paper piping bag, ensuring you have a pencil-sized point to enable you to pipe finely. You could also use a stencil, readily available online, to create similar effects.

VARIATION

WITH LEMON FROSTING As an alternative, top your gingerbread with this lemon frosting for a tangy contrast. Make the Classic Buttercream as instructed on page 298 and add the finely grated zest of 2 lemons and 30ml (1fl oz) of lemon juice to the buttercream at the end before spreading liberally on top of your gingerbread.

Parkin

Serves 16

340g (11¾oz) plain flour
1½ tsp ground mixed spice
1½ tsp ground ginger
1 tsp salt
1½ tsp bicarbonate of soda
340g (11¾oz) oatmeal
225g (8oz) butter
260g (9¼oz) black treacle
170g (6oz) soft brown sugar
220ml (7½fl oz) full-fat milk
2 eggs, lightly beaten

Traditionally made in the North of England, UK, for eating on a cold and frosty Bonfire Night (5th November) along with treacle toffee, this spicy cake has a wonderfully moist treacle flavour. And like few others, parkin improves – in flavour and in texture – the longer you keep it in a sealed tin. So, don't save this cake just for Bonfire Night, eat it – like me – all year.

1 Preheat the oven to 170°C/325°F/gas mark 3, and grease and line a 23cm (9in) square tin with baking parchment.

2 In a bowl, sift together the flour, spices, salt and bicarbonate of soda, and add the oatmeal.

3 In a pan on a medium heat, melt the butter, treacle and sugar until dissolved.

4 Add the milk to the dry ingredients, followed by the egg.

5 Pour the pan contents into the bowl and mix briskly together then pour into the prepared cake tin. Bake in a preheated oven for about 50 minutes, or until a cocktail stick inserted into the centre comes out clean.

6 Remove from the oven, allow to cool for 20 minutes in the tin and then turn out onto a wire rack and strip off the parchment.

7 Just like treacle toffee, don't save it for Bonfire Night, eat whenever you fancy with a cup of tea.

Chocolate and Polenta Cake

Serves 12

320g (11¼oz) butter, softened
320g (11¼oz) caster sugar
30g (1¼oz) cocoa powder,
    sifted
300g (10½oz) ground almonds
160g (5¾oz) fine polenta
    (or cornmeal)
5g (⅛oz) baking powder
4 eggs, beaten
100ml (3½fl oz) full-fat milk
1 tsp almond essence
200g (7oz) Chocolate
    Buttercream (see page 298)
20g (¾oz) cocoa nibs, for
    decoration

In Roman times, polenta was the staple of the mighty Roman Legions, who would eat it in a porridge or baked hard into a 'cake'. Fortunately, we don't have to limit our eating to polenta porridge and instead can use this grain in baking to create a pleasantly crumbly and grainy texture, as in this cake.

1 Preheat the oven to 160°C/310°F/gas mark 2½, and grease a deep 21cm (8in) square cake tin.
2 Cream the butter and sugar together until light and fluffy.
3 Stir in the sifted cocoa powder, ground almonds, polenta and baking powder.
4 Add in the eggs, one at a time, scraping down after each addition until well combined then fold in the milk and almond essence.
5 Spoon the mixture into the prepared tin and bake in a preheated oven for 45 minutes.

6 Remove from the oven, allow to cool for 10 minutes in the tin and then turn out onto a wire rack.
7 Meanwhile, make the chocolate buttercream as instructed on page 298.
8 Once completely cool, spread the buttercream evenly over the top of the cake and sprinkle with cocoa nibs (or if you prefer use something similar to Belgian chocolate vermicelli).
9 Serve with coffee.

Brownies

Makes 16

340g (11¾oz) butter, softened
675g (1lb 8¾oz) caster sugar
540g (1lb 3oz) dark chocolate
(minimum 70% cocoa
solids), melted
6 eggs
1 tsp vanilla extract
150g (5½oz) plain flour
150g (5½oz) cocoa powder
100g (3½oz) whole hazelnuts,
chopped
100g (3½oz) flaked almonds

The all-American chocolatey treat – the Brownie – was created and first baked at the turn of the 20th century in the US. Culinary historians have traced the first printed recipe of a cake 'brownie' (rather than a cookie version) to *The 1906 Boston Cooking-School Cook Book*. Being quick and easy to make keeps Brownies in the top tray bake charts, and with their endless variations they are perfect for most occasions whether for a school lunchbox, a summer picnic or just a yummy snack.

1 Preheat the oven to 160°C/310°F/gas mark 2½, and grease a 24cm (9½in) square cake tin.
2 Soften the butter in a bowl with a spatula and add the sugar and melted chocolate.
3 Slowly beat in the eggs and vanilla extract.
4 Sift the flour and cocoa powder together and fold into the wet mixture.
5 Add the nuts and mix well.
6 Pour the mixture into the prepared tin and bake in a preheated oven for 55 minutes.
7 Remove from the oven, allow to cool for 10 minutes in the tin and then turn out onto a wire rack.
8 When cool, cut into 16 squares and serve.

VARIATION

NUT-FREE BROWNIES If you have any guests who prefer a nut-free version, then simply omit the nuts and you'll still end up with a wonderfully gooey treat.

Pineapple Upside Down Cake

Serves 9

250g (9oz) golden syrup
9 tinned pineapple rings, thoroughly drained
9 glacé cherries
225g (8oz) butter, softened
225g (8oz) caster sugar
6 eggs
½ tsp vanilla extract
400g (14oz) plain flour, sifted
4 tsp baking powder
120ml (4fl oz) full-fat milk, warmed

This well-known cake was invented in the days when all food was cooked over a fire with just one pot. Fruit would be put in the bottom of the pan, covered in sugar and cooked with a simple sweet batter dolloped on top. Once ready it would be turned over onto a plate to show off the fruit. When American home bakers discovered the convenience of tinned fruit (much of it from Hawaii) in the early 20th century, they made it the classic it is today. Rather than the more usual round version, I like to bake mine in a square tin so that everyone gets a complete pineapple ring to themselves.

1 Preheat the oven to 170°C/325°F/gas mark 3, and grease and line a 23cm (9in) square cake tin with baking parchment.
2 Warm the golden syrup slightly, so it is easier to use, and pour into the bottom of the prepared cake tin.
3 Next, place the pineapple rings on the bottom of the tin with a glacé cherry in the centre of each. Set in the fridge for 30 minutes.
4 Cream the butter and sugar together until light and fluffy, and add the eggs one at a time, scraping down after each addition, followed by the vanilla extract.

5 Slowly add the sifted flour and baking powder to the egg mix and incorporate well.
6 Finally, mix the warmed milk slowly into the batter until it achieves a dropping consistency. Pour the batter over the pineapple rings and bake in a preheated oven for 1 hour or until a cocktail stick inserted into the centre comes out clean.
7 Remove from the oven, cool for 10 minutes in the tin and then turn out onto a wire rack and strip off the baking parchment.
8 Make sure each serving has a complete pineapple ring – share out that retro cake love.

Basbousa

Makes 16

For the syrup:
330g (11½oz) caster sugar
220ml (7½fl oz) water
3 tbsp lemon juice

For the cake:
450g (1lb) butter
300ml (10fl oz) yogurt
225g (8oz) caster sugar
350g (12oz) fine semolina
2 tsp baking powder
2 tsp vanilla extract
60g (2oz) blanched almonds, chopped
60g (2oz) shelled pistachios, chopped
toasted almonds, to decorate

Semolina (ground durum wheat) is a food staple used throughout North Africa and the Middle East to make couscous and throughout the world to make pasta. Super-sweet semolina cakes are hugely popular in Libya, Egypt and the rest of the Middle East. Whether it's referred to as Basbousa (Egypt and Libya), Revani (Turkey and Greece) or Namoura (Syria), this tray-baked cake oozes with syrup or honey. Apparently, 'basbousa' can be used for a term of affection, such as 'sweety' or 'my sweet'. You can add a variety of nuts and fruits to a Basbousa, and desiccated coconut is another popular addition.

1 Preheat the oven to 200°C/400°F/gas mark 6, and grease and line a 21cm (8in) square baking tin with baking parchment.
2 First make the syrup. Put all the ingredients in a pan and bring to the boil. Simmer for 10 minutes until syrupy then leave to cool.
3 Melt the butter. Pour the yogurt into a bowl and add two-thirds of the melted butter (set aside the rest), the sugar, semolina, baking powder, vanilla extract and the chopped nuts.

Mix everything thoroughly together.
4 Pour the mixture into the prepared tin, smooth the top using a palette knife and bake in a preheated oven for 20 minutes.
5 Remove from the oven and cut into diamond shapes while still warm and in the tin. Then firmly press a toasted almond into the centre of each piece and return to the oven for a further 15 minutes or until golden brown.
6 Remove from the oven and pour the cold syrup evenly over the Basbousa and return to the oven for a further 2 minutes.
7 Warm the remaining butter, remove the cake from the oven and pour the butter evenly over the cake's surface.
8 Leave to cool, strip off the baking parchment and serve with cream and coffee.

VARIATION

COCONUT BASBOUSA
Replace 30g (1¼oz) of the semolina with 75g (2¾oz) of desiccated coconut. For the syrup replace the water with coconut water and the lemon juice with lime juice.

Millionaire's Shortbread

Makes 16

For the shortbread base:
200g (7oz) butter
100g (3½oz) caster sugar
1 egg yolk
1 tsp double cream
225g (8oz) plain flour

For the caramel:
180g (6½oz) butter
75g (2¾oz) caster sugar
50g (1¾oz) golden syrup
345ml (11⅔fl oz) condensed
    milk

For the topping:
250g (9oz) dark chocolate
    (minimum 60% cocoa
    solids)
50g (1¾oz) butter

This triple-layered perfection has a golden crunch from the shortbread, creamy caramel and bittersweet chocolate to top it all off. Some say it's a Scottish treat while others argue it's British through and through. And whatever you call it, it tastes divine.

1 Preheat the oven to 170°C/325°F/gas mark 3. You'll need a 24cm (9½in) square non-stick tin.
2 First, make the base. Cream the butter and sugar together in a bowl until light and fluffy, then add the egg yolk and cream.
3 Stir in the flour. Using your fingers and thumbs, work the mixture until it resembles fine breadcrumbs. Bring together and work a little on a floured surface. Wrap in clingfilm and place in the fridge to rest.
4 Remove the shortbread mixture from the fridge and roll out until 1cm (½in) thick and press down into the cake tin.
5 Bake in a preheated oven until light brown (about 10–15 minutes). Remove from the oven and leave to cool.
6 Meanwhile, make the caramel. Melt the butter in a pan, add the sugar, golden syrup and condensed milk and stir continuously over a low heat until it turns a caramel colour. Remove from the heat and leave the mixture in the pan. (Test a small amount to see if it will set in the fridge before removing it completely from the heat.) This mixture can 'catch' very easily – if you notice any small black dots, change the pan, as any catching will spoil its flavour.
7 Pour the warm caramel over the cooled shortbread, lightly shaking the tin to ensure an even covering. Leave to cool then chill to set.
8 Meanwhile, melt the chocolate and butter in a heatproof bowl over a pan of simmering water and stir until smooth.
9 Pour the chocolate over the chilled caramel and shortbread. Return to the fridge until set and then slice into squares and serve with coffee or tea.

Fridge Cake

Makes 12

120g (4oz) digestive biscuits
120g (4oz) chocolate
    digestive biscuits
150g (5½oz) milk chocolate
150g (5½oz) dark chocolate
    (minimum 55% cocoa
    solids)
100g (3½oz) butter
150g (5½oz) golden syrup
100g (3½oz) dried apricots,
    chopped
50g (1¾oz) macadamia nuts,
    chopped
50g (1¾oz) cashew nuts,
    toasted
75g (2¾oz) raisins

No baking is required for these yummy squares of chewiness. They just need to be set in the fridge, hence the name; though some people also call this cake 'tiffin'. You can include all sorts of ingredients, so you just need to pick your favourites for the perfect teatime treat.

1 You will need an 18cm (7in) square tin.
2 Place the biscuits in a plastic bag and bash with a rolling pin into small pieces.
3 In a heatproof bowl over a pan of simmering water, melt together the chocolate, butter and golden syrup, stirring occasionally.
4 Remove from the heat and add the biscuits, apricots, nuts and raisins, and mix well.
5 Spoon the mixture into the tin, leave to cool a little and then refrigerate for at least 2 hours.
6 Remove from the tin and cut into squares.

VARIATION

TIFFIN WITH A TWIST For a surprise for your guests, sprinkle in 50g (1¾oz) of popping candy after the raisins. The popping candy starts popping as soon as you take the lid off, so measure it out last and mix in well before chilling.

MILLIONAIRE'S SHORTBREAD

FRIDGE CAKE

Where to Eat Cake...
ROME

Rome is one of the most ancient cities in Europe, full of awe-inspiring and historic places to visit – all the more reason to know of a perfect place to take a well-deserved break for cake. With the many piazzas and streets filled with cafés spilling out onto the pavements, you will be spoilt for choice.

POMPI
Via Albalonga 7, 00183 Rome
www.barpompi.it
The only place in Rome to buy tiramisu, according to the Romans. If you're unlucky and they've run out, then console yourself with one of the many flavours of their home-made gelati (ice cream).

ANDREOTTI
Via Ostiense 54b, 00154 Rome
www.andreottiroma.com
Located in one of Rome's most historic areas, this contemporary café has become a hot spot for traditional Roman pastries (such as cornetti, a local take on a croissant) and extravagant confectionery creations. It's easy to while away an afternoon at an outside table.

BOCCA DI DAMA
Via Arenula 17, 00186 Rome
www.boccadidama.it
This lovely café is run by people who consider cake making a form of art. You'll have to see it to believe it. While you're there tuck into divine cupcakes topped with blueberries or exquisite bon bons with names such as bacio dell'architetto (the architect's kiss).

BAR MIZZICA
Via Catanzaro 30, 00161 Rome
www.mizzica.it
This is the place that sells all things sweet from the island of Sicily and is one of the best kept secrets of Rome. Unfortunately, you can't sit inside, and there may well be a wait for a table outside, but it will be well worth it.

CRISTALLI DI ZUCCHERO
Via di Val Tellina 114, 00151 Rome
www.cristallidizucchero.it
A dream shop for anyone who loves fruit-based tarts and puff pastry – some say it's the best pastry shop in Rome – with all the cakes coming in miniature (as in pop-straight-into-the-mouth) sizes. You can take them home or eat them while relaxing in the local piazza.

ZAMPILLI MARCELLO & C PASTICCERIA
Via Antonio Tempesta 41A, 00176 Roma
No website
The perfect stop for breakfast pastries or cakes to go with your coffee. If you're in Rome during Carnival season (early February), this is the bakery to buy your Frappe and Castagnole (traditional Carnival sweets) from.

SIGNORINI ANTONIO PASTICCERIA
Via di Tor Pignattara 16, 00177 Rome
No website
Renowned for its wonderful celebration cakes, it also does a great line in extremely good-value pastries. It comes highly recommended.

MONDI
Via Flaminia 468, 00191 Rome
www.mondiroma.it
Renowned among the locals as the best place for desserts, this traditional pastry shop sells everything from croissants to cookies and cakes.

VITTI
Piazza di San Lorenzo in Lucina, 33, 00186 Rome
www.caffetteriavittiroma.it
Situated in the intimate square of San Lorenzo, this famous bar and pastry shop offers the best in the world of Italian pastries including rum soaked baba from Naples to bite sized Sacher cakes.

Panforte di Siena

Serves 12

120g (4oz) blanched almonds
100g (3½oz) blanched
    hazelnuts
85g (3oz) unsalted, green,
    shelled pistachios
275g (9¾oz) mixed dried
    fruit, including apricots,
    mixed peel, raisins and
    sultanas
1 tsp ground cinnamon
½ tsp ground ginger
¼ tsp ground cloves
½ tsp ground nutmeg
¼ tsp ground black pepper
100g (3½oz) plain flour
1 rounded tbsp cocoa powder
1 tsp salt
180g (6½oz) clear honey
180g (6½oz) caster sugar
icing sugar, to dust

Originally from Siena in Tuscany, this sticky, sweet, spicy nut cake is usually served in winter, particularly at Christmas. Its recipe is centuries old, dating back to when spices arrived by boat at the nearby port of Pisa. I love the combination of the black pepper and nuts in this recipe, making it deliciously spicy and incredibly moreish.

1 Preheat the oven to 180°C/350°F/gas mark 4, and grease and line a 21cm (8in) square cake tin with baking parchment. You'll also need a baking tray.

2 Arrange the almonds and hazelnuts on a baking tray and bake until lightly golden, about 5–6 minutes. Allow them to cool before chopping them roughly. Turn the oven temperature down to 150°C/300°F/gas mark 2.

3 In a bowl, put the chopped nuts, pistachios and dried fruit and mix well.

4 In a separate bowl, sift the dry ingredients together and mix well. Then add the fruit and nut mixture and combine well.

5 Mix together the honey and sugar in a pan and stir over a low heat until the sugar has dissolved. Bring to the boil and continue to cook until the mixture reaches 115°C/239°F (use a probe thermometer).

6 Pour the honeyed mixture over the fruit and nut mix and stir well.

7 Tip the mixture into the prepared tin and spread out evenly. Bake in the preheated oven for 30–40 minutes until slightly firm.

8 Allow to cool in the tin and then turn out onto a wire rack. Strip off the baking parchment.

9 Cut into delicate finger slices, lightly dust with icing sugar and serve.

Sheet Cake

Serves 30

For the orange sponge:
6 eggs
200g (7oz) caster sugar
160g (5¾oz) plain flour, sifted
25g (1oz) cornflour, sifted
40g (1½oz) butter, melted
½ tsp yellow food colouring
finely grated zest of 2 oranges

For the chocolate sponge:
6 eggs
200g (7oz) caster sugar
160g (5¾oz) plain flour, sifted
60g (2oz) cocoa powder, sifted

This American favourite can be as simple or as complicated as you like. However it comes, it's always popular and is perfect when baking for large numbers of people. And it's helpful to have an extra pair of hands when making this cake – so you can promise your helper the first, and biggest, slice.

1 Preheat the oven to 170°C/325°F/gas mark 3, and line a baking tray with baking parchment.
2 Make the orange sponge first. Whisk the eggs until soft and foamy. Slowly add the sugar and beat until trebled in size.
3 Fold in carefully the sifted flour and cornflour and then fold in the melted butter and finally the food colouring and the orange zest.
4 Use the same method for the chocolate sponge, adding the cocoa with the sifted flour.
5 Glue the baking parchment to the tray with a dot of cake mixture at each corner to prevent it flapping about in the oven.
6 Put each sponge mix into a piping bag with a 3cm (1¼in) nozzle and – this is the fun bit – with a friend, put the two piping bags together and rotate around the tray until you have filled it with the dual-colour sponge mix in a spiral.
7 Bake in a preheated oven for 10 minutes until a cocktail stick inserted into the centre comes out clean.
8 Remove from the oven, allow to cool for

10 minutes and then turn out onto a wire rack and strip off the baking parchment. When removing the parchment, make a nick in the middle of the paper and tear away from the middle, so as not to tear the sponge.
9 Square off the cake with a serrated knife, cut into squares and enjoy with pouring cream.

VARIATIONS

GINGER SHEET CAKE Double the mix of either the chocolate or the orange sponge. Add 2 tablespoons of ground ginger and 100g (3½oz) of stem ginger. Decorate with frosting and walnuts.

LEMON SHEET CAKE Double the orange sponge recipe and replace the orange zest with lemon zest and add 1 teaspoon of lemon oil.

Swiss Roll

Serves 8

500ml (18fl oz) Crème
    Chantilly (see page 296)
6 eggs, separated
250g (9oz) icing sugar
100g (3½oz) cocoa powder,
    sifted
25g (1oz) cornflour
150g (5½oz) seedless
    raspberry jam, warmed

For the sugar syrup:
100g (3½oz) caster sugar
100ml (3½fl oz) water

icing sugar, sifted, to dust
fresh raspberries, to serve

Many countries around the world have their own takes on a Swiss Roll – see the French's on page 270 as the Bûche de Nöel – and it seems that it didn't actually originate in Switzerland. But one thing's for sure, this wonderful teatime treat always elicits the wickedest smile when served.

1 First, make the crème Chantilly as instructed on page 296 and set aside in the fridge.
2 Preheat the oven to 170°C/325°F/gas mark 3, and grease and line a baking tray or Swiss roll tin. I used one 40cm x 30cm (16in x 12in) and I blob a little bit of cake mixture under each corner to stop the paper flapping in the oven.
3 In a large bowl, whisk the egg yolks together with one-third of the icing sugar to create a thick and pale mixture.
4 In a separate bowl, whisk the egg whites until they form soft peaks, then add the rest of the icing sugar.
5 Fold the egg white mixture into the egg yolk mixture, then fold in the cocoa and cornflour.
6 Pour the mixture into the prepared tin and, using a palette knife, spread out the mixture evenly across the tin.
7 Bake in a preheated oven for 20 minutes.
8 Meanwhile, make the sugar syrup. Place the sugar and water in a pan. Cook over a low heat, stirring continuously then boil for a

minute or so. Pass the liquid through a sieve. Remove from the heat and leave to cool.
9 Remove the sponge from the oven. If it's ready, the sponge will spring back to the touch.
10 Turn out immediately onto a clean tea towel. Make a slit in the centre of the baking parchment with a knife. Starting from the slit, carefully peel the baking parchment away from the sponge.
11 While the sponge is still warm, dip a pastry brush into the sugar syrup and dab the sponge until moist but not soaked.
12 Brush on a layer of warmed raspberry jam and smooth the crème Chantilly over the sponge evenly.
13 Pick up the edges of the tea towel furthest away from you and slowly bring it towards you to curl the sponge into a roll. Wrap the tea towel around the rolled sponge and place in the fridge to set and absorb the flavours.
14 Serve sprinkled with icing sugar alongside fresh raspberries and a cup of tea.

Apple Streusel

Serves 6–8

For the dough:
150g (5½oz) plain flour
110g (3¾oz) butter
100g (3½oz) caster sugar
½ tbsp vanilla extract
½ tbsp baking powder
2 eggs

For the topping:
2 apples, peeled, cored and
   sliced
½ tsp ground cinnamon
a pinch of ground cloves
a pinch of ground nutmeg
40g (1½oz) flaked almonds

For the streusel:
30g (1¼oz) butter, melted
60g (2oz) plain flour
75g (2¾oz) caster sugar

Not to be confused with another popular cake – Apple Strudel (see page 230) – 'streusel' is German and literally means 'to scatter'. The streusel refers to the topping, which is scattered over the cake to create a super-crunchy finish, a little like a British crumble (see Rhubarb Crumble Cake page 89). This lovely aromatic cake works just as well as a dessert, too – bonus.

1 Preheat the oven to 160°C/310°F/gas mark 2½, and lightly oil an 18cm (7in) square tin.
2 Mix all the ingredients for the dough in a large mixing bowl until well combined.
3 Spoon the dough into the prepared tin and flatten it using your fingers until it reaches all the corners and is equally distributed.
4 Place the sliced apples on top in two to three rows slightly overlapping each other, and sprinkle over the cinnamon, cloves and nutmeg and, lastly, the flaked almonds.
5 Now, make the streusel. Mix the butter, flour and sugar together with your fingers until the mixture resembles breadcrumbs. Add more flour if you need to reach a crumbly texture.
6 Sprinkle the streusel on the top of the cake and bake in a preheated oven for about 1 hour.

7 Remove from the oven, allow to cool for 30 minutes in the tin and then turn out onto a wire rack.

VARIATIONS

CHERRY STREUSEL When cherries are in season, simply replace the apples with 120g (4oz) stoned cherries.

APRICOT STREUSEL As with cherries, using fresh apricots when in season, simply replace the apples with 120g (4oz) quartered fresh apricots.

Kueh Lapis

Serves 10–12

550g (1lb 3½oz) butter, softened
260g (9¼oz) caster sugar
15 egg yolks
8 egg whites
¾ tsp cream of tartar
85g (3oz) plain flour
4 tsp ground cinnamon
6 tsp full-fat milk

Hailing from Indonesia and Malaysia, kueh is like a cake or a pastry. This version – Kueh Lapis – is one of the more popular cakes served on special occasions. It's a moist, rich cake of 'a thousand layers' and does take time to prepare as each layer is grilled separately, but I can assure you that the outcome is well worth it. I've stuck with a traditional recipe here but recently new flavours, such as chocolate, coffee or prune, have become popular.

1 You will need an 18cm (7in) square cake tin lined with baking parchment.
2 Cream the butter and half the sugar together until light and fluffy. Add the yolks one at a time.
3 Whisk the egg whites with the rest of the sugar and cream of tartar until stiff peaks form.
4 Sift the flour and cinnamon into a bowl.
5 Incorporate a third of the egg white into the egg yolk mix to loosen up the mixture. Then, fold in one-third of the sifted dry ingredients followed by the milk and then the rest of the egg white mixture and combine.

6 Finally, fold in the rest of the dry ingredients.
7 Turn your grill on to a medium heat.
8 Spread a thin layer (2–3 tablespoons) of the mixture into the prepared cake tin and grill for about 4 minutes until nicely brown. Remove from the grill, spread another thin layer of mixture on top and place under the grill as before. Repeat until all the mixture is used up.
9 Leave in the tin to cool completely then turn out onto a serving plate, strip off the baking parchment and slice thinly for your guests. Serve with a strong coffee.

CHEESECAKES

Vanilla Cheesecake

Serves 6

40g (1½oz) butter
100g (3½oz) digestive biscuits, crushed
600g (1lb 5oz) full-fat cream cheese
½ vanilla pod, split and scraped
85g (3oz) caster sugar
75g (2¾oz) soured cream
1 egg

For the blueberry compôte:

500g (1lb 2oz) fresh or frozen blueberries
75g (2¾oz) caster sugar
1 tbsp water

The cheesecake actually dates back to Ancient Greece. Early forms of 'cheese cake' were made with flour, wheat, honey and cheese. Cheesecake was served to Olympic athletes, as a source of energy, and at weddings, as a celebratory dessert. This smooth, rich and easy-to-make cheesecake fits the bill every time and is great with a blueberry compôte.

1 Preheat the oven to 140°C/275°F/gas mark 1 and grease a 15cm (6in) wide x 3.5cm (1½in) deep tart ring and a baking tray.
2 Melt the butter in a pan, pour over the crushed biscuits and mix together. Spread the mixture evenly in the prepared tart ring.
3 In a bowl, soften the cream cheese with a spatula or wooden spoon. In a separate bowl, mix the vanilla seeds with the sugar, then add to the cream cheese. Add the soured cream and egg and beat slowly for a short time – do not overbeat as too much air will result in a soufflé.
4 Fill the ring with the cream cheese mixture and smooth over the top with a palette knife. Bake in a preheated oven for 40 minutes.

5 To see if the cheesecake is cooked, gently push a cocktail stick into the centre – it should come away clean. Remove from the oven and leave to cool for 20 minutes before chilling.
6 Next, make the compôte. Put 200g (7oz) of the blueberries, all the sugar and the water in a pan and slowly bring to the boil. Simmer for 5 minutes, then leave to cool for 10 minutes. Blitz in a blender then pass through a sieve to remove any bits. Return to the pan and gently simmer until reduced by half. Add the remaining blueberries and bring to the boil. Remove from the heat and leave to cool.
7 Remove the ring just before serving, and spoon on some of the blueberry compôte.

New York Cheesecake

Serves 12

For the base:
250g (9oz) digestive biscuits, crushed
50g (1¾oz) butter, melted

For the filling:
1.58kg (3½lb) full-fat cream cheese (preferably Philadelphia)
1 vanilla pod, split and scraped
250g (9oz) caster sugar
250g (9oz) soured cream
2 eggs, beaten

America's very own contribution to the world of cheesecake came after a delicious accident when a New York dairy farmer invented cream cheese in the 19th century. By the 1900s, all New Yorkers loved cheesecake. Each region of the world has its own take on a great cheesecake, but this classic version has a deep, baked, smooth creamy topping and a biscuity base – and always wows a crowd. I like to serve it plain, just as the New Yorkers do, with no toppings or side additions of fruit or chocolate.

1 Preheat the oven to 160°C/310°F/gas mark 2½, and grease well and line (the bottom) of a 23cm (9in) loose-bottomed cake tin with baking parchment.
2 Mix together the crushed biscuits and the melted butter and then spread into the prepared tin. Using the back of a spoon, pat down evenly and chill for at least 20 minutes.
3 Using a spatula, soften the cream cheese in a bowl. Add in the vanilla seeds and sugar, then the soured cream and beaten eggs. Mix well.
4 Remove the base from the fridge and pour the cream cheese mixture on top and smooth the surface with a palette knife.
5 Bake in a preheated oven for 1 hour; the centre should still have a slight wobble. Remove from the oven, cool on a wire rack and strip off the baking parchment.
6 Place in the fridge for at least 1 hour and serve chilled.

Where to Eat Cake...
NEW YORK CITY

New York has long been famous for its bakeries and it's hardly surprising as it was the first stop for many of the immigrants arriving from some of the world's great baking nations. The Germans, Austrians, Hungarians, Poles and Jewish people from all over Eastern Europe settled here, as did many Italians and French, bringing their traditional recipes with them. More recently, the Big Apple saw a bakery boom, which partnered the explosion in the New York restaurant scene, and artisanal bakeries are continuing to spring up all over the city. New Yorkers would argue that they have the best bakeries in the world and whether you're after a cupcake, éclair or a big slice of cheesecake, there are plenty of places where you can recover from the bustle of NYC.

MAGNOLIA BAKERY
401 Bleecker St, New York, NY 10014 and other branches
www.magnoliabakery.com
Home of the cupcake. It started off the huge trend (in 1996) in cupcakes and bakeries to be seen in.

BALTHAZAR BAKERY
80 Spring St (corner of Crosby St), New York, NY 10012
www.balthazarbakery.com
This buzzing and bustling city bakery turns out hand-made French bread and pastries. Many top-end restaurants in New York – including Alain Ducasse, Jean-Georges, Craft, Artisanal and Gramercy Tavern – serve Balthazar breads.

ZUCKER BAKERY
433 East 9th St, New York, NY 10009
www.zuckerbakery.com
Eastern European and Mediterranean bakeshop; and it's good to know that the recipes for pastries are all handed down from family and friends.

ONE CUP TWO CUPCAKES
953 Columbus Ave, New York, NY 10025
www.onecuptwocupcakes.com
As the name implies, this place specialises in cupcake creations for all occasions as well as speciality cakes, gourmet pies and much much more.

LADY MENDL'S TEA SALON
The Inn at Irving Place, 56 Irving Place, New York, NY 10003
www.innatirving.com
Grand tea salon in traditional English style favoured by New Yorkers.

DOMINIQUE ANSEL
189 Spring St, New York, NY 10012
www.dominiqueansel.com
Named as one of the 'top 10 pastry chefs in America', Dominique Ansel produces fine French pastries, ranging from filled choux buns to layer cakes and crunchy crusted canneles.

FRANCOIS PAYARD BAKERY
1293 Third Ave, New York, NY 10021
www.fpbnyc.com
Renowned French chef, François Payard latterly opened this branch of his famous

pâtisserie in the Upper East Side. The famous macarons on offer are both sweet and savoury, with flavours such as squid ink and olive tapenade. Highly original and impeccably produced.

GRANDAISY BAKERY
250 West Broadway, New York, NY 10013
www.grandaisybakery.com
A European-style bakery and shop famed for its Italian pastries – and pizzas. If you're in the mood for a nibble, they also do biscotti, brioche, turnovers and all manner of cakes.

PETROSSIAN
182 West 58th St, New York, NY 10019
www.petrossian.com
Known primarily for their caviar, this international company also sells delicious cakes and bakes from its high-end bakery outlet. Their blueberry tarts are rightly famous.

FINANCIER PÂTISSERIE
62 Stone St, New York, NY 10004
(and other branches)
www.financierpastries.com
Opened in 2002 by restaurateur Peter Poulakakos (of Harry's Café & Harry's Steak) and Executive Pastry Chef Eric Bedoucha (of Bayard's, Lutece and La Grenouille) Financier Patisserie is a charming pastry shop specialising in traditional and signature French Pastries.

ALMONDINE BAKERY
85 Water St between Main and Old Dock Sts, Dumbo, Brooklyn, NY 11201
www.almondinebakery.com
These neighbourhood bakeries offer top-notch French-style breads and pastries, including croissants, baguettes and madeleines, to name but a few. Their croissants are said to be some of the best in New York city.

AMY'S BREAD
75 Ninth Ave (between 15th & 16th Sts), New York, NY 10011
(and other branches, see website)
www.amysbread.com
In 1992, Amy Scherber launched her first bakery. Go for classic cakes as well as her famous raisin semolina loaves.

MOMOFUKU MILK BAR
251 East 13th St, New York, NY 10003
(and other branches)
www.milkbarstore.com
Pastry chef Christina Tosi gives a wildly original spin to homey classics. Try the crack pie, compost cookies or pretzel milk. You won't regret it.

LADY M
41 East 78th St, New York, NY 10075
www.ladym.com
An awesome and mindblowing selection of cakes, tortes and tarts of all kinds are on offer at this confectionery.

BIEN CUIT
120 Smith St, Brooklyn, NY 11201
www.biencuit.com
This award-winning Brooklyn bakery with a French influence first opened its doors in July 2011 and later expanded to Greenwich Village in 2012. Run by a husband-and-wife team (Zachary Golper and Kate Wheatcroft), Bien Cuit provides perfect croissants, baguettes, breads and tarts.

JOYCE BAKESHOP
646 Vanderbilt Ave (between Park Pl and Prospect Pl), Brooklyn, NY 11238
www.joycebakeshop.com
Husband and wife team baking mini cupcakes, mini croissants and individual cakes of all kinds.

EGIDIO PASTRY SHOP
622 East 187th St, Bronx, NY 10458
No website
The pre-eminent Italian pastry shop in the Bronx was established in 1912. Come for pastries and cakes, biscotti and an espresso or for their must-try cannoli.

JUNIORS
Flatbush Ave, Brooklyn, NY 11201
www.juniorscheesecake.com
Known as the home of New York cheesecake, Juniors is the place to go for the best, and is worth the trip to Brooklyn.

BAKED BROOKLYN
359 Van Brunt St, Brooklyn, NY 11231
www.bakednyc.com
Hop on the subway to Brooklyn to sample the huge array of yummy cakes, cupcakes, cookies, brownies and whooopie pies – the menu is extensive.

MANSOURA
515 Kings Highway, Brooklyn, NY 11223
www.mansoura.com
If you're in the mood for something sweet and sticky, here is the best baklava in town.

Fiadone

Serves 8

150g (5½oz) caster sugar
1 tsp vanilla extract
3 eggs
250g (9oz) cottage cheese or
    ricotta
finely grated zest of ½ lemon
1 tsp cornflour, made into a
    paste with 1 tsp water
a pinch of salt

This Corsican cheesecake is really a cross between a flan and a rustic cheesecake and is the most famous and popular cake from the island of Corsica in the Mediterranean. Traditionally, it is made with a Corsican goat's cheese called Brioccu but I've found that ricotta or cottage cheese (which is slightly easier to get hold of) works just as well.

1 Preheat the oven to 170°C/325°F/gas mark 3 and grease an 18cm (7in) loose-bottomed cake tin well.
2 Whisk together the sugar, vanilla extract and the eggs in a bowl until frothy.
3 Add in the cheese, lemon zest, cornflour and salt and mix until well combined.
4 Pour the mixture into the prepared cake tin and bake in a preheated oven for 25 minutes without opening the oven.

5 The Fiadone does not swell, but should be browned on the edges and a cocktail stick inserted into the centre should come out clean.
6 Remove from the oven, allow to cool for 10 minutes in the tin and then turn out onto a wire rack.
7 Keep in the fridge and serve cold with coffee.

Chocolate Cheesecake

Serves 10

40g (1½oz) white chocolate, melted

100g (3½oz) cornflakes, crushed

75g (2¾oz) praline paste

1½ bronze gelatin leaves (or 2 tsp powdered gelatin)

700g (1lb 10oz) full-fat cream cheese

200g (7oz) icing sugar, sifted

160ml (5½fl oz) Grand Marnier liqueur

200g (7oz) dark chocolate (minimum 70% cocoa solids), melted

550ml (19fl oz) double cream, whipped

orange confit or candied orange peel, to decorate (optional)

For me, this recipe is a wonderful alternative to a baked cheesecake. It keeps the super-smooth creaminess of many cheesecakes, so I think the texture is spot on. The Grand Marnier and chocolate are perfectly matched and, with the surprise of the crunchy praline base, it's sure to become your new favourite.

1 You'll need a 25cm (10in) wide x 2.5cm (1in) deep tart ring and a cake board or serving plate.

2 Pour the melted white chocolate over the crushed cornflakes. Add the praline paste and mix thoroughly.

3 Place the tart ring on the board or plate and spoon the cornflake mixture into the ring and press down with the back of the spoon to smooth it evenly. If the mixture sticks to the spoon, dip it in warm water.

4 Soften the gelatin leaves in a bowl of iced water (if using powdered gelatin, mix it into a paste with a little cold water).

5 Meanwhile, in a bowl, soften the cream cheese with a spatula or wooden spoon, then add the sifted icing sugar.

6 In a pan, warm the Grand Marnier, add the softened gelatin leaves (or gelatin paste) and dissolve thoroughly. Remove from the heat and whisk gently into the cream cheese mixture. Then, add the melted chocolate and fold in the whipped cream.

7 Pour the mixture into the ring and smooth over with a palette knife. Leave to set in the fridge for 3 hours.

8 Remove the ring just before serving, and, if you like, decorate with orange confit.

Banana Cheesecake

Serves 8

For the base:
60g (2oz) butter
60g (2oz) caster sugar
120g (4oz) chocolate digestive
    biscuits, crushed

For the filling:
2 ripe bananas
juice and finely grated zest of
    ½ lemon
120g (4oz) caster sugar
250g (9oz) cream cheese
2 eggs, separated
150g (5½oz) soured cream
1½ bronze gelatin leaves
    (or 12g (⅓oz) powdered
    gelatin)
5 tbsp water

For the decoration:
50g (1¾oz) caster sugar
1 large banana, sliced

This super-easy, non-baked cheesecake produces nonetheless impressive results, as you can see opposite. The winning combination of the bananas with the chocolate digestives is always delicious and popular.

1 Grease a 21cm (8in) springform cake tin.
2 For the base, in a pan melt the butter and the sugar together over a gentle heat then stir in the crushed biscuits until fully mixed. Spread evenly over the base of the prepared cake tin and press down firmly. Chill for at least 30 minutes.
3 Break up the bananas into a large mixing bowl along with the lemon juice and zest and half of the caster sugar. Purée with a hand-held blender until smooth.
4 Beat in the cheese, the egg yolks and the soured cream, making sure there are no lumps.
5 Soften the gelatin in iced water, which removes any residue gelatin flavour. Heat up the 5 tablespoons of water in a pan and dissolve the leaves in the hot water. Allow to cool for 10 minutes before adding to the mix.
6 Next, whisk the egg whites until stiff then whisk in the remaining sugar. Fold the egg

whites lightly but thoroughly into the mixture and then spoon into the tin, shaking gently to level the surface.
7 Chill for 3–4 hours or until set.
8 To make the banana decoration, sprinkle half the sugar in a frying pan and heat until it begins to dissolve. When it becomes golden place the slices of banana onto the sugar and then sprinkle over the rest of the sugar. Turn over after 2 minutes once the bananas have turned golden. When golden on both sides tip the slices onto a piece of baking parchment or a silicone mat and space them out evenly so they can cool and don't stick together. Once cool, arrange neatly around the edge of your cheesecake.
9 Slice and serve with a jug of cream.

SMALL
CAKES

Madeleines

Makes 24

For the beurre noisette:
120g (4oz) butter, plus extra
    for melting and greasing
    moulds

For the sponge:
4 eggs
200g (7oz) caster sugar
250g (9oz) plain flour, plus
    extra for flouring moulds
2 tsp baking powder
250g (9oz) full-fat milk
finely grated zest of 1 orange
finely grated zest of 1 lemon

Forever immortalised by Marcel Proust in *À la Recherche du Temps Perdu*, published early in the 20th century, where he recalls his immediate transportation to childhood on tasting a Madeleine. These bite-sized delicate French sponges are made in a distinctive scallop shell mould and are best enjoyed warm from the oven. In France they're often eaten dipped in coffee or tea – and that's how Marcel as a child liked his, apparently. The secret to baking the best Madeleines is not only a hot oven but also well-buttered and floured moulds, so be sure to prepare them carefully.

1 Preheat the oven to 220°C/425°F/gas mark 7, and you'll need a Madeleine mould tray.
2 Make the beurre noisette. Place the butter in a pan and bring to the boil. Keep boiling until it turns a light brown and then remove from the heat. It's worth scraping down the sides of the pan thoroughly to include the residue from the boiling butter. Pour into a cold pan to prevent further cooking and set aside.
3 Place the Madeleine moulds in the freezer for 10 minutes, then remove them and brush quickly with melted butter. Return them to the freezer for 5 minutes, remove and repeat the process, but this time follow with a good drenching of flour. Knock off the excess flour and then return to the freezer for a few more

minutes. They're now ready to use.
4 Meanwhile, whisk the eggs and sugar together in a mixing bowl. Add the flour, baking powder, milk and zests, followed by the cooled beurre noisette. Mix together until everything is well combined.
5 Using a medium piping nozzle, pipe the mixture into the chilled moulds, being careful not to overfill.
6 Bake in a preheated oven for 10 minutes or until golden brown. Then remove and immediately knock out onto a wire rack.
7 Madeleines are delicious served hot – with your favourite topping of custard, icing sugar or even dipped in melted chocolate, but are equally tasty eaten just as they are.

VARIATION

CHOCOLATE MADELEINES
Follow the same method as above but using slightly different ingredients to create some glorious chocolate versions of these delicate sponges.
100g (3½oz) butter, for the beurre noisette
5 egg whites
200g (7oz) icing sugar
25g (1oz) plain flour
25g (1oz) cocoa powder
50g (1¾oz) ground almonds
50g (1¾oz) ground hazelnuts

Blueberry Financiers

Makes 12

For the beurre noisette:
150g (5½oz) butter

100ml (3½fl oz) Stock Syrup
(see page 299)

For the sponge:
6 egg whites
150g (5½oz) caster sugar
60g (2oz) ground almonds
60g (2oz) plain flour, sifted
100g (3½oz) fresh blueberries

For decoration:
65ml (2½fl oz) Apricot Glaze
(see page 299)

I've given these traditional French sponge teacakes a colour boost with the purple blueberries, which pairs well with the sponge's distinctive nutty taste from the beurre noisette. Traditionally, Financiers are made in mini-rectangular moulds as if miniature bars of gold. If you want to take these to the next level (as I've done many times before), you can transform these simple sponges into heavenly delicacies by dipping them straight from the oven into a heady rum and sugar syrup – just see how long you can wait before popping one in your mouth.

1 Preheat the oven to 200°C/400°F/gas mark 6 and you'll need 12 silicone moulds 8cm x 3cm x 3cm (3¼in x 1¼in x 1¼in) – I find silicone moulds are easier to use and clean.
2 Make the beurre noisette. Put the butter in a pan and bring to the boil. Keep boiling until it turns a light brown. Remove from the heat. It's worth scraping down the side of the pan thoroughly to include the residue from the boiling butter. Pour into a cold pan to prevent further cooking and set aside.

3 Make the syrup as instructed on page 299.
4 Beat the egg whites until they start to foam but are not whipped, then add the sugar and beat. Stop and scrape down the sides and beat again to ensure the ingredients are fully combined. Gradually add the ground almonds and flour, beat rapidly for a short time until thoroughly mixed, then add the cooled beurre noisette. Mix together.
5 Add the blueberries to the sponge mixture, making sure the fruits are well distributed.
6 Spoon the mixture into the moulds and place them on a baking tray in a preheated oven for about 20 minutes.
7 Remove from the oven and cool on a wire rack. Brush liberally with the glaze when cool and serve with some afternoon tea.

VARIATIONS
For other versions, substitute the following amounts of whichever takes your fancy for the blueberries above:
150g (5½oz) sultanas
100g (3½oz) chopped apricots
100g (3½oz) chopped pistachios.

Chocolate and Rum Canneles

Makes 20

500ml (18fl oz) full-fat milk
85g (3oz) butter
1 vanilla pod, split and
    scraped
110g (3¾oz) dark chocolate
    (minimum 70% cocoa
    solids), broken up
225g (8oz) icing sugar
10g (¼oz) cocoa powder
85g (3oz) plain flour
2 eggs, plus 2 egg yolks,
    beaten together
20ml (⅔fl oz) dark rum

These little delights have a very distinctive outer edge and originate from Bordeaux in Southwest France. Traditionally, these mini-cakes are baked in copper moulds, which ensure a crispy outer layer with a soft inside. You can buy these moulds from specialist cake suppliers for extra authenticity but you can use silicone moulds too (just make sure they're deep enough) – I've used both with great results all round.

1 Preheat the oven to 180°C/350°F/gas mark 4, and grease 20 moulds of 4cm (1½in) with silicon spray (if you can get hold of deodorised beeswax this would be better for the copper moulds as it helps the caramelisation).
2 Boil together the milk, the butter and the vanilla pod.
3 Break up the chocolate and put in a bowl.
4 Discard the vanilla pod and pour the hot liquid over the chocolate and whisk until the chocolate has melted. Set aside.
5 Sift together the icing sugar, cocoa powder and flour, and add these to the eggs and extra egg yolks and mix everything together well.

6 Now, fold in the chocolatey milk mixture and then add the rum. Mix again. (If you want to postpone your baking you can keep the dough at this stage for 3–4 days in the fridge; simply whisk the mixture thoroughly before baking.)
7 Spoon the mixture into the moulds up to 5mm (¼in) from the top edge.
8 Bake in a preheated oven for 35–40 minutes. Remove from the oven, allow to cool for 10 minutes in the moulds and then turn out onto a wire rack.
9 These little beauties are best eaten on the day they're baked as they will lose their wonderful crispy outer edge overnight.

Macarons

Makes 18

40g (1½oz) plain flour
350g (12oz) icing sugar
210g (7½oz) ground almonds
8 egg whites
85g (3oz) caster sugar
½ tsp food colouring powder
1 tsp flavouring of your choice

These delicate, multicoloured, almondy sweet treats have always been popular in France. Historians can find all sorts of stories about when macarons first put in an appearance from as far back as the 8th century, but it's not until early in the 20th century that we see two macarons sandwiched around a filling. Recently macarons have enjoyed a new lease of life as people all around the world have become entranced by their fabulous array of colours and tastes. They can be difficult to get right but it's worth persevering as they will always bring a smile to the recipient's face.

1 Line a baking tray with baking parchment or use a silicone baking mat.
2 Sift the flour, icing sugar and ground almonds into a bowl.
3 In another bowl, beat the egg whites until soft peaks form and slowly add the caster sugar. Then add any food colouring and food flavouring you desire.
4 Using a metal spoon, fold the dry ingredients into the egg whites until fully combined. Continue to fold until a thick ribbon forms. Be careful not to overfold as the mixture will be too wet to pipe.
5 Fill the piping bag and, using a No.10 piping nozzle, pipe the macarons onto a silicone mat or prepared baking tray.

6 Pipe into approximately 4cm (1½in) rounds evenly spaced across the tray. Tap the tray gently to release any air and leave for about 20 minutes until a skin has formed on the top of the macaron.
7 Meanwhile, preheat the oven to 140°C/275°F/ gas mark 1.
8 Bake in the oven for 8 minutes, then turn the tray around and cook for a further 8 minutes.
9 Remove from the oven and leave to cool on the tray before sandwiching together with your favourite filling. Here I have made Blueberry Macarons filled with a White Chocolate Ganache (see page 297), Raspberry Macarons filled with raspberry jam and Lemon Macarons filled with Chocolate Ganache (see page 297).

Where to Eat Cake...
PARIS

For anyone visiting Paris the first glimpse of one of the numerous boulangerie-pâtisserie window displays is unlikely to be forgotten, and they seem to be all around you. With their eye-catching and sumptuous array of high-quality cakes, pastries and breads, you won't need to wander far to find a place to stop and refuel or just to sample the delightful confections to solve that enduring question: does it taste as good as it looks? Invariably, the answer will be yes. And as the true home of the macaron, the challenge will be to choose a favourite flavour from the many rainbow-coloured displays. This compact French city is best discovered on foot, and that is also the best way to discover the nearest beautiful boulangerie.

LADURÉE
16 Rue Royale, 75008 Paris
(other locations see website)
www.laduree.fr
One of Paris's first tea rooms, its most notable invention is the double-side macaron, that is two almond meringue biscuits stuck together with a smooth ganache filling – pure pleasure.

DES GÂTEAUX ET DU PAIN
63 Boulevard Pasteur, 75015 Paris
www.desgateauxetdupain.com
The best chausson aux pommes in Paris. The owner and chef used to work with Pierre Hermé and makes a different tart for every season using best produce.

ROSE BAKERY
46 Rue des Martyrs. 75009 Paris
30 Rue Debelleyme. 75003 Paris
No website
This super-boho British bakery has locations in the 9th and the 3rd. Its carrot cake is unrivalled.

PIERRE HERMÉ
72 Rue Bonaparte, 75006 Paris
(and other branches, see website)
www.pierreherme.com
Pierre Hermé is renowned for revolutionising the art of French pâtisserie, and in particular has become known as the master of macarons. His quirky flavours include salty caramel, pistachio and strawberry and wasabi. The man to beat, he will always be ahead of the game.

DALLOYAU
101 Rue du Faubourg Saint-Honoré, 75008 Paris
(and other branches, see website)
www.dalloyau.fr
This pâtisserie is a royal gastronomic legacy and family run business. As well as macarons, the 'Opera' cake has been served for over 100 years, with its glorious coffee syrup soaked Viennois biscuit, layered coffee flavoured buttercream and a bittersweet chocolate ganache.

LE CAFÉ LENÔTRE
10 Champs-Élysées, 75008 Paris
www.lenotre.com
Started by the godfather of French pâtisserie, Le Nôtre is an offshoot of the famous cookery school. Visit for a selection of top-notch cakes and bakes.

SADAHARU AOKI

Boutique Lafayette Gourmet
40 Boulevard Haussmann, 75009 Paris
www.sadaharuaoki.com
Combining Japanese flavours with French confectionery has resulted in an almost avant-garde and wonderful selection of pâtisserie from this Japanese chef. The green tea opera cake or the black sesame éclair come highly recommended.

LA PÂTISSERIE DES RÊVES

93 Rue du Bac, 75007 Paris
www.lapatisseriedesreves.com
A beautifully designed concept pâtisserie with innovative interiors and avant-garde cakes. Worth a visit just to experience the glass domes.

BAGELS AND BROWNIES

12 Rue Notre-Dame des Champs, 75006 Paris
No website
This outlet sells some of the best bagels in Paris, plus they also bake moist and chewy chocolate brownies.

BLÉ SUCRÉ

Square Trousseau, 7 Rue Antoine Vollons, 75012 Paris
No website
The best madeleines in Paris, according to many foodies. It is take away only, but still worth seeking out – eat on the hoof.

CAFÉ MAURE A LA MOSQUÉE DE PARIS

39 Rue Geoffroy St Hilaire, 75005 Paris
No website
Its interior is decorated with beautiful Moorish carved wood and tiles, providing an atmospheric setting for mint tea and a superb baklava.

CAFÉ POUCHKINE

Printemps, 64 Boulevard Haussmann, 75009 Paris
www.cafe-pouchkine.fr
The French pastries at this salon de thé in the Printemps department store have a distinctly Russian accent. Go for flavour pairings and ingredients you won't find anywhere else.

POILÂNE

8 Rue du Cherche-Midi, 75006 Paris
www.poilane.com
Respected as *the* sourdough, pain Poilâne is synonymous with quality and consistency. Since the bakery opened its doors in 1932, Poilâne has gone on to become the pain campagne of choice for many chefs. Famous for producing the best bread, the bakery also creates a small and superb selection of sweet treats, including Paris–Brest and apple tartlets.

CAFÉ DE FLORE

172 Boulevard St Germain, 75006 Paris
www.cafe-de-flore.com
Experience Parisian café society from the 1930s with wonderful pastries to boot.

LE LOIR DANS LA THÉIÈRE

3 Rue des Rosiers, 75004 Paris
No website
This cosy tea salon is popular and famous for its tarts, both sweet and savoury.

PÂTISSERIE VIENNOISE

8 Rue de l'École de Médecine, 75006 Paris
No website
Alongside the usual French pastries and cakes appear some more unusual Viennese treats – tortes, tarts and strudels.

AUX CASTELBLANGEOIS

168 Rue Saint-Honoré, 75001 Paris
No website
Incredible tarts to be savoured using the sweetest fruit on a bed of rich cream and flaky pastry.

ANGELINA

226 Rue de Rivoli, 75001 Paris
www.angelina-paris.fr
This beautiful tea salon is believed to serve the best hot chocolate in Paris. Why not sample some accompanied by a slice of its famous Mont Blanc cake (a cake combining meringue, light whipped cream and chestnut cream vermicelli) after a visit to the nearby Louvre museum.

Mustikkapiiraat

Makes 12

For the pastry:
20g (¾oz) fresh yeast
100ml (3½fl oz) full-fat milk
70g (2½oz) caster sugar
400g (14oz) plain flour
60g (2oz) butter, softened
1 egg, plus 1 egg yolk, beaten,
    for brushing
½ tsp ground cardamom
50g (1¾oz) raisins
a pinch of salt

For the filling:
375g (13oz) fresh blueberries
1 tbsp cornflour
40g (1½oz) caster sugar

These Finnish blueberry buns will fill your house with wonderful aromas and it'll be hard to wait for them to be cool enough to eat. Buns and pastries are a huge tradition in Finland – sometimes being eaten at every mealtime. In the summer months, bushes literally groan with edible wild berries, such as blueberries, loganberries and strawberries, which have been incorporated into all sorts of traditional national dishes. I find a little cardamom (another favourite Scandinavian spice) in the dough really does make a difference. Try it and see for yourself.

1 Dissolve the yeast in the milk and with the sugar and set aside for 10 minutes.
2 Using a food mixer with a dough hook, sift in the flour and add the softened butter while mixing slowly, then add the rest of the ingredients.
3 Mix until a smooth dough forms; add a little extra flour if the mixture is too sticky.
4 Cover the bowl with greased clingfilm and leave in a warm place for an hour or until doubled in size.
5 Make the filling by combining all the ingredients together and set aside.
6 Using a floured hand, scrape down the sides of the bowl to bring all the dough together in a ball.
7 Slightly grease your work surface and divide the dough into 12 equal pieces. Now, line a baking tray with baking parchment.
8 Roll each piece into a smooth ball and place on the baking tray. Leave in a warm place for 20 minutes.
9 Meanwhile, preheat the oven to 180°C/350°F/gas mark 4.
10 Using an egg cup, make an indent in the centre of each ball. Spoon the filling into the middle of each bun and brush the pastry with the beaten egg yolk.
11 Bake in a preheated oven for 15 minutes.
12 Remove from the oven and cool on a wire rack. Take off the baking parchment.
13 Best eaten warm straight from the oven and served with coffee.

Banbury Cakes

Makes 12

400g (14oz) Puff Pastry
   (see page 221)
75g (2¾oz) butter
1 tbsp clear honey
¼ tsp freshly grated nutmeg
½ tsp ground cinnamon
120g (4oz) currants
60g (2oz) candied orange peel
plain flour, to dust
1 egg white, beaten, for
   brushing
1–2 tbsp caster sugar

These sweet oval puff pastries stuffed with juicy currants take their name from the town where they originated – Banbury in Oxfordshire, England – and date back to medieval times when they were baked for high days and holidays. Other similar local pastries appeared all over the UK around this time too, such as the Eccles Cake (see opposite), Chorley Cake, Scottish Black Bun (see page 269) and Welsh Cakes (see page 168).

1 Make the puff pastry as on page 221.
2 Line a baking tray with baking parchment.
3 In a bowl, combine the butter and honey, then add the spices. Tip in the currants and candied peel and mix well.
3 Remove the puff pastry from the fridge. Roll out the pastry, on a lightly floured work surface, to 3mm (⅛in) thick then place on a tray covered in baking parchment and refrigerate for 30 minutes. After that time, cut out 12 discs of pastry (I used a 7cm (2¾in) cutter), rerolling the trimmings as you go.
5 Divide the fruity mixture between the 12

discs. Next, bring together the edges of the pastry to enclose the fruit in the middle.
6 Invert the cake and press slightly to flatten into an oval shape, being careful not to split the cake open. Then pop on the lined baking tray and allow to rest for a further half an hour. Preheat the oven to 170°C/325°F/gas mark 3.
7 Next, brush with the beaten egg white, sprinkle with sugar and then bake (on the same tray) for 20–25 minutes until golden.
8 Remove from the oven, take off the parchment and cool on a wire rack. Best eaten while still warm.

Eccles Cakes

Makes 10

500g (1lb 2oz) Puff Pastry (see page 221)
140g (5oz) soft light brown sugar
1 tsp cinnamon
½ tsp mixed spice
140g (5oz) currants
85g (3oz) mixed citrus peel
85g (3oz) butter, melted
plain flour, to dust
1 egg, lightly beaten, for brushing
a little milk, for brushing
caster sugar, for sprinkling

These perfect little pastries hail from the town of Eccles in Lancashire, UK, and were first sold in the town way back in 1793. They're a regional cake, similar to Banbury Cakes (see opposite) and Chorley Cakes. And the look of the currants inside the cake gives these their affectionate nickname of 'squashed fly cakes'.

1 Make the puff pastry as on page 221.
2 Preheat the oven to 180°C/350°F/gas mark 4, and you will need a non-stick baking tray.
3 Mix the sugar, cinnamon, mixed spice, currants and citrus peel together, then add the melted butter.
4 Remove the puff pastry from the fridge. Roll out the pastry, on a lightly floured work surface, to 3mm (⅛in) thick. Transfer to a tray and allow to rest for 30 minutes in the fridge.
5 Cut out into 9cm (3½in) discs (there should be approximately 10). Place on the baking tray for a further 30 minutes in the fridge.
6 Using a tablespoon, spoon out the filling and roll into balls.
7 Place a pastry disc on a floured work surface

and lightly brush the edge with the beaten egg. Press a ball of the mixture into the centre of the disc and gently flatten it with the heel of your hand.
8 Bring the edges of the pastry over the mixture to meet in the middle and press down. Turn over the disc and gently press down again. Repeat for the remaining discs.
9 Place the cakes on the baking tray, brush with milk and sprinkle with caster sugar.
10 Bake in a preheated oven for 20 minutes until nice and golden.
11 Remove from the oven and turn out onto a wire rack.
12 Enjoy with a slice of Lancashire cheese and a cup of tea – the traditional way.

Fat Rascals

Makes 10

275g (9¾oz) plain flour, plus extra for dusting

1½ tsp baking powder

120g (4oz) butter, cubed

85g (3oz) currants

85g (3oz) caster sugar

50g (1¾oz) mixed citrus peel

175g (6¼oz) soured cream

1 egg and 1 egg yolk, beaten, plus 1 egg, beaten, for brushing

glacé cherries and blanched almonds, to decorate

Also known as a Yorkshire Turf Cake, this teatime treat is a bit like a scone and dates from Elizabethan times. The Fat Rascal is now inextricably linked with the famous tea rooms, Bettys (originally of York and Harrogate) when they began baking and selling these little cakes in the early 1980s.

1 Preheat the oven to 180°C/350°F/gas mark 4, and grease a baking tray.

2 Sift the flour and baking powder into a bowl, add the butter and rub in together until it resembles breadcrumbs.

3 Add the currants, sugar and citrus peel, followed by the cream and eggs. Mix well until fully combined.

4 On a floured surface, roll out the mixture to 2cm (¾in) thickness and cut out with a 7cm (2¾in) cutter.

5 Glaze with a beaten egg and firmly push in the glacé cherries and blanched almonds in the time-honoured pattern. Transfer to the baking tray and bake in the preheated oven for 15–20 minutes or until golden brown.

6 Remove from the oven and transfer to a wire rack to cool.

7 Serve warm or cold with clotted cream or jam and butter.

Where to Eat Cake...

Harrogate

BETTYS CRAFT BAKERY
Bettys Tea Rooms
1 Parliament Street,
Harrogate, Yorkshire
HG1 2QU
and other branches
www.bettys.co.uk
Bettys has been serving tea since 1919 and Fat Rascals are a specialty; you'll be spoilt for choice with over 300 breads, cakes and chocolates.

Rock Cakes

Makes 10

100g (3½oz) butter, cubed
200g (7oz) self-raising flour, sifted
a pinch of salt
100g (3½oz) caster sugar
25g (1oz) glacé cherries
30g (1¼oz) currants
25g (1oz) sultanas
1 egg
4 tbsp full-fat milk

For many of us, Rock Cakes bring back memories of childhood baking, as they do not require great skill and were often the first attempts at making cakes of some sort. These cakes are a cross between a scone and a buttery cake and were publicised during the Second World War in the UK as they could be made with fewer eggs and sugar (which were being rationed at the time) than traditional cakes. These delicious small cakes can be rustled up in no time – helpers with little hands may well want to join in – just take care not to overcook them, as that way lies dental disaster.

1 Preheat the oven to 180°C/350°F/gas mark 4, and grease two baking trays.
2 Rub the butter into the flour mixed with the salt until the mixture resembles breadcrumbs.
3 Stir in the sugar and dried fruit until evenly distributed throughout.
4 Beat the egg with the milk and add it to the mixture. Mix well until fully combined.
5 Drop dessertspoonfuls on to the baking trays, and bake in a preheated oven for 15–20 minutes until lightly browned.
6 Remove from the oven and transfer to a wire rack to cool.
7 Serve with a cup of tea and a lemonade for the little helpers.

Welsh Cakes

Makes 20

450g (1lb) plain flour
1 tsp baking powder
a pinch of ground allspice
a pinch of salt
120g (4oz) butter
120g (4oz) lard or vegetable
   shortening
210g (7½oz) caster sugar
110g (3¾oz) raisins
2 eggs, beaten
full-fat milk, to mix

In Wales, UK, these little cakes were originally cooked on a heated bake stone and served to travellers on their arrival at an inn. Known as 'pice ar y maen' in Welsh, which translates as 'cakes on the stone', these variations of a drop scone are a wondrous versatile treat that can be served hot or cold, with tea or coffee, jam or ice cream, as a snack or a dessert. How will you eat yours?

1 Sift together the flour, baking powder, allspice and salt.
2 Rub in the butter and the lard/shortening until the mixture resembles breadcrumbs.
3 Add the sugar and the raisins.
4 Beat the eggs and add to the mixture, with a little milk to make a fairly stiff dough.
5 On a lightly floured surface, roll out the dough to a thickness of about 2cm (¾in) deep.
6 Using a 6cm (2½in) pastry cutter, stamp out rounds of dough.
7 Cook on a greased griddle or heavy-based frying pan for about 3 minutes on each side until golden brown. Cook in batches and keep warm in the oven.
8 Best served warm, sprinkled with a little caster sugar.

Singing Hinnies

Makes 16

475g (1lb 1 oz) plain flour
¼ tsp bicarbonate of soda
½ tsp cream of tartar
½ tsp salt
120g (4oz) butter, cubed
120g (4oz) lard or vegetable
   shortening, cubed
50g (1¾oz) currants
50g (1¾oz) raisins
50g (1¾oz) sultanas
50ml (2fl oz) full-fat milk
a knob of clarified butter, for
   cooking

This curiously named scone is typical of the north of England. The singing refers to the sound of the sizzling as the dough hits the frying pan. These are delicious any time – and can be whipped up in no time – but are particularly good served as a breakfast time cake.

1 Preheat the oven to 170°C/325°F/gas mark 3.
2 In a bowl sift together all the dry ingredients. Add the butter and lard/shortening and rub together until it resembles breadcrumbs. Then mix in all the dried fruit.
3 Pour in the milk until the mixture becomes a firm dough.
4 Roll out the dough to a thickness of 2.5–3cm (1–1¾in) and then cut into rounds using a 7cm (2¾in) cutter.
5 Heat a frying pan on a moderate heat, then add the clarified butter. Depending on the size of your pan, you'll need to cook them in batches. Add the Singing Hinnies to the pan and cook until brown on each side.
6 Remove the hinnies to a baking tray and bake in the preheated oven for 10–15 minutes until cooked through.
7 Serve warm with butter.

SINGING HINNIES

VARIATIONS

BUTTERMILK SCONES
These scones are really rich and really moist and make a lovely alternative to standard classic scones; plus they have a lot of vanilla in, so it makes them almost a shortbread scone. See below for ingredients and give them a try.
1 Split and scrape the vanilla pods and add the seeds to the sugar. Mix well to incorporate all the vanilla seeds.
2 Then follow the main method below.

FRUIT SCONE Follow the Scone recipe below and after step 3 add 225g (8oz) of sultanas or raisins for a fruity number.

Scones

Makes 15

900g (2lb) self-raising flour
4 tsp baking powder
a pinch of salt
60g (2oz) caster sugar
200g (7oz) butter, cubed
550ml (19fl oz) full-fat milk
1 egg, beaten, for brushing

Buttermilk Scones
Makes 12

4 vanilla pods
110g (3¾oz) caster sugar
550g (1lb 3½oz) self-raising
    flour
4 tsp baking powder
225g (8oz) butter
600ml (1 pint) buttermilk
1 egg, beaten, for brushing

There's many an argument about how to say 'scone' in the UK where they are a favourite teatime treat. Does it rhyme with 'gone' or 'stone'? And, should you put the clotted cream on first (as in Devon cream tea) or the jam on first (as in Cornish cream tea)? However you say it and however you serve it, these little cakes are easy to rustle up for impromptu visitors and can be adapted to what you have in the cupboards; they can be as simple or fancy as you like.

1 Preheat the oven to 180°C/350°F/gas mark 4, and line a baking tray with baking parchment or use a silicone mat.
2 Sift the flour, baking powder and salt together into a bowl and stir in the sugar.
3 Rub in the butter until the mixture resembles breadcrumbs and then fold in the milk until a dough forms.
4 On a lightly floured surface, roll out the dough to a thickness of 4cm (1½in). Using a floured 7cm (2¾in) pastry cutter, stamp out the scones and place on the baking tray or silicone mat.

5 Bring together the leftover dough, then roll out again and cut out until all the dough is gone; do be careful, though, not to overwork the dough.
6 Lightly brush the tops with beaten egg and bake for 15 minutes until risen.
7 Remove from the oven, take off the baking parchment and cool on a wire rack.
8 Serve the scones warm from the oven with clotted cream and your favourite jam.

Scotch Pancakes

Makes 30

1½ tsp white wine vinegar
450ml (15¾fl oz) full-fat milk
330g (11½oz) plain flour
1½ tsp baking powder
3 eggs
50ml (2fl oz) vegetable oil

These little pancakes are also known as 'drop scones' because dollops of the mixture are dropped from the spoon into the pan, or griddle, which is how they were traditionally cooked. And Scotch Pancakes have been cooked on cast-iron griddles in Scotland, UK, since the 16th century. They can be served at any time of day and are traditionally spread with butter and jam (like toast) and must be eaten straight away – though, that's not normally much of a problem.

1 Mix the vinegar into the milk and leave for a few minutes.
2 Sift the flour and the baking powder together in a bowl.
3 Add in the eggs and the vegetable oil and mix together. Then add in the milk mixture.

4 Heat a heavy non-stick frying pan or griddle and drop in tablespoonfuls of the mixture. When bubbles appear in the centre (after about 2 minutes) flip over for another 2 minutes.
5 Cook in batches and keep warm in the oven or just serve up as they're finished.
6 Serve immediately with your favourite topping – maple syrup, honey, black cherry jam or whatever takes your fancy. I like to eat mine straight from the pan with lashings of maple syrup.

Russian Tea Cakes

Makes 18

235g (8½oz) butter, softened
290g (10¼oz) icing sugar, plus
    extra to dust
2 tsp vanilla extract
330g (11½oz) plain flour,
    sifted
110g (3¾oz) ground
    hazelnuts

These tea cakes are popular throughout the whole of Eastern Europe and particularly Russia, where during the 17th century taking tea with a sweet cake was an important and routine part of the day. These sweet cakes go by many names – Mexican Wedding Cakes and Viennese Sugar Balls, among others – and when drenched in icing sugar they look like little snowballs.

1 Preheat the oven to 180°C/350°F/gas mark 4, and line a large baking tray with baking parchment.
2 Cream the butter and sugar together until light and fluffy, and then add the vanilla extract.
3 Add in the sifted flour and hazelnuts and mix until all the ingredients are well combined.
4 Cover the dough in clingfilm and chill in the fridge for at least 1 hour.
5 Remove the dough from the fridge and divide into ping-pong-sized balls.

6 Roll each ball between the palms of your hands until smooth and place on the baking tray spaced 1cm (½in) apart.
7 Bake in a preheated oven for about 20–25 minutes or until light golden.
8 Remove from the oven, take off the baking parchment and cool on a wire rack.
9 While still warm, roll the tea cakes in the icing sugar and allow to cool.
10 Serve with a lovely light blend of tea in the afternoon.

Pineapple Coconut Cakes with Pineapple Syrup

Makes 8

130g (4½oz) butter, softened
150g (5½oz) caster sugar
2 eggs
175ml (6fl oz) buttermilk
225g (8oz) self-raising flour,
    sifted
100g (3½oz) desiccated
    coconut
150g (5½oz) fresh or canned
    pineapple, diced

For the pineapple syrup:
700g (1lb 10oz) fresh or
    canned pineapple, diced
270g (9½oz) caster sugar
juice of 6 limes
100ml (3½fl oz) water
100ml (3½fl oz) white rum

Flavours that grow together generally go together, so I have used pineapple and coconut in these deliciously moist mini-cakes using flavours from the Caribbean. These flavours are also popular in Australia and New Zealand.

1 Preheat the oven to 170°C/325°F/gas mark 3. Grease eight small fluted petit-Brioche tins (11cm x 5cm (4¼in x 2in) and place on a baking tray.
2 Cream the butter and sugar together until light and fluffy. Then, slowly add the eggs and the buttermilk and combine well.
3 Stir in the sifted flour, coconut and pineapple, then spoon the mixture into the prepared tins.
4 Bake in a preheated oven for 20 minutes or until golden and a cocktail stick inserted into the centre comes out clean.

5 Meanwhile, make the syrup. Combine the pineapple, sugar, lime juice and water in a pan and stir over a medium-high heat until the sugar dissolves. Bring to the boil and simmer for 15 minutes or until syrupy. Cool, add the rum and pour through a fine-mesh sieve, discarding solids. Cool completely.
6 Remove the cakes from the oven, pour over half the syrup, then turn them out of their tins and cool on a wire rack.
7 Serve with the remaining syrup and some sliced pineapple on the side.

RUSSIAN TEA CAKES

PINEAPPLE COCONUT CAKES

PINEAPPLE COCONUT CAKES

RUSSIAN TEA CAKES

Malpuas

Makes 15

500ml (18fl oz) full-fat milk, for the rabri
320g (11¼oz) caster sugar
175ml (6fl oz) water
¼ tsp ground cardamom
pinch of saffron
250g (9oz) plain flour
¼ tsp baking powder
300g (10½oz) condensed milk
200ml (7fl oz) full-fat milk
ghee (or clarified butter), for frying

These wonderfully sweet flatcakes are an Indian tradition served during festivals and holidays. Each region has its own take on these pancakes, adding banana or coconut or a touch of cardamom (as here). They are similar to pancakes and can be eaten plain or dressed with fruit, drizzled with flavoured syrups or sprinkled with chopped nuts.

1 Boil together the milk and 100g (3½oz) of the sugar in a pan until reduced by about two-thirds. Sieve and chill. This is the rabri.
2 Put the rest of the sugar in a pan with the water and boil until it becomes a thick syrup.
3 Tip the syrup from the pan into a bowl and add the cardamom and saffron.
4 To make the flatcakes, in a bowl sift the flour and baking powder together and add the condensed milk and milk and whisk to a smooth batter.

5 Heat up a non-stick frying pan or griddle and melt 1 teaspoon of ghee or clarified butter. Ladle the batter until a roughly 10cm (4in) diameter pancake forms and cook until bubbles appear in the middle. Flip over and cook the other side until golden brown.
6 Serve drizzling liberally with the sugar syrup and rabri or, for an authentic experience, immerse in the syrup after cooking and then pour rabri over the top.
7 Serve hot with a cup of camomile tea.

Tippaleipä

Makes 10

7 egg whites
1 egg yolk
150g (5½oz) caster sugar
175g (6¼oz) plain flour, sifted
500ml (18fl oz) vegetable oil,
    for deep-frying
icing sugar, for dusting

In Finland the first of May is a day of celebration all over the country, to mark the beginning of spring. Vappu is the name given to the carnival-like street festivals that spring up in every town and city. Tippaleipä are doughnut-like delights or 'funnel cakes', so called as the batter is poured through a funnel during their preparation (see also Churros, page 178), that are eaten on this day. And, if you want a truly authentic experience then buy some Sima – a lemon-and-sugar-based yeast drink – the traditional accompaniment to Tippaleipä.

1 Beat half the egg whites with the egg yolk and sugar until blended, then stir in the sifted flour to make a batter.
2 In a separate bowl, whisk the other half of the egg whites until stiff peaks form then fold in to the batter.
3 Pour the oil into a deep, wide heavy-based pan and heat it until it reaches 190°C/374°F. Cover a baking tray with kitchen paper.
4 Pour the batter into a piping bag and use a No. 4 nozzle or use a large plastic food bag and snip off the corner. Now, take care and pipe swirls of the batter into the hot oil to create a bird's nest shape.
5 Fry, turning to get an even colour, for about 30 seconds on each side until golden brown.
6 Remove with a slotted spoon and drain on the kitchen paper. Continue to cook the rest of the dough in batches.
7 Dust with icing sugar and serve straightaway with some Sima.

Sfenz

Makes 10

For the dough:
2 eggs, beaten
20g (¾oz) caster sugar
2 tbsp vegetable oil
½ tsp baking powder
160g (5¾oz) plain flour
roughly grated zest of 1
    orange
30g (1¼oz) ground almonds
¼ tsp orange-flower water
500ml (18fl oz) vegetable oil,
    for deep-frying

For the syrup:
410g (14½oz) caster sugar
¼ tsp lemon juice
¼ tsp orange-flower water
¼ tsp vanilla extract
150ml (5fl oz) water

The very first doughnuts were most likely prepared by the ancient Egyptians, and Sfenz originate from their neighbours the Libyan Jews of North Africa. Deep-fried doughnuts, such as Sfenz, are often served as the traditional sweet treat during the Jewish festival of Hannukah.

1 Mix together all the ingredients for the dough (except the deep-frying oil) adding additional flour, if necessary.
2 Pull off balls of the dough and roll in the palm of your hand until about the size of a chestnut (roughly 30g (1¼oz)).
3 Press down on the ball with your fingers to form a circle. Dip a No. 10 piping nozzle into some flour, to prevent it sticking to the dough, and push it through the dough to push out a hole in the centre of the doughnut. Reuse all the 'centres' to make a final doughnut.
4 Leave for 10 minutes then re-cut the central hole, otherwise the dough expands to fill it.

5 Pour the oil into a deep, wide heavy-based pan and heat it until it reaches 170°C/338°F. Have ready a plate covered with kitchen paper.
6 Add the doughnuts a few at a time and deep-fry until brown on both sides, about 3 minutes. They will rise to the top of the oil and turn over while they are cooking.
7 Remove with a slotted spoon and drain on the kitchen paper. Continue to cook the rest of the dough in batches.
8 Make the syrup by putting all the ingredients in a pan. Heat gently until the contents become syrupy. Keep the syrup on a low heat while dipping each doughnut into the syrup. Remove to a serving plate and allow to cool.

Sonhos

Makes 12

150ml (5fl oz) water
60g (2oz) butter
2 tsp caster sugar
a pinch of salt
100g (3½oz) strong flour
3–4 eggs, whisked (only add
    the 4th egg if the mix is
    still stiff)
500ml (18fl oz) vegetable oil,
    for deep-frying
icing sugar, to dust

These super-light doughnuts originated as a Christmas speciality. 'Sonhos' literally translates from the Portuguese as 'dreams' and these small cakes sure are little dreamy doughnuts. Because they're so delicious, you can now get them year round, not just at Christmas.

1 Place the water, butter, sugar and salt in a pan and bring to the boil, making sure the butter is completely melted.
2 Add the flour and stir in with a wooden spoon – it is important to cook the flour fully so don't hurry this process. The dough should come away easily from the side of the pan.
3 Place the dough in a food mixer and, while beating, add the eggs one at a time, scraping down the bowl after each addition. Add egg until the mixture is suitable for deep frying – if it's too wet you won't be able to use it. Cover the bowl with clingfilm and leave to rest in the fridge for 1–2 hours.

4 Pour the oil into a deep, wide heavy-based pan and heat it until it reaches 170°C/338°F. Have ready a baking tray or plate covered with kitchen paper.
5 Deep-fry dessertspoonfuls of the dough until golden brown, then remove with a slotted spoon and drain on the kitchen paper. Cook the rest of the dough in batches.
6 Serve the Sonhos warm, lightly dusted with some icing sugar.

Makes 15

For the Churros:
345ml (11⅔fl oz) boiling
    water
50g (1¾oz) butter, melted
½ tsp vanilla extract
250g (9oz) plain flour
1 tsp baking powder
a pinch of salt
500ml (18fl oz) vegetable oil,
    for deep-frying

For the chocolate sauce:
200g (7oz) dark chocolate
    (minimum 70% cocoa
    solids), broken up
50g (1¾oz) milk chocolate,
    broken up
2 tbsp golden syrup
300ml (10fl oz) double cream

For the cinnamon sugar:
100g (3½oz) caster sugar
2 tsp ground cinnamon

Churros

These super-crunchy, deep-fried dough sticks, sprinkled with sugar, and often served with hot chocolate for dipping are hugely popular in Spain as well as in Mexico and South America. Each region has its own slight take on Churros – whether it's in the shape and thickness of the dough or whether it's filled with fruit, chocolate or custard (as in Cuba or Brazil). The word 'churros' comes from a Spanish breed of sheep whose horns are similar in shape.

1 Pour the water into a jug and add the melted butter and vanilla extract.
2 In a separate bowl, sift together the flour, baking powder and salt.
3 Make a well in the centre and pour in the buttery water mixture and slowly beat together until there are no lumps. Allow to rest for 10 minutes while you make the sauce.
4 Put all the sauce ingredients into a pan and heat slowly until everything has melted. Keep warm until ready to use.
5 Pour the oil into a deep, wide heavy-based pan and heat it until it reaches 170°C/338°F. Have ready a baking tray or plate covered with kitchen paper.

6 Mix the sugar and cinnamon together.
7 Fill a piping bag with the rested Churros mixture and, using a large star nozzle, pipe two strips directly into the pan of hot oil, snipping the end of the mixture with scissors, once desired length is reached (they have to fit across the pan).
8 Fry until golden brown and, turning to get an even colour, then remove with a slotted spoon and drain on the kitchen paper.
9 Continue to cook the rest of the dough in batches.
10 Sprinkle over the cinnamon sugar and serve the Churros alongside bowls of the chocolate sauce for dipping.

Where to Eat Cake...
MADRID

Spain has a strong café culture. Whether it's a traditional sort for a café con leche at the bar or a milkshake in a funky modern place, everyone in Spain goes out to cafés. It's inside these cafés in Madrid where you'll find the real Spain – in all its forms and also where you'll find plenty of pastries and sweet treats to enjoy.

CONVENTO DE LAS CARBONERAS
Plaza del Conde de Miranda 3, 28005 Madrid
No website
The Carboneras nuns make a selection of speciality cakes and biscuits including mantecados, yemas and almond biscuits. As this is a closed convent you have to buy them through a grille.

CAFÉ DEL REAL
Plaza de Isabel II, 2, 28013 Madrid
No website
Come for the cosy atmosphere and to mingle with the locals while tucking into carrot or chocolate cake and coffee, or if you prefer something stronger there's a bar.

LA MALLORQUINA
Calle Mayor, 2, 28013 Madrid
No website
This is one of the oldest bakeries in Madrid and is famous for its napolitanas and rosquillas as well as a selection of pastries and croissants. Heads up, it's always busy.

ANTÍGUA PASTELERÍA DEL POZO
Calle del Pozo, 8, 28012 Madrid
No website
What used to be baked and eaten just around the days of Epiphany can now be bought and eaten all year round. We are talking here of the ring-shaped Rosco de Reyes with its sugar and glazed fruits. Plus, they also make flaky pastries filled with custard or pumpkin jam.

HAPPY DAY BAKERY
Calle del Espíritu Santo 11 (corner with Jesús del Valle), 28004 Madrid
www.happydaybakery.es
This bakery is full-on American-style, slap bang in the middle of Madrid. Expect cupcakes galore, muffins and giant cookies.

HORNO SAN ONOFRE
Calle de San Onofre, 3, 28004 Madrid (and other branches)
www.hsonofre.com
Honouring the tradition of including a bean and a coin in their famous Rosco de Reyes (or King Cake), this bakery is also famed for its Tarta de Santiago (see page 274).

CHOCOLATERÍA SAN GINÉS
Pasadizo de San Ginés 5, 28013 Madrid
www.chocolateriasangines.com
It's the only place to come for 'chocolate y churros' since it opened in 1894. And it's open all day every day, to serve anyone's yearning for some sweet sticky dough sticks and dipping chocolate.

LA DUQUESITA
Calle Fernando VI, 2, 28004 Madrid
www.laduquesita.es
Marvel at the window display and try one of the uniquely seasonal pastries and cakes, such as San Anton Muffins.

HARINA
Plaza de la Independencia 10, 28014 Madrid
www.harinamadrid.com
Great bread and freshly baked buns and cakes from recipes handed down through the generations.

ORIOL BALAGUER
Calle de José Ortega y Gasset, 44, Madrid
www.oriolbalaguer.com
Intense chocolate confections, cakes and pastries – elegant sculptures. Other branches too elsewhere in Spain.

Muffins

Makes 12 of each

Blueberry Muffins
75g (2¾oz) butter, melted
3 eggs
220ml (7½fl oz) buttermilk
finely grated zest of 1 lemon
finely grated zest of 1 orange
450g (1lb) plain flour, sifted
1 tsp baking powder
75g (2¾oz) caster sugar
1 tsp salt
225g (8oz) fresh or frozen
  blueberries

Chocolate Chip Muffins
150g (5½oz) butter, melted
2 eggs
345ml (11⅔fl oz) full-fat milk
200g (7oz) dark chocolate,
  melted
500g (1lb 2oz) plain flour
1 tsp baking powder
150g (5½oz) caster sugar
½ tsp salt
½ tsp bicarbonate of soda
350g (12oz) chocolate chips

Cherry and Ricotta Muffins
120g (4oz) butter, melted
2 eggs
345ml (11⅔fl oz) full-fat milk
150g (5½oz) ricotta 500g (1lb
2oz) plain flour
1 tsp baking powder
300g (10½oz) caster sugar
1 tsp salt
2 tsp bicarbonate of soda
200g (7oz) glacé cherries (use
  fresh cherries when in
  season)

There are so many delicious varieties of muffins it was hard to choose just three for this book. Muffins have been a staple food in North America for the last hundred years but they have only really gained popularity in Europe since the 1990s. Most bakeries will have an enormous variety to choose from as the basic muffin recipe is so adaptable. Muffins are best eaten freshly baked at any time of day.

1 Preheat the oven to 180°C/350°F/gas mark 4, and place 12 paper muffin cases in a muffin tin.
2 Put all the wet ingredients – melted butter, eggs, buttermilk (or milk), zests, melted chocolate and ricotta, followed by the dry ingredients – flour, baking powder, sugar, salt and bicarbonate of soda into a large bowl and mix together lightly. Do not over-mix as this will make the muffins heavy.
3 Next, fold in the lumpier ingredients – blueberries/chocolate chips/cherries.

4 Fill each muffin case three-quarters full with the mixture.
5 Bake in a preheated oven for 20–25 minutes or until a cocktail stick inserted into the centre comes out clean.
6 Remove from the oven, allow to cool for a few minutes in the tin and then turn out onto a wire rack.

Cupcakes

Cupcakes originated in the United States in the 19th century with the name deriving from the teacup, as they were weighed and baked in cups. They soon became popular as they were so easy to make and quick to bake. Now, of course, we have individual muffin tins as well as a huge array of colourful cases to make the baking even easier. Today's cupcakes can be mini works of art, with the huge range of toppings available, and they are no longer just the preserve of children's parties, with professionals making them ever more sophisticated.

Vanilla Cupcakes

Makes 8

2 eggs
175g (6¼oz) caster sugar
140g (5oz) plain flour, sifted
small pinch of salt
½ tsp baking powder
80ml (3fl oz) double cream
50g (1¾oz) butter, melted
few drops of vanilla extract
250g (9oz) Classic
    Buttercream (see page 298)

1 Preheat the oven to 180°C/350°F/gas mark 4 and place eight paper cases in a muffin tin.
2 In a food mixer, whisk the eggs with the sugar until fully blended. Add the sifted flour, salt and baking powder and whisk together.
3 Mix in the cream then fold in the melted butter. Finally, add a few drops of vanilla extract and mix.
4 Fill the muffin cases three-quarters full.

5 Bake in a preheated oven for 20 minutes until golden brown or until a cocktail stick inserted into the centre comes out clean.
6 While they're cooling, make the buttercream as instructed on page 298.
7 Once the cupcakes are cool, decorate with the buttercream and sprinkle on the decorations.

Double Chocolate Cupcakes

Makes 6

85g (3oz) butter, softened
225g (8oz) soft brown sugar
2 eggs
40g (1½oz) ground almonds
100g (3½oz) self-raising flour,
    sifted
2 tsp cocoa powder
60g (2oz) dark chocolate
    (minimum 70% cocoa
    solids), melted
250g (9oz) Chocolate
    Buttercream (see page 298)

1 Preheat the oven to 180°C/350°F/gas mark 4 and place six paper cases in a muffin tin.
2 Cream the butter and sugar together until light and fluffy, and add the eggs one at a time.
3 Add the ground almonds, sifted flour and cocoa powder, followed by the melted chocolate and mix well.
4 Fill the muffin cases three-quarters full with the mixture.
5 Bake in a preheated oven for 20 minutes until golden brown or until a cocktail stick inserted into the centre comes out clean.
6 Now, make the chocolate buttercream, following the instructions on page 298.
7 Once the cupcakes are cool, decorate with the buttercream and sprinkle on gold stars.

Raspberry Cupcakes

Makes 8

1 Vanilla Cupcake recipe (see page 182)
1 tsp raspberry flavouring

For the raspberry buttercream:
250g (9oz) Classic Buttercream (see page 298)
200g (7oz) fresh raspberries
75g (2¾oz) caster sugar
1 tbsp water

1 Follow the instructions on page 182 in the Vanilla Cupcake recipe but instead of the vanilla extract use the raspberry flavouring.
2 While they're cooling, make the buttercream, as instructed on page 298.
3 Meanwhile, place the raspberries, sugar and water in a pan and bring to the boil. Simmer for 5 minutes then blitz in a blender and pass through a sieve.

4 Return the liquid to the pan and reduce by about half, before adding to the buttercream and mixing together.
5 Refrigerate for about 30 minutes before filling a piping bag with the buttercream, using a large star nozzle, and top each cupcake. Sprinkle with preferred decoration.

Raspberry and Coconut Cupcakes

Makes 6

120g (4oz) butter, softened
225g (8oz) caster sugar
3 eggs, lightly beaten
75g (2¾oz) plain flour, sifted
75g (2¾oz) self-raising flour, sifted
75g (2¾oz) desiccated coconut
75g (2¾oz) soured cream
a small pinch of salt
150g (5½oz) fresh raspberries, set aside 12 for decoration
180g (6½oz) Cream Cheese Frosting (see page 298)
flaked coconut, to decorate

1 Preheat the oven to 180°C/350°F/gas mark 4 and place six paper cases in a muffin tin.
2 Cream the butter and sugar together until light and fluffy, and add the eggs one at a time.
3 Add the sifted flours and coconut, followed by the soured cream and a pinch of salt. Gently fold in the fresh raspberries.
4 Fill the muffin cases three-quarters full with the mixture.
5 Bake in a preheated oven for 40 minutes until golden brown or until a cocktail stick inserted into the centre comes out clean.
6 Meanwhile, make the cream cheese frosting as instructed on page 298. You'll need 20–30g (¾–1¼oz) of frosting per cupcake.
7 Remove the cupcakes from the oven, allow to cool for 5 minutes in the tin and then turn out onto a wire rack.
8 Once the cupcakes are cool, decorate with the topping, sprinkle with flaked coconut and pop two raspberries on top of each cupcake. Voilà!

VANILLA

RASPBERRY & COCONUT

DOUBLE CHOCOLATE

RASPBERRY

Whoopie Pies

Makes 12 pies
(24 pieces)

These are not, of course, pies but actually two small cakes or biscuits sandwiched together with a sweet filling. They originate from America, have been around for nearly 100 years and are still as popular as ever. Legend has it they are so named because children exclaimed 'whoopee' when they saw them! Serve any flavour combination – or all three if you've got room – with a cold glass of milk.

Chocolate with Marshmallow Filling

70g (2½oz) butter, softened
210g (7½oz) soft brown sugar
1 egg
275g (9¾oz) plain flour, sifted
1½ tsp bicarbonate of soda
85g (3oz) cocoa powder
a pinch of salt
200ml (7fl oz) milk
1 tsp vanilla extract

For the marshmallow filling:

3 leaves of gelatin or 10g
  (¼oz) powdered gelatin
100g (3½oz) caster sugar
50g (1¾oz) golden syrup
40ml (1½fl oz) water
2 egg whites
a pinch of salt
1 tsp vanilla extract

Lemon with Lemon Curd Filling

120g (4oz) butter, softened
210g (7½oz) caster sugar
2 tsp lemon zest
1 egg
180g (6½oz) plain flour, sifted
1 tsp bicarbonate of soda
120ml (4fl oz) buttermilk
2 tsp Limoncello or lemon
  flavouring
½ tsp yellow food colouring
100g (3½oz) good-quality
  lemon curd, for the filling

For the cakes or biscuits

1 Preheat the oven to 170°C/325°F/gas mark 3.
2 Cream the butter and sugar together until light and fluffy. Mix in the lemon zest if making the lemon cakes.
3 Add the egg and then the dry ingredients – sifted flour, bicarbonate of soda, cocoa powder and salt – alternating with the milk (or other liquid if making the lemon cakes) and combine well. Add in the vanilla extract and mix well.
4 Fill a piping bag with the mixture and, using a No. 10 nozzle, pipe 2.5–3cm (1–1¼in) dots of mix onto baking parchment or a silicon mat.
5 Bake in a preheated oven for 10 minutes.
6 Remove from the oven and leave to cool on a wire rack.

For the marshmallow filling

1 Soak the gelatin in iced water to remove any excess gelatin flavour, and set aside.
2 In a pan mix together the sugar, golden syrup and water and heat until a temperature of 115°C/239°F is reached.
3 In another bowl, whisk the egg whites until stiff peaks form and slowly add salt and vanilla extract and then the syrup in three separate additions as it reaches 118°C/244°F.
4 Drain the gelatin, add to a pan with 2 tablespoons of water and heat until dissolved. Once dissolved pour onto the whipped egg white mixture and continue whisking until the mixture is cooled.
5 When ready to use, transfer to a piping bag with a No. 8 nozzle and pipe onto a chocolate biscuit and then sandwich on the second half. Repeat with the remaining biscuits and filling until they're all done.

Lemon with Lemon Curd Filling

1 When ready to assemble, transfer the lemon curd to a piping bag with a No. 8 nozzle and pipe onto a lemon biscuit and then sandwich on the second half. Repeat with the remaining biscuits and filling until they're all done.

Vanilla with Passionfruit Filling

120g (4oz) butter
110g (3¾oz) caster sugar
110g (3¾oz) dark brown sugar
1 egg
300g (10½oz) plain flour, sifted
1 tsp bicarbonate of soda
1½ tsp baking powder
120ml (4fl oz) buttermilk
2 tsp vanilla extract

For the passionfruit filling:

2 passionfruits, cut in half and flesh and seeds scooped out
50g (1¾oz) butter
1 tbsp lemon juice
2 eggs, beaten
100g (3½oz) caster sugar
2 tsp cornflour

Vanilla with Passionfruit Filling

1 Pulse the passionfruit two or three times to separate the flesh from the seeds.
2 Place the pulp, butter, lemon juice, eggs and sugar in a pan and sift the cornflour in.
3 Stir over a medium heat for 5 minutes or until the mixture thickens.
4 Remove from the heat and chill in the fridge.
5 When ready to use, transfer to a piping bag with a No. 8 nozzle and pipe onto a vanilla biscuit and then sandwich on the second half. Repeat with the remaining biscuits and filling until they're all done.

Shannon Bennett's Lamingtons

Makes 20

For the sponge:
6 eggs
150g (5½oz) caster sugar
150g (5½oz) plain flour, sifted

For the red berry jam:
40g (1½oz) caster sugar
180g (6½oz) frozen red
    berries
½ tsp pectin

For the cream:
250ml (8½fl oz) double cream
25g (1oz) caster sugar

For the chocolate glaze:
250g (9oz) icing sugar
250g (9oz) cocoa powder
water

300g (10½oz) desiccated
    coconut, to coat

I have known Shannon since we worked together at The Restaurant Marco Pierre White in London in the 1990s and I really wanted to include a recipe from my old friend in this book. He has since gone on to become one of Australia's most exciting and acclaimed chefs. His restaurant Vue de Monde is located at the top of Melbourne's iconic Rialto building and has won Australian Restaurant of the Year on several occasions, as well as numerous other prestigious awards. Shannon has become renowned around the world for his dedication to cutting-edge cuisine, is also an accomplished author having written four books, and more recently has opened two Vue spin-offs in Melbourne. Here is his recipe for an age-old Ozzie favourite.

1 Preheat the oven to 180°C/350°F/gas mark 4, and grease and line two 21cm x 25cm (8in x 10in) cake tins with baking parchment.
2 Whisk the eggs and sugar in a food mixer, until pale and tripled in volume.
3 Then remove the bowl from the machine and by hand mix the sifted flour into the egg mixture until the mixture is uniform.
4 Divide the mixture in half and, using a spatula, evenly spread one half of the mixture to the corners of the cake tin. Repeat with the second half of the mixture in the other cake tin.
5 Bake in a preheated oven for 10 minutes or until firm to the touch and golden.
6 Remove the sponges from the oven and allow to cool in the tins and remove the parchment.
7 Cut both sponges in half, there should be: two for cream, one for jam, and one for the top.
8 Now, make the red berry jam. Place 25g (1oz) of sugar and the red berries into a heavy-bottomed pan and bring to the boil. Mix the pectin and 15g (½oz) of the sugar until uniform. Once boiling, add the pectin-sugar mixture, bring the jam to 106°C/223°F, remove from the heat and allow to cool. (You could always use a good-quality seedless raspberry jam.)
9 Now, make the cream. Simply whip the cream with the sugar and set aside.

10 Spread the cream evenly over two of the sponges and set aside ready for use.
11 Now, start to assemble. Place one of the sponge sheets with the cream evenly spread onto a work surface, place another plain sponge on top to sandwich the cream between.
12 Spread a generous amount of the jam over the top of the second sponge. Place the other sheet of sponge that is spread with cream over the jam.
13 Finally, place the last sponge on top of the third sponge. The layers will then be: sponge, cream, sponge, jam, sponge, cream, sponge.
14 Place the cake in the freezer until it becomes firm to the touch (30 minutes) before cutting into cubes of 4cm (1½in) and set aside.
15 Next, make the chocolate glaze. Sift and mix the dry ingredients, then add water while mixing until the desired texture is reached.
16 With a wire rack ready, place the prepared Lamington cubes into the chocolate mixture, making sure all sides are coated. Then place the dipped Lamingtons onto the rack until the mixture no longer runs off. Next dip these into a bowl of desiccated coconut. Coat fully with the coconut and arrange on a platter.

Where to Eat Cake...
MELBOURNE & SYDNEY

Melbourne is quite rightly famed for its vibrant café culture and eclectic food styles, and in recent years it seems like its Eastern cousin of Sydney has been catching up. Together these cities reflect the growing desire for coffee, tea and cake culture that is spreading throughout Australia. Coffee drinking – and the never-ending quest for a decent coffee – has become an integral part of the local lifestyle and as a result there has been an explosion of neighbourhood coffee shops, bakeries and pâtisseries in both cities. It seems that locals expect more than the perfect macchiato or brew of chai, they now want all manner of cakes, pastries and tarts to go with their regular cuppa. And this new band of artisan cafés and pâtisseries are only too happy to help.

MELBOURNE

CAFÉ VUE
401 St Kilda Rd, Melbourne 3004
www.vuedemonde.com.au
Funky décor and great food offer a modern take on French classics from renowned chef Shannon Bennett.

BURCH & PURCHESE SWEET STUDIO
647 Chapel St, South Yarra 3141
www.burchandpurchese.com
The wonderfully exquisite and extravagant sweet creations of the chef and owner Darren Purchese are definitely not to be missed.

LET THEM EAT CAKE
147–149 Cecil St, South Melbourne 3205
www.letthemeatcake.com.au
A delightful boutique pastry shop whose cake creations are a wonder to behold. The dark chocolate tart is divine.

LITTLE CUPCAKES
7 Degraves St, Melbourne 3000
(and other branches)
No website
Passionate about cupcakes, this bakery sells over 20 different flavours of both mini and standard-sized cupcakes. Their light creamy frosting tops off a variety of flavours including chocolate, carrot, pistachio and Red Velvet.

CHIMMYS
342–344 Bridge Rd, Richmond 3121
www.chimmys.com.au
Rapidly becoming a Richmond institution, this delightful bakery sells award-winning pastries, cakes and desserts. Expect classic favourites, such as Black Forest Gâteau and Lemon Meringue, mixed in with gluten-free offerings, such as their Framboisine Cake, or delectable tarts.

CHEZ DRE
285–287 Coventry St, South Melbourne 3205
www.chezdre.com.au
Tucked away in a little side alley, this café is full of buzz with great home-made pastries and cakes. Be prepared to wait.

LE PETIT GÂTEAU
458 Little Collins St, Melbourne 3000
www.lepetitgateau.com.au
Pierrick Boyer, Le Petit Gâteau's Head Pastry Chef, has brought his extensive international experience to bear in this inner-city gem of a café in Melbourne. Sip a hot chocolate before diving into one of many of his creations or irresistible classics, such as passionfruit and chocolate gâteau or a Cosmopolitan (here it's a cake not a cocktail).

BRUNETTI CAKES
380 Lygon St, Carlton 3053
www.brunetti.com.au
Famed for its mouth-watering cakes, Brunetti is a true Carlton institution and has a loyal local following. If you find it hard to choose between the macarons and pastries, then opt for a gelato and a coffee while planning a return trip.

A LITTLE BIRD TOLD ME
Near RMIT, 29 Little La Trobe St, Melbourne 3000
No website
Sunny and hip café serving gluten-free friendly delights as well as wonderful home-made goodies; and amazing coffee.

CASA & BOTTEGA
64 Sutton St, North Melbourne 3051
www.casabottega.com.au
Mouth-watering delights await you at this little bit of Italy down-under.

IL FORNAIO
2 Acland St, St Kilda 3182
www.ilfornaio.com.au
This rustic little bakery and café is a sanctuary of sweetness with divine desserts the starring rather than supporting role to the main courses.

LAURENT BOULANGERIE PÂTISSERIE
306 Little Collins St, Melbourne 3000
www.laurent.com.au
You'll see the amazing front windows of this chain of boulangeries dotted throughout Melbourne. Founded by chef Laurent Boillon, who trained at the world-famous Lenôtre in Paris, these bakeries serve up smooth cheesecakes, pies, tarts, tortes and confectionery as well as fantastic breads.

ADRIANO ZUMBO
296 Darling St, Balmain 204
www.adrianozumbo.com
Adriano Zumbo has trained with the best pastry chefs in the New World and the Old World. His unique and unconventional approach to pâtisserie and his wacky selection of pastries and cakes – all with equally wacky names, like Eric is Bananaman or the Jun and Jill Cake – mean that no trip to Sydney is complete without a trip here to sample his wares.

KNEAD BAKERS
396 Burwood Rd, Hawthorn 3122
No website
Artisan rustic bakery producing traditional sourdough; they supply over 40 cafés and shops locally. Swing by any day for sweet and savoury delights all made by the team with organic flour. It's a popular spot, though, so get here early.

SYDNEY

SUGARLOAF PÂTISSERIE
37 President Ave, Kogarah 2217
www.sugarloafonline.com
This small pâtisserie serves a carnival of South American sweet treats, such as caramel churros and dulce de leche sweets.

FERNANDES PÂTISSERIE
516 Marrickville Rd, Dulwich Hill 2203
No website
A friendly place that serves up classic Portuguese sweets and tarts. It's reputed to serve the best traditional custard tart (pasteis de nata) in Sydney; but get there early as they often sell out by lunchtime.

BLACK STAR PASTRY
277 Australia St, Newtown 2042
www.blackstarpastry.com.au
Make a trip to come and see the hugely eclectic array of offerings, and all at great prices, at this maverick pâtisserie. Try the orange cake with Persian fig or the chocolate popcorn cake. And everything here is made in the tiny kitchen out the back of its even tinier shopfront.

CROQUEMBOUCHE PÂTISSERIE
1635 Botany Rd, Banksmeadow 2019
www.croquembouche.com.au
If it's tarts you're after, then this is the place. This pâtisserie serves a wondrous selection of delicious classic European tarts and pastries – you'll soon see (well, taste) why this little place has had to expand its premises within six months of opening.

PASTICCERIA PAPA
145 Ramsay St, Haberfield 2045
www.ppapa.com.au
Whether it's the famed ricotta cheesecake, profiteroles, panzerotti or biscotti you're after, you'll find that along with much much more, all freshly made, at this Sicilian bakery. Plus, there's great espresso and even gelato if it's hot outside.

SHANGRI-LA HOTEL
176 Cumberland Street, The Rocks 2000
www.shangri-la.com/sydney
Overlooking Sydney Harbour, this hotel serves up a super-chocolatey High Tea. See if you can eat your way through three tiers of chocolate cakes, macarons, bavarois and brownies.

BOURKE STREET BAKERY
633 Bourke St, Surry Hills 2010
www.bourkestreetbakery.com.au
One of the original artisan bakeries to open in Sydney. Their tasty pastries, including the signature ginger crème brulée tart, will make up for the inevitable queue!

Fondant Fancies

Makes 9

3 egg yolks
240ml (8fl oz) full-fat milk
drop of vanilla extract
300g (10½oz) plain flour, sifted
300g (10½oz) caster sugar
2 tsp baking powder
a small pinch of salt
170g (6oz) butter, melted

For the buttercream:

20ml (⅔fl oz) water
30g (1¼oz) caster sugar
1 egg yolk
70g (2½oz) butter, cubed
½ tsp vanilla extract

For the fondant:

40g (1½oz) caster sugar
20ml (⅔fl oz) water
500g (1lb 2oz) ready-made
    fondant icing
few drops of different food
    colourings

Despite also being known as French Fancies the idea for these pretty little cakes probably originated from Viennese pâtissiers, who would create the most delicate of cakes to impress their clientele in the days when taking tea was a social occasion and an important part of the day.

1 Preheat the oven to 180°C/350°F/gas mark 4, and grease and line a 18cm (7in) square x 10cm (4in) deep tin with baking parchment.
2 Mix the egg yolks, milk and vanilla together in a bowl.
3 Slowly add the flour, sugar, baking powder and salt.
4 Beat everything together then add the melted butter and mix in thoroughly.
5 Pour the mixture into the prepared tin and bake in a preheated oven for 20 minutes or until a cocktail stick inserted into the centre comes out clean.
6 Remove from the oven, allow to cool for a few minutes in the tin and then turn out onto a wire rack and strip off the baking parchment. Place in the fridge to cool completely and firm up.

7 Next make the buttercream. Mix the water and sugar in a pan and bring to the boil. When it reaches 120°C/248°F whisk the egg yolk on a low speed. Remove the sugar from the heat and pour slowly into the egg yolk while continuing to whisk. Now, whisk on a high speed until the mixture begins to cool down. Add the cubed butter and the vanilla extract and mix thoroughly.
8 Remove the cake from the fridge and then slice off the top horizontally and neaten and square off the sides before cutting into nine square pieces. Place on a wire rack and spoon a blob of buttercream on the top of each fancy.
9 Now, for the fondant. In a pan, place the sugar and water and boil until it becomes a syrup. Cool a little.
10 In a different pan, warm the fondant icing slightly with just enough sugar syrup to make the fondant malleable (about body temperature), which will give a lovely finish.
11 Pour the fondant (using a small ladle) over each fancy (while sitting on a wire rack), covering the top and all the sides completely. Allow to set. For an extra decorative touch, pipe with swirls of icing.

LEAVENED CAKES

Brioche

Makes 12 mini-brioches

1 tbsp warm water

15g (½oz) fresh yeast

4 eggs, plus 1 egg yolk for brushing

330g (11½oz) strong flour

10g (¼oz) salt

25g (1oz) caster sugar

200g (7oz) butter, softened, plus extra, to grease

nibbed sugar, to decorate

This rich buttery bread has been baked in Paris since the 17th century and I have been using this particular recipe for over 20 years. You do need quite a bit of time to prepare this delightful treat but the results are well worth it; you may never buy ready-made brioche again.

1 Pour the warm water into a mixing bowl. Tip the yeast into the bowl and whisk until dissolved.

2 Whisk 2 eggs together in a bowl, then add the flour, salt and sugar before the remaining eggs. The mixing is best done in a food mixer with a dough hook, or the paddle attachment if you don't have a dough hook; you really do need a machine to help with this recipe.

3 Mix on speed 1 for 5 minutes, scrape the mixture down and increase the speed to number 2 for 10 minutes until the gluten has been stretched.

4 Now, slowly add the butter a little at a time until fully combined, scraping down every few minutes (this should take about 4–5 minutes).

5 Place in a floured bowl, cover with clingfilm and leave to rest overnight in the fridge.

6 Grease 12 small fluted petit-Brioche tins (11cm x 5cm (4¼in x 2in)) on a baking tray.

7 The next day, remove from the fridge and weigh out 85g (3oz) balls of dough for each mould. Stamp each ball flat on a floured worktop and fold in on itself, beginning furthest away from you. Then roll back into a ball and place in the greased mould. Repeat with the rest and leave to prove in a warm area until they have doubled in size.

8 Meanwhile, preheat the oven to 180°C/350°F/gas mark 4.

9 Brush each brioche with the beaten egg yolk, sprinkle with nibbed sugar and place in the oven for 10–15 minutes.

10 Remove from the oven and allow to cool in the moulds on a wire rack.

11 Best eaten while still warm. Delicious!

Chelsea Buns

Makes 12

For the yeast starter:
15g (½oz) caster sugar
85g (3oz) strong flour
300ml (10fl oz) full-fat milk,
    slightly warmed
25g (1oz) fresh yeast

For the dough:
675g (1lb 8¾oz) strong flour
a pinch of nutmeg
140g (5oz) butter, cubed
1 egg
85g (3oz) caster sugar, plus
    extra for sprinkling
finely grated zest of 1 lemon

For the decoration:
50g (1¾oz) butter, melted
50g (1¾oz) caster sugar
2 tsp ground cinnamon
50g (1¾oz) currants
65ml (2½fl oz) Stock Syrup
    (see page 299)

The Chelsea Bun might once have originated in the eponymous area of London, England, but its popularity extends way beyond the city's limits to the entire UK. This sweet and sticky currant bun makes a perfect mid-morning snack and revealing an entire batch on a tray from the oven will make you feel like a domestic god/goddess.

1 To make the yeasty mix, stir the sugar and flour into the slightly warmed milk in a pan then add the yeast. Keep it warm until it froths up and then drops.

2 To make the dough, sift the flour and nutmeg together in a bowl then rub in the butter until it resembles breadcrumbs. Next make a well in the centre of this dry mixture.

3 Whisk the egg, sugar and lemon zest into the yeasty mixture then tip this into the well and mix until the dough is smooth, silky and slightly elastic. Allow it to rest for 1 hour wrapped in clingfilm.

4 Grease and line a baking sheet with baking parchment.

5 On a lightly floured surface, roll out the dough to a square shape about 4cm (1½in) thick, then brush with melted butter. Sprinkle sugar, cinnamon and currants over its surface.

6 Roll up the dough (think Swiss roll), then brush the outside of the roll with more of the melted butter.

7 Cut the roll into pieces about 4cm (1½in) wide and place cut side down on the prepared baking sheet. Make sure that you place them evenly in rows so they can 'batch' together during their proving time, 45–60 minutes. They're ready to bake when they have doubled in size and all the buns are touching each other.

8 Meanwhile, preheat the oven to 190°C/375°F/gas mark 5 and make the stock syrup, as instructed on page 299.

9 Bake in a preheated oven for 8–12 minutes until golden brown.

10 Remove from the oven, brush with the stock syrup, sprinkle with caster sugar, remove from the baking parchment and transfer to a wire rack to cool.

Kanelbulle

Makes 20

75g (2¾oz) butter, melted
250ml (8½fl oz) full-fat milk
25g (1oz) fresh yeast
¼ tsp salt
85g (3oz) caster sugar
1 tsp ground cardamom
525g (1lb 2½oz) plain flour,
   sifted

For the filling:

40g (1½oz) butter, softened
2½ tbsp caster sugar
1 tbsp ground cinnamon
1 egg, beaten, for brushing
blitzed nibbed sugar and
   flaked almonds, to decorate

The humble cinnamon bun, or as the Swedes say 'kanelbulle', is one of the more famous bakes associated with Sweden – it even has its own national day on 4th October. The cardamom in the dough gives a lovely spicy kick to the sweetened pastry and, topped with almonds and sugar, they are a perfect partner for your mid-morning coffee – or 'fika' as they say in Sweden.

1 Preheat the oven to 190°C/375°F/gas mark 5, and you'll need paper muffin cases and a baking tray.
2 Melt the butter and milk together in a pan.
3 In a bowl, first dissolve the yeast with a little of the warm butter–milk mixture and then add the rest of the mixture, the salt, sugar, cardamom and the sifted flour. Mix until a dough forms.
4 Knead the dough for 5 minutes until the mixture is soft and pliable. Then, leave in a warm place until doubled in size.
5 On a floured work surface, knead the dough before rolling out to a rectangle about 25cm x 45cm (10in x 18in) in size.
6 Spread with softened butter and sprinkle with the sugar and cinnamon.

7 Roll up from one long side to form a giant long bun and then cut into about 20 pieces.
8 Place each piece in a muffin case on a baking tray and then leave in a warm place for about 20 minutes.
9 Brush with the beaten egg, sprinkle with nibbed sugar and flaked almonds and then bake in a preheated oven for 8–9 minutes.
10 Remove from the oven, allow to cool for 10 minutes and then transfer cases to a wire rack to cool completely.
11 Serve with coffee.

Iced Buns

Makes 12

For the bun dough:

30g (1¼oz) powdered milk
345ml (11⅔fl oz) water
60g (2oz) fresh yeast
2 eggs
1.1kg (2lb 6½oz) plain flour, sifted
½ tsp salt
140g (5oz) caster sugar
140g (5oz) butter, cubed
65ml (2½fl oz) Stock Syrup (see page 299)

For the decoration:

250g (9oz) ready-made fondant icing
food colouring of your choice
food flavouring of your choice, such as lemon essence

The sight and taste of these sticky sweet buns instantly transport Brits back to childhood, as the slight tingling of the icing hits your teeth followed by the super-soft buns beneath dissolving in your mouth. As popular with adults as they are with kids, Iced Buns are a perfect between-meal treat or for serving at children's parties and picnics.

1 To make the dough, whisk the powdered milk into the water then dissolve the yeast in it and finally add the eggs.
2 In a large bowl, mix the sifted flour and salt with the sugar then rub in the butter using your fingertips until it resembles breadcrumbs.
3 Make a well in the centre then add the yeast liquor in several bursts until a firm but supple dough is formed. Continue to mix until it is fully combined.
4 Wrap the dough in clingfilm and allow to prove in a warm place. After 40 minutes, knock back the dough and leave to prove for a further 20 minutes.
5 Grease and line a baking tray with baking parchment.
6 Divide the dough into 12 pieces and lightly roll each into a finger shape and carefully place on the prepared tray in nice straight lines, allowing room to expand around each bun.

7 Allow to prove again for 45–60 minutes until the buns have doubled in size. Meanwhile, preheat the oven to 190°C/375°F/gas mark 5.
8 Bake in a preheated oven for 7–9 minutes until they are golden brown. Meanwhile, make the stock syrup as instructed on page 299.
9 Remove from the oven and immediately glaze with the syrup then take off the baking parchment and transfer to a wire rack to cool.
10 To prepare the fondant, place it in a saucepan and add a little water; you could add some food colouring for a visual effect if you like. Warm the fondant through until soft, pliable and shiny.
11 When the iced buns are completely cold, dip the top of each bun into the prepared fondant, flavoured with a spot of lemon essence, if you like. Wipe off any residue with a palette knife and allow the fondant to set.

Loukamades

Whether you spell it Loukamades, Loukoumathes, Lokma or Lokmades, mounds of these little honey doughballs adorn bakeries throughout Greece and Turkey. These aromatic deep-fried doughnuts are drizzled with a spiced honey syrup – they are tooth-tinglingly sweet. Rumour has it that they were presented to the winners of the Olympic Games in Ancient Greece.

Makes 20

500ml (18fl oz) warm water
20g (¾oz) fresh yeast
1 tbsp sugar
450g (1lb) self-raising flour, sifted
1 tsp salt
½ tsp ground cinnamon
500ml (18fl oz) vegetable oil, for deep-frying

For the syrup:
200ml (7fl oz) water
175g (6¼oz) caster sugar
1 stick cinnamon
5 cloves
1 tbsp rosewater

1 You'll need a cup filled with cold oil and some teaspoons handy for the frying.
2 In a bowl, use 100ml (3½fl oz) of the water to mix with the yeast and the sugar until dissolved. Leave in a warm place for 15 minutes.
3 After that, slowly add the sifted flour, salt and cinnamon and the remaining warm water until you have a wet batter.
4 Cover the bowl with clingfilm and leave to prove in a warm place for 40 minutes.
5 To make the syrup, place all the ingredients, except the rosewater, in a pan and boil for 10 minutes. Switch off the heat and stir in the rosewater. Leave to cool and then discard the spices.
6 Pour the oil into a deep wide heavy-based pan and heat it until it reaches 170°C/338°F. Have ready a baking tray or plate covered with kitchen paper.

7 Wet your hand with water and place in the bowl of batter. Take a handful of the batter, make a fist until a ball of the mixture pops out of the top of your hand. Use a teaspoon to scrape off the ball and drop it straight into the hot oil; be careful not to splash yourself in the hot oil. (After each batch remember to wet your hand and to frequently dip the teaspoon into the cup of cold oil as this will help the batter slip off the spoon.) Continue to do this until the pan is full of frying balls.
8 Deep-fry for 3 minutes, turning occasionally, until the balls are golden brown.
9 Remove with a slotted spoon to the paper-lined tray or plate. Repeat until all the batter is cooked.
10 When cool, transfer to a serving plate and then drizzle with the cooled syrup (or use honey if you prefer). Scatter toasted almonds over, too, if you like.

Kolache

Makes 30

5g (⅛oz) fresh yeast
20ml (⅔fl oz) warm water
20g (¾oz) caster sugar
350g (12oz) plain flour, plus
    extra for dusting
¼ tsp salt
60g (2oz) butter, cold and
    cubed
1 egg, plus 1 egg, beaten, for
    brushing
1 tsp lemon juice
120ml (4fl oz) evaporated milk
3 apples, peeled and cubed

VARIATION

For a savoury version,
replace the apple in
each kolache with
a tablespoonful of
goat's cheese.

These slightly sweet pastries hold a good dollop of fruit within (I used apple) and make an ideal breakfast; if you prefer, bake a savoury version filled with meat or cheese. Kolache originate from Czechoslovakia (or what is now the Czech Republic and Slovakia) in Eastern Europe, and date as far back as the 1700s where they were served at weddings. Kolache – which translates as 'cookie' – also appear in bakeries in America, particularly in the South, where a large Czech population settled and where they hold annual Kolache festivals.

1 In a bowl, dissolve the yeast in the warm water with half of the sugar.
2 Sift the flour with the salt and the rest of the sugar and place in a mixer. On a low speed, slowly add the cubed butter until it starts to form crumbs. Or, by hand, rub in the butter until it resembles breadcrumbs.
3 Whisk the egg into the yeast mixture and add to the bowl, followed by the lemon juice and the evaporated milk until a smooth dough forms.
4 Tip the mix out onto a lightly floured surface, bring the dough together, wrap in clingfilm and refrigerate for at least 2 hours or preferably overnight.
5 Preheat the oven to 180°C/350°F/gas mark 4,

and line a baking tray with baking parchment.
6 Remove the dough from the fridge and, on a lightly floured work surface, roll out to a rectangle about 3–4 mm (⅛in) thick.
7 Divide into 30 squares and place on the lined baking tray. Place a tablespoon of apple into the middle of each square and fold two opposite corners of the dough over the apple and pinch together.
8 Leave in a warm place for 15–20 minutes.
9 Lightly brush with beaten egg and bake in a preheated oven for 10–12 minutes.
10 Remove from the oven, take off the baking parchment and cool on a wire rack and then serve warm with coffee.

Bath Buns

Makes 12

For the bun dough:
30g (1¼oz) powdered milk
345ml (11⅔fl oz) warm water
60g (2oz) fresh yeast
2 eggs, plus 1 egg for cracking
1.1kg (2lb 6½oz) plain flour,
    sifted, plus extra, for
    dusting
½ tsp salt
140g (5oz) caster sugar
140g (5oz) butter
85g (3oz) sultanas
30g (1¼oz) candied mixed
    peel
nibbed sugar, for decoration
65ml (2½fl oz) Stock Syrup
    (see page 299)

A regional recipe from Bath in Southwest England, these buns date back to the 17th century. Discussion and debate is ongoing as to which is the original recipe and who invented it – we will probably never know, but suffice to say this version is a great bun whatever the time of day.

1 To make the dough, whisk the powdered milk into the warm water then dissolve the yeast in it and finally add the eggs.

2 In a large bowl, mix the sifted flour and salt with the sugar then rub in the butter using your fingertips until it resembles breadcrumbs.

3 Make a well in the centre then add the yeast liquor in several bursts until a firm but supple dough is formed. Continue to mix until it is fully combined.

4 Wrap the dough in clingfilm and allow to prove in a warm place. After 40 minutes, knock back the dough and leave to prove for a further 20 minutes.

5 Grease and line a baking tray with baking parchment.

6 On a lightly floured work surface, gently flatten the dough and liberally sprinkle the fruit and peel over its surface.

7 Next, crack an egg over the fruited dough and smear it all over, so everything is covered.

8 With a dough scraper (or a metal spatula if you don't have a dough scraper), begin to 'chop and fold' the mixture into itself, so that you end up with evenly coated pieces of fruit and dough.

9 Divide the dough into 12 pieces and lightly form each into a ball by cupping your hands around it, then dropping it onto the prepared tray, allowing room to expand around each bun.

10 Sprinkle each bun with nibbed sugar and allow to prove again for 60–90 minutes until the buns have doubled in size. Meanwhile, preheat the oven to 190°C/375°F/gas mark 5.

11 Bake in a preheated oven for 8–10 minutes until they are golden brown, turning the tray around after 6 minutes.

12 Meanwhile, make the stock syrup as instructed on page 299.

13 Remove the buns from the oven and immediately glaze with the syrup (for a lovely glossy finish) then transfer the buns from the baking parchment to a wire rack to cool.

Kouign Amann

Serves 8

12g (⅓oz) fresh yeast
175ml (6fl oz) tepid water
200g (7oz) caster sugar, plus extra for rolling out
260g (9¼oz) strong flour, sifted, plus extra for dusting
½ tsp salt
110g (3¾oz) butter, cubed and chilled, plus extra 2 tbsp melted butter

It's difficult to pronounce the name of this cake without being given the phonetic – koo-ween a-mon – since it's in the old Breton language, rather than French. And this butter cake is a little piece of heaven. It may resemble a sweet puff pastry but it is made of bread dough, with layers of butter and sugar folded in; the resulting cake is crisp on the outside yet chewy inside.

1 In a bowl, dissolve the yeast in the tepid water with a pinch of sugar. Stir briefly, then let stand for 10 minutes until bubbles appear.
2 Place the sifted flour and salt into the bowl of a food mixer and, using the dough hook, slowly add the yeast mixture on a low speed until fully mixed. Then, increase the speed to medium for 4–5 minutes until the dough has become nice and elastic. Place in a greased bowl, cover with clingfilm and leave in a warm place for 1 hour.
3 Remove from the bowl and on a lightly floured surface, roll the dough into a rectangle about 25cm x 30cm (10in x 12in).
4 Bring the dough around so that the short side of the rectangle is facing you. Sprinkle 50g (1¾oz) sugar vertically down the middle third of the dough. Sprinkle the cubed butter over the sugar. Fold the left-hand third of the pastry over the top of the butter and sprinkle 25g (1oz) sugar over the pastry then fold the right-hand side over and sprinkle another 25g (1oz) sugar.

Fold the top third towards you and the bottom third up to cover the fold you have just made.
5 Place on a plate lined with parchment paper and chill in the fridge for 30 minutes.
6 Remove from the fridge and roll out again to the same size but using caster sugar instead of flour on your work surface. Repeat the whole process again and chill for a further 30 minutes.
7 Preheat the oven to 200°C/400°F/gas mark 6, and grease and line a 21cm (8in) springform tin with baking parchment.
8 Roll out for a final time on a sugared surface to the size of the prepared cake tin and place inside. Pour the melted butter over the top and bake for 30 minutes until nicely caramelised.
9 Remove from the oven, cool for 10 minutes in the tin and then turn out onto a wire rack and strip off the baking parchment.
10 If you like, you can make the dough the day before and leave in a cake tin overnight, then you can serve with coffee at breakfast.

Cinnamon Bear Claws

Makes 12

25g (1oz) fresh yeast
50g (1¾oz) caster sugar
90ml (3¼fl oz) warm water
575g (1lb 4oz) plain flour, plus
    extra for dusting
250g (9oz) butter, very cold
    and cubed
120ml (4fl oz) evaporated milk
a pinch of salt
2 eggs, plus 1 egg yolk for
    brushing

For the filling:
1 egg white
200g (7oz) almond paste (or
    marzipan)
100g (3½oz) icing sugar
1½ tsp ground cinnamon

flaked almonds, to decorate
nibbed sugar, to decorate

With a bit of forethought, you can wow your guests with freshly baked pastries with their mid-morning coffee. These sweet, yeasted, flaky pastries evolved from Danish pastries and are popular in the US. The curved pastries are slashed before cooking, so after baking they look like a bear's claws.

1 Dissolve the yeast and the sugar in the water and set aside for 10 minutes.
2 Sift the flour into the bowl of a food mixer with a paddle attachment or into a bowl. Either use the machine or your fingers to rub in the butter until it resembles breadcrumbs.
3 Add the evaporated milk, salt and eggs to the mix and combine thoroughly.
4 Next, either using the dough hook or your own hands, mix all the ingredients again to stretch the dough for a further 2–3 minutes.
5 Cover the dough with clingfilm and refrigerate overnight.
6 Line a baking tray with baking parchment.
7 Remove the dough from the fridge and, on a lightly floured surface, roll the dough out to a rectangle about 30cm x 40cm (12in x 16in); we're aiming for a thickness of 5mm (¼in).
8 Turn the dough one turn clockwise, then fold the right third over and the left third over that. Do this – fold over, chill then roll out – three times, chilling for 30 minutes after rolling out.
9 Roll out again to the same size and repeat the process. Chill for 1 hour.

10 Make the filling by beating all the ingredients together in a bowl until smooth.
11 Remove the dough from the fridge and, on a lightly floured work surface, roll out to a rectangle about 30cm x 40cm (12in x 16in) and 5mm (¼in) thick. Spread the filling over the top.
12 Cut in half lengthways and roll each piece up lengthways. With the seam on the bottom, use a rolling pin gently to roll along the top of the dough to flatten slightly and then cut each length into six pieces.
13 With a small knife cut four or five slits into each pastry to create your 'claws'.
14 Place on the prepared baking tray, curving them slightly as you place them. Leave in a warm place for 30 minutes or until they have risen a little.
15 Preheat the oven to 180°C/350°F/gas mark 4.
16 Brush with a beaten egg yolk and place a flaked almond on each toe, sprinkle with nibbed sugar and bake in a preheated oven for 15 minutes.
17 Remove from the oven and cool on a wire rack. Serve with a cup of coffee.

Hot Cross Buns

Makes 12

1 tsp mixed spice
1 tsp ground ginger
60g (2oz) currants
30g (1¼oz) sultanas
15g (½oz) candied mixed
    peel
15g (½oz) powdered milk
200ml (7fl oz) water
40g (1½oz) fresh yeast
1 egg
500g (1lb 2oz) plain flour,
    sifted
1 tsp salt
75g (2¾oz) caster sugar
75g (2¾oz) butter, cubed

Pastry for the cross:
120g (4oz) plain flour
1 tsp baking powder
40g (1½oz) shortening or
    butter
100ml (3½fl oz) water

65ml (2½fl oz) Stock Syrup
    (see page 299)

'One a penny, two a penny, Hot Cross Buns' – so goes the old English song about this bun traditionally made just in the week before Easter Sunday, with the pastry cross symbolising the crucifixion of Jesus. Nowadays, people long for these spiced sweet buns not just at Easter and so bakeries make them year round. I tend to make mine from New Year onwards, when I toast them and spread them with a little butter – delicious.

1 Mix all the spices and fruits together in a bowl and set aside.
2 To make the dough, whisk the powdered milk into the water then dissolve the yeast in it and finally add the egg.
3 In a large bowl, mix the sifted flour and salt with the sugar then rub in the butter using your fingertips until it resembles breadcrumbs.
4 Make a well in the centre then add the yeast liquor in several bursts until a firm but supple dough is formed. Continue to mix until it is fully combined.
5 Wrap the dough in clingfilm and allow to prove in a warm place. After 40 minutes, knock back the dough, add the fruit and spices and mix gently without breaking up the fruit. Cover with clingfilm again and leave to prove for a further 20 minutes.

6 Grease and line a baking tray with baking parchment.
7 Divide the dough into 12 pieces and round each piece up to a bun shape. Allow to rest for 10 minutes. Ensure the dough is unbroken and place buns on a prepared baking tray. Be sure to position the buns in straight lines, allowing plenty of room to prove. (It's also easier for you to pipe the crosses on them if the rows line up.)
8 Allow to prove for 60–90 minutes until the buns have doubled in size. Preheat the oven to 190°C/375°F/gas mark 5.
9 Make the crossing paste. Sift the flour and baking powder together then rub in the shortening or butter until the mixture resembles breadcrumbs. Mix in the water and continue mixing until the paste is smooth and pipeable (add extra water if you need to). Then, pour the paste into a piping bag with a No. 4 plain nozzle.
10 When the buns are proved, pipe the crosses on them, by piping continuous straight lines along the centre of the tops of the buns, without breaking the flow. Go first along the length of the tray, then when all of the rows have a line down the centre, turn the tray 90° and pipe straight lines across the centre of the buns, again without breaking the flow across each column of buns. When you have finished, your buns should look like they are under a white grill.
11 Bake in a preheated oven for 8–10 minutes until they are golden brown, turning the tray around after 6 minutes. Meanwhile, make the stock syrup as instructed on page 299.
12 Remove from the oven and immediately glaze with the syrup then take off the baking parchment and transfer to a wire rack to cool.

Rum Baba

Makes 18–20

20g (¾oz) fresh yeast
200ml (7fl oz) full-fat milk
450g (1lb) plain flour, sifted
40g (1½oz) caster sugar
2 tsp salt
6 eggs
zest of 1 lemon
100g (3½oz) butter, softened
120g (4oz) pistachios,
    chopped (optional)

For the syrup:
1 litre (1¾ pints) water
500g (1lb 2oz) caster sugar
zest of 1 lemon
zest of 2 oranges
100ml (3½fl oz) good-quality
    dark rum

The original form of babas was much taller, similar to the Babka (see page 262), but since the 1840s the Rum Baba has been baked in this shape and with fruit and rum. Don't let these little cakes be forever stuck in the 1970s. Liberate them for the 21st century and enjoy with a little red fruit and cream.

1 Preheat the oven to 170°C/325°F/gas mark 3, and grease 18–20 small Savarin moulds well.
2 Whisk the yeast into the milk and leave in a warm area for 30 minutes.
3 Mix together the flour, sugar, salt, eggs and lemon zest, and then add the yeast mixture.
4 Lastly, add the soft butter little by little into the mixing bowl and mix together well (use the paddle attachment if using a food mixer).
5 Transfer the mixture into a piping bag with a No.6 nozzle. Pipe into the prepared Savarin moulds and leave in a warm area for about 30 minutes or until doubled in size.
6 Place in a preheated oven for approximately 10 minutes until golden brown and then turn out onto a wire rack to cool.

7 To make the syrup, put all the ingredients into a pan and bring to the boil. Turn off the heat and cool to about 45°C/113°F before dunking each of the babas into the warm syrup. Turn the babas in the syrup to ensure they are completely covered in the syrup.
8 Top with chopped pistachios and serve with red berries and crème Chantilly (see page 296).

VARIATION
Use Limoncello instead of rum in the syrup for a citrus flavour or try with Malibu and serve with tropical fruits.

Easter Bun Ring

Serves 8

1 tsp mixed spice
1 tsp ground ginger
60g (2oz) currants
30g (1¼oz) sultanas
15g (½oz) candied mixed
    peel
15g (½oz) powdered milk
200ml (7fl oz) water
40g (1½oz) fresh yeast
1 egg
500g (1lb 2oz) plain flour,
    sifted
1 tsp salt
75g (2¾oz) caster sugar
75g (2¾oz) butter, cubed
65ml (2½fl oz) Stock Syrup
    (see page 299)

For the decoration:
250g (9oz) fondant icing
2 drops lemon essence
glacé cherries
flaked almonds

The English word for 'bun' most likely originated from the Greek word 'boun', which described a circular ceremonial cake that was offered to the gods. Easter has been for a long time a mixture of religious and pagan traditions – for instance, Saxons ate buns with a cross on to honour the goddess of light, Eostre. So, this Easter Bun Ring seems a perfect teatime offering, hitting the same spicy fruity notes traditional at this time in the UK.

1 Mix all the spices and fruits together in a bowl and set aside.
2 To make the dough, whisk the powdered milk into the water then dissolve the yeast in it and finally add the egg.
3 In a large bowl, mix the sifted flour and salt with the sugar then rub in the butter using your fingertips until it resembles breadcrumbs.
4 Make a well in the centre then add the yeast liquor in several bursts until a firm but supple dough is formed. Continue to mix until fully combined.
5 Wrap the dough in clingfilm and allow to prove in a warm place. After 40 minutes, knock back the dough, add the fruit and

spices and mix gently without breaking up the fruit. Cover with clingfilm again and leave to prove for a further 20 minutes.
6 Grease and line a baking tray with baking parchment.
7 Divide the dough into two pieces and roll out to two even lengths. Allow to rest for 10 minutes. Ensure the dough is unbroken and place on a prepared baking tray and twist the two lengths together and form into a circle.
8 Allow to prove again for 60–90 minutes until it has doubled in size. Meanwhile, preheat the oven to 190°C/375°F/gas mark 5.
9 Bake in a preheated oven for 20 minutes until golden brown, turning the tray around after 10 minutes. Meanwhile, make the stock syrup as instructed on page 299.
10 Remove from the oven and immediately glaze with syrup then take off the baking parchment and transfer the bun ring to a wire rack to cool.
11 To prepare the fondant, place it in a saucepan and add a little water. Warm the fondant through until soft, pliable and shiny, and flavour with a spot of lemon essence, if you like. Then pour into a roasting tin, ready for dipping the ring in.
12 When the Easter ring is completely cold, dip into the prepared fondant wipe off any residue with a palette knife, dot on glacé cherries, sprinkle over some flaked almonds and allow the fondant to set.
13 Stand back and admire before slicing to share with friends and family.

Lardy Cake

Serves 16

For the bread dough:
15g (½oz) fresh yeast
200ml (7fl oz) warm water
350g (12oz) plain flour, sifted
1½ tsp salt
5g (⅛oz) lard

For the filling:
180g (6½oz) lard, softened
180g (6½oz) caster sugar
180g (6½oz) currants
100g (3½oz) candied mixed
    peel

When my Grandma used to make this cake she would call it 'fat cake'! Don't let that stand in the way of you trying this traditional English tea bread – it is deliciously moist and perks up any afternoon cup of tea with a sugary, fruity hit. The recipe just doesn't work if you substitute butter for the lard, so I'm afraid it's not suitable for vegetarians. Shame, though all the more for us!

1 Preheat the oven to 180°C/350°F/gas mark 4.
2 In a bowl dissolve the yeast in a small amount of warm water and whisk together.
3 Add the flour and the remaining water and mix in a food mixer on low speed until fully combined, or in a bowl with your hands.
4 Next, add the salt and the lard and continue to mix on a low speed for about 8 minutes. Cover the bowl with lightly oiled clingfilm and leave to rise for 1 hour at room temperature.
5 Knock back the dough and roll out on a floured surface to a rectangle about 35cm x 20cm (14in x 8in).
6 Mix the lard and the sugar together in a bowl, then add the dried fruit and peel.
7 With the long edge of the rectangle nearest you on the work surface, spoon the mixture onto the right-hand side covering two-thirds of the rectangle then fold the remaining third of the rectangle over the mixture. Fold the right-hand side third over the folded sections and roll the whole cake out to approximately the size of the original rectangle again. Repeat the folding a second time and then leave to prove for 30 minutes at room temperature.
8 Place on a baking tray and bake in a preheated oven for about 30–35 minutes.
9 Remove from the oven and cool on a wire rack. Turn over after 10 minutes.
10 Cut into finger slices and eat warm or cold.

Chocolate Kugelhopf

Serves 8

For the chocolate ganache:
180g (6½oz) dark chocolate, finely chopped
80ml (3fl oz) double cream

For bowl 1:
40g (1½oz) strong flour
12g (⅓oz) fresh yeast
10g (¼oz) caster sugar
80ml (3fl oz) full-fat milk

For bowl 2:
60g (2oz) butter
40g (1½oz) caster sugar
1 egg and 2 egg yolks

For bowl 3:
160g (5¾oz) strong flour, sifted
½ tsp salt

For the decoration:
25g (1oz) whole almonds, toasted
85g (3oz) Apricot Glaze (see page 299) (optional)

The ring-shaped Kugelhopf seems to have many wondrous spellings – Guglhupf, Kougelhof, Gugelhopf – and its popularity spans from Alsace, France, to Germany and Austria. Its origins have many claims; one from Alsace tells of a Mr Kugel who baked a brioche-like cake in a turban shape for the three Magi, who stopped for sustenance. I have added chocolate ganache here for extra richness, I'm sure the Three Kings would approve.

1 Grease a 17cm x 9cm (6½in x 3½in) Kugelhopf (or Bundt) tin.
2 First make the ganache. Put the chopped chocolate in a bowl. Then pour the cream into a saucepan, bring to the boil and pour onto the chocolate and stir until it has all melted; cover with clingfilm and allow to rest in a cool place until you need it (not the fridge).
3 In bowl 1, combine all the ingredients, cover with clingfilm and place in a warm area for 20 minutes.
4 Meanwhile, cream the butter and sugar for bowl 2 until light and fluffy and then slowly add the egg yolks until fully combined, scraping down two or three times.
5 Sift the flour and salt into a separate bowl and then add the 'yeast starter' from bowl 1 and the creamed mix from bowl 2. In your food mixer, use the dough hook and mix for 10 minutes.
6 Cover the bowl and place somewhere warm for an hour or until doubled in size. Then, knock back the mixture with your hand while in the bowl and then tip the dough onto a floured surface.
7 Using a rolling pin, roll out into a rectangle 40cm x 25cm (16in x 10in), 5mm (¼in) thick. Place on a baking tray and pop in the fridge for 30 minutes.

8 Remove from the fridge and, using a palette knife, spread the chocolate ganache evenly over the sheet of dough.
9 Starting at the top, roll the long edge towards you to form a swiss roll shape. The length of the rolled Kugelhopf will depend on the size of the mould, join the ends together to form a ring shape. Place a whole almond in each ridge of the greased tin.
10 Place the dough piece smooth side down and with the edge of the rolled section facing upwards into the prepared mould.
11 Prove the Kugelhopf for about 1½ hours in a warm place covered with clingfilm. The dough will double in size again. Use the indentation test (the dough will spring back when gently prodded) to tell when the dough is fully proved.
12 Preheat the oven to 180°C/350°F/gas mark 4.
13 Place the mould directly into the preheated oven and bake for about 35 minutes. Remove from the oven and allow to cool for 10 minutes in the mould before turning out, right way up, onto a wire rack.
14 If you want a shine to your Kugelhopf, then make the glaze as instructed on page 299 and brush liberally over the cake. Serve with a glass of sweet white wine.

PASTRIES

Macanese Egg Tarts

Makes 8

200g (7oz) Puff Pastry (see page 221)

For the filling:
2 eggs
85g (3oz) caster sugar
120ml (4fl oz) full-fat milk
250ml (8½fl oz) double cream

Central Macau bustles with food stalls selling a variety of Macanese and Cantonese treats on this island near Hong Kong. These egg custard tarts are a common sight and are very similar to Pastéis de Nata, the Portuguese egg tart, famously made at the monastery in Belem, just outside Lisbon. Macau has many Portuguese influences left over from its colonial days and these are one of the most tempting and most popular.

1 Make the pastry as instructed on page 221.
2 Grease a 12-hole deep muffin tin.
3 Remove the pastry from the fridge. Roll out on a lightly floured surface to 3mm (⅛in) thickness and cut out eight pastry discs of 8cm (3¼in) diameter.
4 Line eight holes of the muffin tin with the eight discs of pastry and chill for 30 minutes.
5 Remove from the fridge and line each pastry case with squares of clingfilm (it fits in the muffin tin easier than baking parchment) and fill with baking beans. Preheat the oven to 170°C/325°F/gas mark 3.

6 Bake blind in a preheated oven for about 15 minutes until lightly brown on the bottom. Remove from the oven and leave to cool for 30 minutes. Remove the beans and clingfilm.
7 Turn up the oven to 190°C/375°F/gas mark 5. Meanwhile, make the custard filling. Whisk the eggs together with the sugar and sieve into a bowl that contains the milk and cream.
8 Fill the tartlets with the custard and bake in a preheated oven for 10–15 minutes or until the surface turns a wondrous brown and the custard has lost its wobble.
9 Serve warm with an espresso.

How To Make Pastry

Here you will find recipes for the most commonly used pastry doughs. I have included a recipe for puff pastry, which I really believe is worth trying to make (although ready-made versions are pretty good). You can't beat its buttery lightness and the satisfaction of making your own is immense.

I use cold butter for my pastry but always bash it with a rolling pin to soften before adding it to the dough. Always roll on a lightly floured surface and just sprinkle a scattering of flour over your dough pat before you begin to roll. If your kitchen is very hot or it is a very hot day, cool down your work surface for a few minutes before you start (use a large roasting dish filled with ice). Enjoy making pastry!

Shortcrust Pastry

The most adaptable pastry of all – strong, easy to roll and versatile. Perfect for cooking liquids in, such as quiche and for topping pies.

Makes 500g (1lb 2oz)
235g (8½oz) plain flour, sifted
10g (¼oz) salt
180g (6½oz) butter, cubed
65ml (2½fl oz) water

1 Using a dough hook attachment put the flour, butter and salt in the bowl and slowly mix while adding the water until an even paste is formed. If you're doing it by hand, rub the butter into the salt and flour with your fingertips until it resembles fine breadcrumbs, then add the water until an even paste is formed.
2 Wrap the dough in clingfilm and allow to rest in the fridge, preferably overnight or for at least 2 hours. Remove from the fridge 30 minutes before you need it.

Variation: Sweet Shortcrust Pastry
If making sweet pastry feels a little daunting, this is a great pastry to start with. Perfect for puddings and pies. Add 20g (¾oz) caster sugar with the flour, butter and salt and follow the instructions above.

Sweet Pastry

A classic recipe that will enhance any tart with its melt in the mouth flavour as well as showing off the filling beautifully.

Makes 700g (1lb 10oz)
225g (8oz) butter
85g (3oz) icing sugar, sifted
2 egg yolks
20ml (⅔fl oz) water
300g (10½oz) plain flour, sifted

1 Cream the butter and sugar together. Then add the egg yolks and half the water and mix.
2 Mix in the sifted flour slowly, then add the rest of the water.
3 Knead slowly on a cool, floured work surface.
4 Wrap the dough in clingfilm and allow to rest in the fridge, preferably overnight or for at least 2 hours. Remove from the fridge 30 minutes before you need it.

Choux Pastry

This recipe will give you enough pastry to make the Croquembouche on page 286. You can scale down this recipe, but be sure to keep the proportions the same.

Makes 2.8kg (6lb 3oz)
1 litre (1¾ pints) water
400g (14oz) butter
20g (¾oz) caster sugar
a pinch of salt
600g (1lb 5oz) strong white flour
16–18 eggs, whisked, plus 3 egg yolks, beaten, for brushing

1 Place the water, butter, sugar and salt in a pan and bring to the boil, making sure the butter is melted.
2 Add the flour and stir in with a wooden spoon over the heat – it is important to cook the flour fully, so don't hurry this process. The dough should come away easily from the side of the pan.
3 Place the dough in a food mixer and, while beating, slowly add enough egg to make it suitable for piping. (Or beat by hand, add the eggs while using a wooden spoon and then whisk for 5–10 minutes.)
4 Cover the bowl with clingfilm and leave to rest in the fridge before transferring to a piping bag.

Puff Pastry

You'll need to account for a lot of chilling time in this recipe, so make it well ahead of when you need it. It is hard to make this recipe any smaller as you would need to halve an egg yolk, so I would suggest making the full amount and freezing any left over. It will keep happily in the freezer for up to 3 months.

Makes approximately 1kg (2¼lb)

50g (1¾oz) plus 450g (1lb) butter
150ml (5fl oz) water
1¼ tsp salt
1 egg yolk
½ tsp white wine vinegar
320g (11¼oz) plus 175g (6¼oz)
    plain flour, sifted

1 In a small pan, melt 50g (1¾oz) of the butter then whisk in the water, salt, egg yolk and vinegar.
2 In a mixer with a dough hook attachment, place 320g (11¼oz) of flour and pour in the contents of the pan. Mix slowly until it is all fully combined. If you want to make it by hand or don't have a mixer, then put the flour in a bowl, make a well in the centre of the flour then pour in the contents of the pan and knead well with your hands. This is called the detrempe.
3 Tip out the dough and form into a ball with your hands. Wrap the dough in clingfilm and allow to rest in the fridge, for at least 3 hours.
4 Soften the 450g (1lb) portion of butter and add to the 175g (6¼oz) of flour in a mixer with a dough hook attachment and mix until fully combined.

5 Place on a lightly floured surface and shape into a square. As before, wrap the dough in clingfilm and allow to rest in the fridge, for at least 3 hours.
6 Remove both the pats of pastry from the fridge. On a lightly floured surface roll out the detrempe into a square twice the size of the square of dough.
7 Place the smaller square into the centre and fold the corners in to meet in the centre, like an envelope. Roll out to a rectangular shape about 2cm (¾in) thick.
8 Fold it into thirds, starting with the shortest edge furthest away from you. This is known as a simple turn. Turn the dough 90° and roll again to about 2cm (¾in) thick.
9 Turn the dough 90° again and fold the ends to meet in the centre and then fold over itself again from left to right. This is called a book turn.
10 Wrap in clingfilm and allow to rest in the fridge, for at least 3 hours.
11 On a lightly floured surface, roll out to a rectangle 2cm (¾in) thick and do a simple turn then roll again and do a book turn. Refrigerate until you need to roll it out for your recipe.
12 Remove from the fridge 30 minutes before you need it.

Rough Puff Pastry

I wanted to include a simple puff recipe for those occasions when a light buttery pastry is needed but you don't need to achieve the even height and lift of traditional puff pastry, for example when making Tarte Tatin or Eccles Cakes. Rough puff, or quick puff, as it is sometimes known will still teach you the basic turning skills as the dough needs to be turned to incorporate the butter.

Makes approximately 600g (1lb 5oz)

250g (9oz) plain flour
1 tsp salt
250g (9oz) butter, cubed
120ml (4fl oz) water

1 Sift the flour and salt into the bowl of a food mixer.
2 Using a dough hook attachment on a low speed, slowly add the cubed butter until the butter is mixed throughout but still in pieces. Then add the cold water until a dough is formed.
3 Turn out onto a lightly floured surface, wrap in clingfilm and rest for at least 1 hour.
4 Return to the floured surface and roll the dough with the rolling pin to form a rectangle about 21cm x 50cm (8in x 20in).
5 Bring the top third over and fold the bottom third over that, turn the dough 90° to the left and roll out again, repeating the whole process twice. Always turn the pastry in the same direction after each turn. As with all types of pastry, always turn a quarter of a turn to the left after a few rolls to keep it nice and even, because you always have one arm stronger than the other.
6 When all the rolling and folding is done, rest the pastry overnight in the fridge before using. Whenever you roll out rough puff, always rest for a good hour after rolling and after cutting to eliminate any shrinkage that occurs during cooking.

Blueberry Maids of Honour

Makes 6

For the blueberry compôte topping:
500g (1lb 2oz) fresh or frozen blueberries (thawed if using frozen)
75g (2¾oz) caster sugar
1 tbsp water

375g (13oz) Sweet Pastry (see page 220)
300g (10½oz) full-fat cottage cheese
50g (1¾oz) ground almonds
50g (1¾oz) caster sugar
finely grated zest of 1 lemon
2 egg yolks
25g (1oz) butter, melted
100g (3½oz) fresh or frozen blueberries

Rumour has it that it was England's King Henry VIII who, in the 16th century, loved these melt-in-the mouth tarts when he first discovered them, being eaten by Anne Boleyn and her maids of honour (ladies in waiting), and who then demanded the secret be kept under lock and key at Richmond Palace. Whether this is true or not isn't known for sure, but what is known is that they taste wonderful. I've used blueberries here but try them with blackcurrants when they're in season – they're sublime.

1 First, make the compôte. Place 200g (7oz) of the blueberries with the sugar and water in a pan and bring slowly to the boil. Simmer for 5 minutes, then leave to cool for 10 minutes. Blitz in a blender, then pass through a sieve. Return to the pan and gently simmer until the quantity is reduced by half. Add the remaining blueberries and bring to the boil. Remove from the heat and allow to cool before using.
2 Make the pastry as instructed on page 220.
3 Preheat the oven to 170°C/325°F/gas mark 3, and grease a 12-hole deep muffin tin.
4 Remove the pastry from the fridge. Roll out on a lightly floured surface to 3mm (⅛in) thickness and cut out six discs of 12cm (4½in)

diameter. Line six holes of the muffin tin with the six discs of pastry and line each pastry case with clingfilm (it fits in the muffin tin better than baking parchment) and fill with baking beans.
5 Bake blind in a preheated oven for about 15 minutes until lightly brown on the bottom. Remove from the oven and leave to cool. Remove the clingfilm and baking beans. Turn the oven down to 150°C/300°F/gas mark 2.
6 Meanwhile, make the filling. Tip the cottage cheese into a bowl and stir in the almonds, sugar, lemon zest, egg yolks and butter. Then, fold in the blueberries.
7 Spoon the mixture into the pastry cases and bake for 20 minutes until the filling is golden and the pastry is crisp and brown.
8 Remove from the oven and allow to cool slightly before transferring to a wire rack to cool completely.
9 When cool, simply spoon the sweet compôte on top and serve.

Where to Eat Cake ...
LONDON

The tradition of taking afternoon tea with friends and family dates back to 1840. It was Anna Maria, the Duchess of Bedford, who first admitted to feeling a tad peckish in the long hours between luncheon and dinner. Her butler brought her a few bits of bread and cakes with some tea; and soon her afternoon tea parties were quite the thing. When Queen Victoria took to this new trend, the rest, as they say, is history. But London offers much more than afternoon tea options – although, it has to be said, there is nothing more quintessentially British than taking afternoon tea. In recent years, London's interest in all things baked has rocketed and has embraced all cultures. Now, you can easily locate a Swedish cinnamon bun, an American whoopie pie or a classic millefeuille, whenever the mood takes you.

PEYTON AND BYRNE
Unit 11, The Undercroft, St Pancras International, London NW1 2QP and other branches
www.peytonandbyrne.co.uk
A stylish bakery offering a modern take on traditional British baking.

PEGGY PORSCHEN
116 Ebury St, London SW1W 9QQ
www.peggyporschen.com
With its signature pastel pink building on a corner of Belgravia, it's hard to miss this most fabulous of cake shops. Renowned for baking and decorating cakes for celebrities, such as Stella McCartney and Elton John, Peggy Porschen's Parlour serves up superb cakes with great aplomb and, needless to say, she has a loyal and committed cake-loving following.

PRIMROSE BAKERY
69 Gloucester Ave, London NW1 8LD
42 Tavistock St, London WC2E 7PB
www.primrosebakery.org.uk
It's all about the cupcakes, cupcakes, cupcakes here. This super-cute bakery with a retro vibe serves up delightfully scrumptious and sugar-coated cakes.

PATISSERIE VALERIE
44 Old Compton St, London W1D 4TY
www.patisserie-valerie.co.uk
This London favourite first opened in Soho in 1926 by the Belgian-born Madame Valerie. Whichever branch you happen upon in London, you'll be sure to marvel at the amazing window displays of individual pastries and towers of croquembouche, all of them top-notch. Their croissants are said to be the best in London.

HUMMINGBIRD BAKERY
133 Portobello Rd, Notting Hill, London W11 2DY
(and other branches, see website)
www.hummingbirdbakery.com
From humble beginnings in London's Notting Hill in 2004 has come the Hummingbird Bakery empire, now with branches all over the city. This all-American-style bakery offers an amazing array of cupcakes, layer cakes, brownies, pies, cheesecakes, muffins and whoopie pies – it's credited with first bringing these little delights to the UK.

BEA'S OF BLOOMSBURY
44 Theobalds Rd, London WC1X 8NW
(and other branches, see website)
www.beasofbloomsbury.com
This fabulous tea room offers spectacular layer cakes, special occasion cakes and unique cupcakes (using Italian buttercream, fluffy Italian meringue or fudge toppings).

CLARIDGES
Brook St, London W1K 4HR
www.claridges.co.uk
Experience tea and cake within the all-pervading atmosphere of genteel refinement. Sadly, you'll need to book up to three months in advance. But the experience is well worth the wait.

FORTNUM & MASON
181 Piccadilly, London W1A 1ER
www.fortnumandmason.com
If you're after a traditionally English afternoon tea with impeccable service and delectable cakes, then look no further than here. You'll need to book well ahead but they have several restaurants that can accommodate any yearnings for a cucumber sandwich or scones with jam and clotted cream.

OTTOLENGHI
287 Upper St, London N1 2TZ
(and other branches, see website)
www.ottolenghi.co.uk
A celebrity chef with a huge following, Ottolenghi ensures his café windows are full of amazing meringues, colourful cakes and pastries. Sink your mouth into sinful miniature tarts or luscious tray bakes.

KONDITOR & COOK
22 Cornwall Rd, London SE1 8TW
(and other branches, see website)
www.konditorandcook.com
This small artisanal bakers of bread and cakes (including their magic cakes, which can spell out any message) has a massive following in the capital.

SKETCH
9 Conduit St, London W1S 2XG
www.sketch.uk.com
Situated in the same building as the Michelin-starred restaurant, the afternoon tea experience in Sketch's parlour is a treat for all the senses, from the super-stylish room to the delightfully decadent food at this quirky and eccentric pâtisserie.

ST JOHN'S BAKERY
72 Druid St, London SE1 2DU
www.stjohngroup.uk.com/bakery
A welcome addition to the London artisan bakery scene from the stable of Fergus Henderson, this bakery has become renowned for its high-quality cakes and bakes; the doughnuts are legendary.

NORDIC BAKERY
14A Golden Square, London W1F 9JG
(and other branches, see website)
www.nordicbakery.com
As the name suggests, traditional Scandi fare, such as cinnamon buns and blueberry buns, is served up in a calm, stylish space and on authentic Nordic designerware.

CAKE BOY
Kingfisher House, Juniper Drive, London SW18 1TX
www.cake-boy.com
Master Pâtissier Eric Lanlard's lush cake boutique also houses a cookery school and serves up a tempting array of sweets, miniature cakes and luscious tarts.

The Classic Turnover

Makes 12 turnovers

500g (1lb 2oz) pastry
  (Sweet or Puff, see pages
  220 and 221)
1 egg, beaten, for brushing

Each of the fillings below
makes enough for 4 turnovers.

For the apple, cinnamon and brown sugar filling:
3 apples
1 tsp ground cinnamon
3 tbsp brown sugar

For the red fruit filling:
40g (1½oz) caster sugar
200g (7oz) raspberry purée
120g (4oz) blackberries
120g (4oz) blueberries
120g (4oz) raspberries

For the tropical filling:
110g (3¾oz) pineapple
110g (3¾oz) mango
1 banana
1½ kiwi fruit
juice of 1 lime
20g (¾oz) coconut cream

Countries all over the world enjoy their own take on a filled pastry. Whether you're eating empanadas in Venezuela or Mexico or hortopitakia in Greece or the classic turnover in the UK or US, such little parcels of lusciousness are irresistible. What's more, they're oh-so easy to make, can be sweet or savoury and keep really well in your freezer, so you can have a regular supply to hand to heat up whenever the mood takes you.

1 Preheat the oven to 180°C/350°F/gas mark 4 and line a baking tray with baking parchment.
2 To make the turnovers, roll out your pastry on a lightly floured surface and cut 12 discs to the required size (I used a 14cm (5½in) saucer to cut round).
3 First, brush a little egg around the edge of one half of the disc. Place a large tablespoonful of your chosen filling (see steps 6–8) on the same half and fold over the other half of the disc and close, pinching the edges to secure.
4 Brush the outside of the turnovers with beaten egg and rest in the fridge for 30 minutes. Remove and bake on the prepared baking tray in a preheated oven for 20 minutes or until golden brown.
5 Remove from the oven, take off the baking parchment, transfer to a wire rack and allow to cool. Devour without burning your tongue!

6 For the apple, cinnamon and brown sugar filling: Peel and cube the apples and put in a pan with the cinnamon and the sugar. Cook until the mixture has pulped slightly but not completely. Allow to cool.
7 For the red fruit filling: Put the sugar and raspberry purée into a pan and heat until it turns jammy, then chill. Halve the blackberries and add along with the blueberries and raspberries to the red fruit jam. Mix together, ready to spoon into the turnovers.
8 For the tropical filling: Dice the pineapple, mango, banana and kiwi and mix with the lime juice and coconut cream.

Kaab el Ghazal

Makes 18

No feast day or holiday in Morocco would be complete without these traditional delicacies – Gazelle Horns – and they're one of the country's most popular pastries. The French 'Corne de Gazelle' describes 'gazelle horns' while the Arabic name 'Kaab el Ghazal' translates as 'gazelle ankles'.

For the filling:
225g (8oz) ground almonds
175g (6¼oz) icing sugar
1 tsp ground cinnamon
3 tbsp orange-flower water

For the pastry:
225g (8oz) plain flour
2 tbsp melted butter
3 tbsp orange-flower water
1 egg, beaten, for brushing

1 First, make the filling. Mix together the almonds, icing sugar and cinnamon.

2 Add the orange-flower water until the mixture binds together.

3 Knead until smooth and then divide in two and roll each half into a thin pencil (about 1.5cm (⅔in) thick).

4 Cut each half into nine pieces and roll each piece into a cigar shape using your fingers and taper the ends.

5 To make the pastry, sift the flour into a bowl and make a well. Add in the melted butter and the orange-flower water.

6 Fold in the flour and gradually add cold water until a dough forms. Ideally use a dough hook attachment and knead for 10 minutes in a food mixer; if you don't have one, then knead by hand for 10 minutes (time it as it can feel like a long time). Rest for an hour in the fridge.

7 Preheat the oven to 180°C/350°F/gas mark 4, and line two baking trays with baking parchment.

8 Remove from the fridge. Place the dough on a lightly floured surface and divide in two. Roll out one half to a strip about 10cm (4in) wide by 75cm (29½in) long.

9 Lay the pastry with its long side nearest you and place half of the filling 'sausages' towards the top edge of the pastry.

10 Brush the top of the pastry with beaten egg, end to end, leaving about 5cm (2in) between each sausage of filling.

11 Fold the pastry over and press the edges together, sealing in the filling.

12 Pinch the pastry up to form a ridge on the top and curve the ends round to form a crescent shape, to look like a horn. Use a pastry cutter to trim the shape neatly.

13 Crimp the edges and the ridge with a fork and brush the outside with beaten egg.

14 Repeat with the rest of the dough and filling.

15 Leave in the fridge for 20 minutes then bake in a preheated oven for 10 minutes.

16 Remove from the oven and leave to cool on a wire rack.

17 Serve with a glass of apple tea.

Feng Li Su

Makes 4

500g (1lb 2oz) Sweet Pastry
(see page 220)

For the pineapple paste:
270g (9½oz) fresh pineapple,
    diced
360g (12½oz) cantaloupe
    melon, diced
150g (5½oz) caster sugar
1 egg, beaten, for brushing

These pineapple cakes have a lovely buttery crust with a sweet pineapple filling. In Taiwan, pineapple is synonymous with prosperity, so these little pineapple cakes are often given to friends and family during celebrations as well as being used as a religious offering during holidays.

1 Make the pastry as instructed on page 220.
2 When you're ready to bake, grease four miniature loaf tins – I used ones 10cm x 6cm x 4cm (4in x 2½in x 1½in) – and place on a baking tray.
3 Separately blitz the pineapple and the melon to a purée. Put both purées in a pan and on a low heat cook for about 20 minutes until most of the moisture has disappeared. Add the sugar and cook for a further 15 minutes until the mixture becomes thick and shiny. Remove from the heat and allow to cool.
4 Remove the pastry from the fridge and leave for about 20 minutes before using.
5 Meanwhile, preheat the oven to 180°C/350°F/ gas mark 4.

6 Divide the pastry into four and, on a lightly floured work surface, roll out to a thickness of 3mm (⅛in).
7 Cut the pastry into rectangles about 21cm x 60cm (8in x 24in). Then, line the tins with the pastry, leaving enough pastry to fold over for a lid.
8 Fill with the fruit purée and, using a little beaten egg around the edges, fold the pastry lid over the top. Lightly press down with your finger and trim any excess with scissors.
9 Bake in a preheated oven for 15–20 minutes.
10 Remove from the oven, allow to cool for 10 minutes in the tin and then turn out onto a wire rack. Serve with some fragrant tea.

Millefeuille

Serves 6

300g (10½oz) Puff Pastry (see page 221)
icing sugar, for drenching

For the white chocolate mousse:
100g (3½oz) Crème Pâtissière (see page 296)
50g (1¾oz) white chocolate, melted
200ml (7fl oz) double cream, whipped until it ribbons

For the dark chocolate mousse:
30ml (1fl oz) water
40g (1½oz) caster sugar
2 egg yolks
85g (3oz) dark chocolate, melted
150ml (5fl oz) double cream, whipped until it ribbons

On a trip to France you will behold the sight of this classic pastry delicacy in every pâtisserie window. But it's not only enjoyed in France, forms of this multi-layered delight can be eaten from Chile to China and from South Africa to Sweden. Millefeuille – literally meaning 'thousand of layers' – refers to the layers in the puff pastry, which are sandwiched together with whatever filling takes your fancy. It could simply be crème pâtissière or whipped cream but here I've used a rich combination of white and dark chocolate mousse.

1 Preheat the oven to 180°C/350°F/gas mark 4, and line a baking tray with baking parchment.
2 Remove the pastry from the fridge and roll out, on a floured work surface, into a rectangle about 3mm (⅛in) thick and transfer to the baking tray.
3 Place another layer of baking parchment and another baking tray on top to prevent the pastry rising and bake in a preheated oven for 15 minutes until slightly brown.
4 Remove from the oven, take off the top layer of baking parchment and the baking tray and allow to cool. Meanwhile, turn up the oven to 220°C/425°F/gas mark 7.
5 Once completely cool, cover the pastry with finely sifted icing sugar and place in a preheated oven until the sugar glazes, about 5 minutes or so.
6 Remove from the oven and allow to cool once more.
7 Cut the pastry into rectangular strips (about 15) 3cm x 8cm (1¼in x 3¼in) and set aside.
8 Now, make the white chocolate mousse. Whip the cold crème pâtissière into a cream and add the melted chocolate. Then whisk in the whipped double cream.
9 Next make the dark chocolate mousse. Heat the water and sugar together. When it reaches 116°C/240°F start whisking the egg yolks until they become pale. Once the sugar syrup has reached 118°C/244°F add to the egg yolks in three batches whisking in between. Whisk the mixture until cooled to room temperature and add the melted chocolate and whisk vigorously until fully incorporated. Then whisk in a third of the ribboned cream and then fold in the rest.

10 Place the mousse mixtures in piping bags and, using a star nozzle, pipe the mousse onto one strip of pastry (what is now the bottom layer of millefeuille).
11 Alternate with the white and dark chocolate mousses until you've used all the pastry strips. (Each millefeuille is three layers of pastry with one layer of white chocolate mousse and one layer of dark chocolate mousse.) Transfer the millefeuilles to the fridge and allow to set (about 20 minutes).
12 Serve with a glass of chilled champagne.

Apple Strudel

Serves 8

75g (2¾oz) brown sugar
5 apples, chopped and cubed
  (I use Braeburn apples)
½ tsp ground cinnamon
75g (2¾oz) sultanas
2 sheets of ready-made filo
  pastry
75g (2¾oz) butter, melted
30g (1¼oz) demerara sugar,
  to decorate

VARIATION

PEAR STRUDEL
For a more delicate
strudel, replace the
apple with 4–5 Comice
pears.

'Cream coloured ponies and crisp apple strudels…' were some of Maria's favourite things in *The Sound of Music*, set in Salzburg in Austria where these layered filo pastries are traditionally eaten, and in nearby Bavaria. 'Strudel' means 'whirlpool' as the pastry dough is spiralled around itself. And even though Apple Strudel will be the most familiar, you can make strudel with all kinds of fillings (sweet and savoury) – walnuts, pumpkin, cabbage and quark, among other ingredients.

1 Preheat the oven to 180°C/350°F/gas mark 4 and you will need a baking tray.
2 In a bowl, mix together the brown sugar, apples, cinnamon and sultanas.
3 On a sheet of baking parchment on a work surface, place the two sheets of filo as overlapping diamond-shapes and glue them together using the melted butter.
4 Square off the bottom of the sheets with a knife and then brush all the pastry with the melted butter.
5 Place the strudel mix, leaving a 2cm (¾in) gap, along the bottom edge of the filo. Using the baking parchment to help you roll up the pastry, start with the edge nearest you and roll away from you to create a fairly tight 'sausage'.
6 Brush the top with melted butter and then seal the ends by folding them in on themselves. Sprinkle with the demerara sugar along the length of the strudel and bake in a preheated oven for 30–40 minutes.
7 Best served straight from the oven, with fresh cream or vanilla ice cream.

Danish Pastries

Makes 30

75g (2¾oz), plus 500g (1lb 2oz) butter
825g (1lb 13oz) plain flour, sifted
10g (¼oz) salt
50g (1¾oz) caster sugar
40g (1½oz) fresh yeast
300ml (10fl oz) full-fat milk, cold
3 eggs, plus 1 egg, beaten, for brushing
500ml (18fl oz) Crème Pâtissière (see page 296)
600g (1lb 5oz) fruit, such as tinned apricot halves or sliced tinned pears
apricot jam, to glaze

Although they're called Danish, these pastries originated from traditional Viennese pastries, which use a sweet yeast pastry, as do croissants, and turn out like puff pastry. But the Danish tag stuck as they became so popular in Denmark and now they're popular worldwide. You can make these pastries in all sorts of shapes and with many different fillings. I like cherry best of all.

1 Preheat the oven to 170°C/325°F/gas mark 3, and line a large baking tray or two smaller ones with baking parchment.
2 Melt 75g (2¾oz) of butter, cool and set aside.
3 Put the flour, salt and sugar in a large bowl.
4 Dissolve the yeast in the milk and then add the eggs and milk to the flour mixture.
5 Add in the melted butter and mix together in a food mixer using a dough hook until you have a smooth dough.
6 Cover the bowl with clingfilm and chill in the fridge for 30 minutes.
7 On a lightly floured surface, roll out the dough to a rectangle 1cm (½in) thick.
8 Cut the 500g (1lb 2oz) of butter into eight or so slices and lay them over the middle of the dough, in a rectangle.
9 Fold the pastry over the top, bottom and then

sides until the butter is completely covered. Then, press the edges down. Roll the dough out again to a rectangle 1cm (½in) thick.
10 Turn the dough one turn clockwise, then fold the right third over and the left third over that. Do this (fold over, chill, then roll out) three times, chilling for 30 minutes after each rolling out.
11 Meanwhile, make the crème pâtissière following the recipe on page 296.
12 Remove the dough from the fridge and cut in half. Roll both pieces nice and thin, about 3mm (⅛in) thick. Now, cut one rectangle into squares of 10cm (4in); these are your bases.
13 From the other rectangle, cut out 5cm (2in) squares and place on your bases. Brush the edges of the pastry with beaten egg.
14 Spoon a tablespoon of crème pâtissière into the centre of each pastry and top with your fruit then dot with 1 teaspoon of apricot jam.
15 Twist the two opposite corners of pastry, place on a baking tray and allow to rise until doubled in size then bake in a preheated oven for 20 minutes until golden and risen.
16 Remove from the oven and leave to cool on a wire rack. Best served warm with a coffee.

VARIATION

JAM DANISH For a jammy Danish, follow the recipe up to step 13, then cut out circles of the second sheet of pastry with a 7cm (2¾in) pastry cutter and place these in the middle of your square bases. Brush the edges of the pastry with beaten egg and place a heaped tablespoon of jam or compôte in the centre of each. Then return to step 15 above but don't twist the corners.

M'hanncha

Serves 10

For the filling:
85g (3oz) butter
250g (9oz) caster sugar
375g (13oz) ground almonds
50g (1¾oz) chopped
    pistachios
1 drop almond essence
½ tablespoon ground
    cinnamon
zest of 1 lemon
zest of 1 orange
80ml (3fl oz) orange-flower
    water
2 eggs
25g (1oz) plain flour

For the pastry:
5 sheets of ready-made filo
    pastry
120g (4oz) butter, melted
2 eggs yolks, beaten, for
    brushing
icing sugar, toasted flaked
    almonds and chopped
    pistachios, to decorate

Give yourself plenty of time to make this scented, nutty pastry cake as it's quite fiddly. But serve it as the Moroccans do at a family celebration and you'll have a very happy audience for sure. The orange-flower water gives a delightful flavour to this M'hanncha, alongside the almonds and pistachios. And once you've mastered the art of baking this cake, you can make 'snakes' big enough to feed your entire family.

1 Preheat the oven to 170°C/325°F/gas mark 3, and cover a baking tray in foil.
2 In a food mixer with the beater attachment or in a bowl, soften the butter with a wooden spoon, add the sugar, ground almonds, chopped pistachios, almond essence, cinnamon, zests and orange-flower water. Mix together and then beat in the eggs and flour.
3 On baking parchment lay out the sheets of filo pastry, slightly overlapping them as diamond shapes. Lightly brush each sheet with melted butter.
4 Trim the diamond points nearest you along the work surface to neaten up the pastry and then spoon the filling about 5cm (2in) from the edges nearest you all the way along in a sausage-like shape.
5 Carefully pick up the pastry edges nearest

you and roll over the sausage and keep rolling until the whole 'snake' is complete. As you near completion, gently concertina the snake slightly to prevent the pastry breaking.
6 Coil the snake up very gently, taking care not to split the filo, then lift the parchment with the snake onto the baking tray.
7 Brush the top of the snake with the beaten egg yolks and bake in a preheated oven for 30–40 minutes or until the pastry is golden and crisp.
8 Remove from the oven and allow to cool before taking off the baking parchment and moving the snake to a serving plate and sprinkle with plenty of icing sugar, toasted flaked almonds and chopped pistachios.
9 Serve with a large jug of Almond Crème Anglaise (see page 296).

SWEET EXTRAS Dip in melted chocolate while still warm for a dramatic and decadent palmier.

FOR A SPICIER SWEETNESS Mix a little ground cinnamon into the dipping caster sugar before the palmiers go into the oven.

SAVOURY PALMIERS To make a savoury version, use flour instead of sugar throughout the recipe and once you have rolled out your pastry spread a thin layer of tapenade or a cheese such as Parmesan or Gruyère before rolling up. Egg wash the whole palmier before baking.

Palmiers

Makes 12

500g (1lb 2oz) Puff Pastry (see page 221)
plenty of icing sugar, for dusting and rolling
caster sugar, for dipping

I used to make these traditional versatile French pastries many years ago as a petit-four when I was Chef patissière at Le Gavroche, London. These Palmiers, albeit a larger version of those I used to make, can be made with a multitude of fillings and served in a multitude of ways; as a savoury canapé, at a picnic or as a sweet petit-four after dinner.

1 Preheat the oven to 190°C/375°F/gas mark 5, and locate a non-stick (ideally silicone) baking mat or a baking tray lined with baking parchment.
2 On a lightly icing-sugared surface, and continually using liberal amounts of sifted icing sugar, roll out your pastry to a 21cm x 40cm (8in x 16in) rectangle.
3 Neaten and square off the edges. (If you are using a filling, spread it thinly onto the pastry at this point.)
4 With the shortest side nearest you on the worktop fold the top edge towards the middle and fold the bottom edge up towards the middle to meet the top edge. Press over the meeting point lightly and gently roll over the whole pastry using a rolling pin.

5 Fold over the top edge again, but this time all the way to the bottom edge and gently roll over the whole pastry, to ensure the layers are properly stuck. Use liberal amounts of icing sugar where needed.
6 Wrap the pastry shape in clingfilm and freeze for about 30 minutes.
7 Remove from the freezer and cut into 1cm (½in) pieces, dip in caster sugar and press firmly onto your non-stick mat – cut side down. Open the 'legs' of the palmier slightly once on the mat.
8 Cook until golden brown – approximately 15 minutes – turn over and cook for a further 2 minutes.
9 Remove from the oven and cool on a wire rack. Serve any time of day.

Kateifi

Makes 12

For the filling:
110g (3¾oz) ground almonds
½ tsp ground cinnamon
¼ tsp ground cloves
1 large egg, beaten
50ml (2fl oz) double cream
2 tbsp caster sugar

For the pastry:
300g (10½oz) kateifi pastry or
    filo pastry, finely shredded
75g (2¾oz) butter, melted

For the syrup:
500ml (18fl oz) water
450g (1lb) caster sugar
1 stick of cinnamon
4 whole cloves
strip of lemon peel
1 tsp lemon juice
chopped pistachios,
    to decorate

This shredded filo pastry is also known as Knafeh or Kadayif, depending on whether you are referring to the Turkish, Greek or Arabic pastries. It looks a little like Shredded Wheat (the breakfast cereal, that is) and is available from most local Greek or Turkish stores. The finished pastries are sweet and syrupy with a delicious spicy almond filling.

1 Preheat the oven to 200°C/400°F/gas mark 6 and lightly grease a baking tray.
2 To make the filling, mix all the ingredients together in a bowl.
3 Tear off a handful of the kateifi (or shredded filo) and pull apart until it measures about 15cm (6in). Spoon a dessertspoonful of the filling on one end and roll up into a cylinder shape. Continue in this way until all the filling is used.
4 Place all the Kateifi, join side down, on the prepared baking tray and pour a little melted butter over each one.
5 Bake in a preheated oven for 25 minutes.
6 Meanwhile, make the syrup. Heat the water, sugar, cinnamon, cloves and lemon peel. Boil for 5 minutes, then add the lemon juice and continue boiling for a further 5 minutes.

7 When the Kateifi are ready, remove from the oven and spoon over the strained syrup straightaway and sprinkle over the pistachios. Allow to cool before serving.

VARIATION

KATEIFI WITH ORANGE-FLOWER WATER Add
1 tablespoon of orange-flower water and thin strips of orange peel to the syrup, and pour over as above.

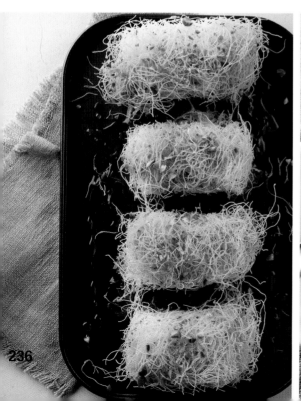

Baklava

Serves 12

225g (8oz) almonds, chopped
225g (8oz) walnuts, chopped
100g (3½oz) pistachios, chopped
85g (3oz) caster sugar
2 tsp ground cinnamon
½ tsp ground cloves

For the pastry:
200g (7oz) butter, melted
300g (10½oz) filo pastry

For the syrup:
300g (10½oz) caster sugar
a pinch of ground cinnamon
300ml (10fl oz) water
2 tbsp rose water
2 tbsp lemon juice

Once enjoyed only by the wealthy this aromatic Greek favourite (although it's also said to be Turkish or Iranian in origins) is now accessible to everyone and, despite appearances, is actually very easy to make. Your efforts at creating your own version of this pastry layered cake stuffed with nuts and cinnamon and then sweetened with a sugar syrup will be rewarded in full when you take your first bite. Perfect with a coffee, any time of day.

1 Preheat the oven to 180°C/350°F/gas mark 4.
2 Mix all the nuts, sugar, cinnamon and cloves together and divide into two bowls.
3 Grease a 23cm (9in) square tin with melted butter. Cover the base of the tin with a double layer of filo pastry and brush again with melted butter. Sprinkle over half the nutty sugar mixture then cover with another double layer of filo and brush again with melted butter.
4 Sprinkle the remaining nutty sugar mixture, then cover with a triple layer of filo. Cut into portions.

5 Bake in a preheated oven until crispy and light brown (about 30 minutes).
6 Meanwhile, make the syrup. Put all the ingredients in a pan and bring to the boil until the liquid becomes syrupy.
7 Remove from the oven and immediately pour over the hot syrup to flood the pastry. Leave to soak overnight and then refrigerate.
8 Serve cold for a super-chewy texture.

Éclairs

Makes 9

150ml (5fl oz) water
60g (2oz) butter
2 tsp caster sugar
a pinch of salt
100g (3½oz) strong white flour
2–3 eggs, whisked, plus 1
   egg yolk, beaten, for
   brushing

For the fillings:

250ml (8½fl oz) Crème
   Pâtissière (see page 296)
- For the chocolate éclair:
   20g (¾oz) dark or milk
   chocolate, melted
- For the coffee éclair:
   1 tbsp espresso coffee
- For the bergamot and rose
   éclair:
   ¼ tsp bergamot flavouring

For the fondant topping:

100g (3½oz) fondant icing
- For the chocolate éclair:
   1 tsp cocoa powder mixed
   with a little water and then
   added to the fondant
- For the coffee éclair:
   2 tsp espresso
- For the bergamot and rose
   éclair:
   4 drops of rose water
   red food colouring (use a
   cocktail stick to add a tiny
   amount to make a delicate
   pink)

Don't be afraid of making choux pastry – many people are – it really isn't hard and your guests will be so impressed (as will you) when you present a selection of these luscious filled treats. The most common éclair is a chocolate one but, of course, they can be filled with any variety of cream or custard fillings, which can be made well in advance. Here I have made a selection of three éclairs – chocolate, coffee, and bergamot and rose.

1 First, make the crème pâtissière as instructed on page 296 and refrigerate.
2 Preheat the oven to 250°C/480°F/gas mark 9, and line a baking tray with baking parchment or use a silicon mat.
3 Place the water, butter, sugar and salt in a pan and bring to the boil, making sure the butter is melted.
4 Add the flour and stir in with a wooden spoon – it is important to cook the flour fully, so don't hurry this process. The dough should come away easily from the side of the pan.
5 Place the dough in a food mixer and, while beating, slowly add enough egg to make it suitable for piping – if it's too wet you won't be able to pipe it. (If you don't have a mixer, then beat by hand, add the eggs while using a wooden spoon and then whisk to beat for 5–10 minutes.)
6 Cover the bowl with clingfilm and leave to rest in the fridge.
7 Fit a piping bag with a No. 12 nozzle and fill with the cooled choux pastry mixture.
8 Secure the baking parchment on the tray with a little dot of mixture at each corner. Slowly pipe the mixture in lines about 8cm (3¼in) long. Remember to squeeze only the top of the bag as you pipe and end the piping by pressing the nozzle firmly against the tray to break off the mixture cleanly.
9 Space the éclairs at least 3cm (1¼in) apart.
10 Using a pastry brush dipped in beaten egg yolk smooth over any rough edges of the éclair to neaten.

11 Place in a preheated oven and turn the oven off as soon as you put the éclairs in. Leave for 15 minutes.
12 Switch the oven back on and heat to 180°C/350°F/gas mark 4 and cook for a further 30–40 minutes until the choux is nearly dry inside. I test mine by breaking one open – if it isn't cooked through continue cooking the rest for a further 10 minutes.
13 Remove from the oven, take off the baking parchment and cool on a wire rack.
14 Remove the Crème Pâtissière from the fridge and divide it (I portioned it into thirds for this selection of flavours) and add each flavouring, as you like.
15 To fill the éclair, first ensure the flat side is the top and then make a small hole at both ends using a small sharp knife towards the underside of the éclair. Using a piping bag with a No. 2 nozzle, pipe the éclairs with the filling until it begins to come out of the other end, then stop.
16 Divide the fondant into thirds, warm in a pan with each flavouring, you may need a little Stock Syrup (see page 299) to soften it. Warm through until soft and shiny.
17 Take the éclair and dip the flat side into the fondant. Leave to set on a wire rack ensuring it won't fall over.
18 Serve to your guests with a wide smile and a proud heart that it's all your own work.

Paris–Brest

Serves 8

For the pastry:
150ml (5fl oz) water
60g (2oz) butter
2 tsp caster sugar
a pinch of salt
100g (3½oz) strong flour,
    sifted
3–4 eggs, whisked, plus 1
    egg, beaten, for brushing
30g (1¼oz) flaked almonds,
    to decorate

For the filling:
500ml (18fl oz) Crème Légère
    (see page 297)
icing sugar, to dust

Many people will have heard of the annual Tour de France bicycle race, but fewer will have heard of another that goes from Paris to Brest and back and takes place every four years; the race first took place in 1891 (making it one of the oldest cycling events). This choux pastry delight was baked to commemorate the race, with its wheel-shaped pastry and super-light filling. The pastry remains popular today and is sold in French pâtisseries.

1 Place the water, butter, sugar and salt in a pan and bring to the boil, making sure the butter is completely melted.
2 Add the flour and stir in with a wooden spoon – it is important to cook the flour fully, so don't hurry this process. The dough should come away easily from the side of the pan.
3 Place the dough in a food mixer and, while beating, slowly add enough egg to make it suitable for piping – only add the fourth egg if the mixture is still stiff; if it's too wet you won't be able to pipe it. Cover the bowl with clingfilm and leave to rest in the fridge for 1–2 hours.
4 Preheat the oven to 230°C/455°F/gas mark 8, and grease and flour a baking tray.
5 Place the choux pastry in a piping bag with a No. 10 piping nozzle.

6 On a sheet of baking parchment, draw a 21cm (8in) diameter circle (you can use a plate as a size guide). Turn the parchment over before piping on the choux pastry mixture, so the pen doesn't bleed into the mixture.
7 Use a small dot of the mixture to 'glue' the parchment down so it doesn't flap in the oven.
8 Pipe a ring of choux pastry just inside the circle. Pipe a second circle inside the first one, just touching. Rest for 15 minutes in the fridge.
9 Remove from the fridge and pipe a third circle on top of the join in the previous rings.
10 Brush the pastry with beaten egg and smooth over the joins using a pastry brush.
11 Sprinkle the top with the flaked almonds and place in a preheated oven and immediately turn off the oven.
12 Leave for 10–12 minutes. Then turn the oven back on to 180°C/350°F/gas mark 4 for a further 15 minutes, then turn off again and leave for another 10 minutes.
13 Turn the oven back on at 180°C/350°F/gas mark 4 and cook for a further 40 minutes. All the while, the oven door must remain closed otherwise the choux will flatten.
14 Remove from the oven, take off the baking parchment and cool on a wire rack. While the choux is cooling make the crème légère as instructed on page 296 and transfer into a piping bag with a large star nozzle (No. 15).
15 When the choux is cool, slice it horizontally in half and remove the top half. (If you notice any raw choux, remove it with a spoon.)
16 Pipe the filling around the choux ring in concentric rings until full. Replace the top half and dust with icing sugar.
17 Set for 25 minutes in the fridge and then serve with a little amaretto.

TARTS

Tarte Tatin

Serves 2–3

85g (3oz) butter
3 apples (I like to use
    Braeburns)
85g (3oz) caster sugar
120g (4oz) Puff Pastry (see
    page 221)
ice cubes, in a roasting tin
    with water for an ice bath

VARIATION

PEAR TATIN Use
6 small pears, halved
and cored, in place of
the apples.

This upside-down French tart has been made since the Tatin sisters created it in the 1880s and sold it in their hotel in a little town a couple of hours south of Paris. Today, this tart is often served as a dessert but it is such a classic recipe I had to include it in this book. I have been making Tarte Tatin for over 25 years and was awarded the Egon Ronay Dessert of the Year 1992 for this recipe. I have to admit that it has become my most requested recipe from my friends and family.

1 Slice the butter thinly and lay on the bottom of a stainless-steel rimmed 15cm (6in) copper pan (if you don't have one, use a shallow heavy-bottomed, ovenproof pan). Leave for 15 minutes.

2 Meanwhile peel the apples. Slice the apples in half lengthwise, core and remove the stalks.

3 Smooth over the butter with your fingers so that it becomes a nice even layer, then sprinkle over the sugar.

4 With the bottom side of the apple facing the inside of the pan, trim the top end of the apple so that five halves fit evenly around the edge of the pan.

5 Cut the remaining half into a disc and place in the centre of the apples.

6 Remove the pastry from the fridge and, on a lightly floured surface, roll it out to a 3mm (⅛in) thick circle and prick with a fork.

7 Place the pan on the centre of the puff pastry and cut around leaving a 1cm (½in) border. Then lay the pastry on top of the apples and lifting each apple half at the outside edge tuck the pastry in, like tucking in a baby. Allow to rest at room temperature for 30 minutes.

8 Cut a circle out of foil and place over your gas burner, making a hole allowing the burner to poke through and the foil not to be covered by the flame – this prevents any caramel spilling over and marking your hob.

9 On a medium to high heat, place the pan and cook until a caramel appears and begins to turn a light golden brown.

10 Place the pan in the DIY ice bath to stop the caramel cooking and leave until it has set (about 15 minutes). Meanwhile, preheat the oven to 170°C/325°F/gas mark 3.

11 When the caramel has set, place the pan in a preheated oven for 40 minutes or until the pastry is cooked. The secret of a good Tatin is to cook the pastry thoroughly (it's very important), so that it stays crisp; no one likes a soggy bottom.

12 Remove from the oven and allow to rest in the pan for at least an hour so the flavours intensify. Turn out onto a serving plate when ready and serve warm or cold with crème fraîche, ice cream or pouring cream.

Marco Pierre White's Harvey's Lemon Tart

Serves 8

For the lemon filling:
250ml (8½fl oz) double
 cream
9 eggs
350g (12oz) caster sugar
345ml (11⅔fl oz) fresh
 lemon juice
finely grated zest of
 2 lemons

500g (1lb 2oz) Sweet Pastry
 (see page 220)

Marco Pierre White is a British chef, restaurateur and television personality. He is highly acclaimed for his contributions to contemporary cuisine and was the youngest chef to be awarded three Michelin stars at the age of just 33.

Marco says 'This is my most preferred pudding and a wonderful way to finish a meal. Any chef worthy of his name will have a lemon tart on his menu and this one has been with me since Harvey's, my first ever restaurant – we made it twice a day: in the morning just before lunch service and again in the early evening around 7pm just before dinner, so it was always fresh and aromatic. I suggest you don't make it any smaller as it tends to disappear rather quickly. I generally allow my lemon tart to speak for itself, but you could serve it with a little whipped cream, if you like.'

1 Make the sweet pastry as instructed on page 220 and then chill for 24 hours.
2 In a large bowl, whisk the cream until it forms a ribbon.
3 In a separate bowl, whisk the eggs and the sugar until smooth.
4 Add the lemon juice to the egg and sugar mixture and then pour this through a sieve onto the cream.
5 Whisk everything together and then add the lemon zest. Allow to stand in the fridge for 2 hours and mix thoroughly again before using.
6 Take the pastry out of the fridge and, on a lightly floured surface, roll it out to about 3mm (⅛in) thickness. Dust with flour as you roll to prevent it from sticking. Place a 25cm (10in) wide by 4cm (1½in) deep tart ring on top of the pastry and cut a circle 2cm (¾in) bigger than that all the way round.
7 Line a baking tray with baking parchment. Place the tart ring on the prepared baking tray and place the pastry over the top of the ring. With thumbs and forefingers, gently push the pastry down all around to the edges of the ring. Chill for 2 hours.
8 Preheat the oven to 170°C/325°F/gas mark 3.
9 Remove the pastry case from the fridge. Line the base and sides with baking parchment and fill with baking beans. Bake blind for about 25–30 minutes until the inside of the tart becomes slightly golden.
10 Remove from the oven, allow to cool slightly and carefully remove the beans and baking parchment.
11 Turn the oven down to 130°C/250°F/ gas mark ½.
12 Pour the chilled lemon filling into the warm pastry case (this will ensure that the case is sealed) and bake in a preheated oven for about 30 minutes. There should still be a slight wobble in the centre when it is cooked.
13 Remove from the oven and remove the tart ring once completely cool and set.

VARIATION

CHOCOLATE AND CHERRY
BAKEWELL Use black cherry
jam instead of the raspberry jam. And
replace 50g (1¾oz) of the self-raising
flour with 50g (1¾oz) cocoa powder
in the Bakewell mix. Use pitted fresh
cherries pushed evenly into the
mixture before baking.

Bakewell Tart

Serves 8

300g (10½oz) Sweet Pastry
(see page 220)

For the Bakewell mix:
250g (9oz) butter, softened
250g (9oz) caster sugar
120g (4oz) ground almonds
60g (2oz) rice flour, sifted
60g (2oz) self-raising flour,
    sifted
3 eggs
550g (1lb 3½oz) seedless
    raspberry jam, warmed
180g (6½oz) flaked almonds
Crème Anglaise (see page
    296), to serve

Hailing from the town of Bakewell in Derbyshire in the UK, it was the
Bakewell Puddings baked in the town that made it famous in the mid
nineteenth century. More commonly eaten as a Bakewell Tart now, this is my
tried-and-tested recipe. This twist on the classic Bakewell Pudding works
well when it's dressed down for afternoon tea or up for a dessert after dinner.
I like to serve it hot or cold with some crème Anglaise.

1 I like to make both the pastry and the
Bakewell mix a day ahead to give it time to
rest and prevent the soufflé effect during
baking, but if you're pushed for time just a
few hours ahead should be enough. Make the
sweet pastry as instructed on page 220 and
then chill for 24 hours.
2 For the Bakewell mix, cream the butter and
sugar together until light and fluffy, then add
the ground almonds and sifted flours. Whisk
together well, then slowly whisk in the eggs
until fully combined. Place in the fridge to rest.
3 Take the pastry out of the fridge and, on a
lightly floured surface, roll it out to about 3mm
(⅛in) thickness. Dust with flour as you roll to
prevent it from sticking. Place a 25cm (10in)
wide by 1cm (½in) deep tart ring on top of the
pastry and cut a circle 2cm (¾in) bigger than
that all the way round.
4 Line a baking tray with baking parchment.
Place the tart ring on the prepared baking tray
and place the pastry over the top of the ring.
With thumbs and forefingers, gently push the

pastry down all around to the edges of the ring.
Chill for 2 hours.
5 Preheat the oven to 170°C/325°F/gas mark 3.
Remove the Bakewell mix from the fridge and
allow to come to room temperature.
6 Remove the pastry case from the fridge. Line
the base and sides with baking parchment and
fill with baking beans. Bake blind for about
25 minutes until lightly brown on the bottom.
Remove from the oven and leave to cool.
Remove the beans and parchment.
7 Turn the oven down to 160°C/310°F/gas
mark 2½. Spread the raspberry jam over the
pastry, then cover with the Bakewell mix. Bake
for 10 minutes. Then remove briefly from the
oven to liberally sprinkle on the flaked almonds
and return to bake for a further 30 minutes or
until the tart is firm to the touch.
8 While the tart is baking, make the crème
Anglaise (see page 296) and keep in the fridge.
9 Remove from the oven, allow to cool for
20 minutes in the tin and then turn out onto
a wire rack and strip off the parchment.

Tarte aux Pommes

Serves 8

500g (1lb 2oz) Sweet Pastry
(see page 220)
15 Golden Delicious or similar
apples, peeled and cored
85g (3oz) caster sugar
30g (1¼oz) butter
65ml (2½fl oz) Apricot Glaze
(see page 299)

This classic French tart – now popular around the world – has many regional variations depending on where you are in France when you eat it. Some regions prefer to use a frangipane filling (see page 297) while others use an apple compôte (which I prefer), so it's really up to you whether you want the almond flavour with your apples or not.

1 Make the sweet pastry as instructed on page 220 and then chill for 24 hours.
2 Remove the pastry from the fridge and leave for about 20 minutes before using.
3 On a lightly floured surface, roll the pastry out to about 3mm (⅛in) thickness. Dust with flour as you roll to prevent it from sticking. Place the tart ring on top of the pastry and cut a circle 3cm (1¼in) bigger than that all the way round.
4 Place the tart ring on a baking tray lined with baking parchment and place the pastry over the top of the ring. With thumbs and forefingers, gently push the pastry down all around to the edges of the ring. Chill for 2 hours.
5 Preheat the oven to 170°C/325°F/gas mark 3.
6 Remove the pastry case from the fridge. Line the base and sides with baking parchment and fill with baking beans. Bake blind for about 25–30 minutes until the inside of the tart becomes slightly golden.
7 Remove from the oven, allow to cool slightly and carefully remove the beans and parchment.

8 Turn the oven down to 150°C/300°F/gas mark 2.
9 Dice five apples and add to a pan with the sugar and butter. Cook on a low heat until a rough purée forms. Set aside to cool.
10 Peel, halve and core the remaining apples and, using a mandolin, slice the apples lengthwise 3mm (⅛in) or thinner if you can.
11 Smooth the apple purée around the bottom of the pastry case and place the sliced apples in decreasing circles in the tart overlapping each one about 3mm (⅛in). As you reach the centre fill with any bits of apple to form a mound in the centre to create your last circle.
12 Bake in a preheated oven for 1 hour 15 minutes.
13 Near the end of the baking time, make the apricot glaze as instructed on page 299.
14 Remove from the oven and immediately glaze with the warmed apricot jam.
15 Serve the tart warm with vanilla ice cream or crème Chantilly (see page 296).

Oliver Peyton's Strawberry and Marjoram Cream Tart

Serves 8

For the filling:
500ml (18fl oz) full-fat milk
15g (½oz) fresh marjoram
120g (4oz) caster sugar
2 eggs, beaten
60g (2oz) plain flour, sifted
10g (¼oz) cornflour
120ml (4fl oz) double cream, whipped until it ribbons

For the pastry:
360g (12½oz) butter, softened
150g (5½oz) icing sugar
4 egg yolks
40ml (1½fl oz) water
500g (1lb 2oz) plain flour, sifted

For the decoration:
350g (12oz) fresh strawberries
150g (5½oz) redcurrant jelly

Oliver Peyton is a renowned restaurateur and the founder of Peyton and Byrne bakery outlets throughout London, UK, which, over the years, have been as much applauded for their architectural achievements as their gastronomic standards. I was lucky enough to be invited by Oliver to help start up the Peyton and Byrne bakery and spent a happy two years there indulging my love of baking.

1 Infuse the milk with the marjoram in a pan and bring to the boil with 25g (1oz) of the sugar.
2 Put the eggs and the rest of the sugar in a bowl and whisk in the sifted flour and cornflour.
3 Pour the milk mixture, through a sieve, onto the egg mixture.
4 Pour the mixture back into the pan, whisking continuously and cook for 10 minutes and then allow to cool.
5 Spread on to a baking tray and cover with clingfilm and place in the fridge to set for at least 30 minutes.
6 Remove and place into a mixer bowl with a paddle attachment and beat until softened with no lumps and then fold in the ribboned cream. Transfer into a piping bag.
7 To make the pastry, cream the butter and sugar together until light and fluffy. Add the egg yolks and a little of the water.
8 Slowly add the flour and the rest of the water until a dough forms. Wrap the dough in clingfilm and chill for at least 3 hours, preferably overnight. Remove from the fridge 30 minutes before you need to roll out.
9 On a lightly floured surface, work the pastry a little first to stretch the gluten then roll it out to about 3mm (⅛in) thickness. Dust with flour as you roll to prevent it from sticking. Place a 25cm (10in) wide by 3cm (1¼in) deep tart ring on top of the pastry and cut a circle 2cm (¾in) bigger than that all the way round.

10 Line a baking tray with baking parchment. Place the tart ring on the prepared baking tray and place the pastry over the top of the ring. With thumbs and forefingers, gently push the pastry down all around to the edges of the ring. Chill for 1 hour.
11 Preheat the oven to 170°C/325°F/gas mark 3.
12 Remove the pastry case from the fridge. Line the base and sides with baking parchment and fill with baking beans. Bake blind for about 20 minutes until the inside of the tart becomes slightly golden.
13 Remove from the oven, allow to cool completely and carefully remove the beans and baking parchment.
14 Transfer the filling into a piping bag and, using a No.10 nozzle, pipe circles starting in the centre of the pastry case until it is filled.
15 Slice the strawberries in half and overlap them in concentric circles until the tart is completely covered.
16 Heat the jam in a small pan with 20ml (⅔fl oz) of water and brush over the top of the strawberries. Remove the tart ring after going round the edge with a sharp knife.
17 Set in the fridge for at least 1 hour and serve chilled.

Pithiviers with Prunes

Serves 8

50ml (2fl oz) Stock Syrup
  (see page 299)
50ml (2fl oz) brandy
50ml (2fl oz) rum
100g (3½oz) prunes, pitted

For the frangipane:
150g (5½oz) caster sugar
130g (4½oz) butter, softened
zest of 1 orange, finely grated
zest of 1 lemon, finely grated
1 vanilla pod, split and
  scraped
200g (7oz) ground almonds
30ml (1fl oz) cognac
25g (1oz) plain flour
2 eggs

For the pastry:
2 x 375g (13oz) Puff Pastry
  (see page 221)
1 egg, beaten, for brushing

Pithiviers may well have originated in the town of the same name in France. They are usually made with puff pastry and often enclose a savoury filling. Conjure up your own imaginary trip to France with the baking aromas of this version, using a combination of frangipane and prunes that have been steeped in brandy and rum for several days – it's a super-sweet treat.

1 Preheat the oven to 180°C/350°F/gas mark 4, and line a 30cm (12in) square baking tray with baking parchment.
2 Make the stock syrup as instructed on page 299, mix with the brandy and rum, pour over the prunes and allow to soak for up to a week.
3 On the day you want to bake, first make the frangipane. Cream the sugar, butter, orange and lemon zests and vanilla seeds together until pale and fluffy.
4 Add the ground almonds and cognac, mix to combine and then sift and stir in the flour.
5 Add the eggs one at a time, beating well after each addition.
6 Drain the prunes from their soaking mixture, coarsely chop half of them and fold into the frangipane mixture. Rest for 1 hour.
7 On a lightly floured surface, roll out one lot of pastry to a 3mm (⅛in) thickness. Allow to rest.
8 Cut a 23cm (9in) diameter circle from one pastry sheet and transfer to the baking tray.

9 Spread the frangipane mixture over this pastry, mounding it in the centre and leaving a 2cm (¾in) border at the edge.
10 On a lightly floured surface, roll out the other pastry to a 3mm (⅛in) thickness. Cut a 27cm (10½in) diameter circle (the lid). Allow to rest.
11 Brush the edges with the beaten egg and place the lid carefully on top of the filling. Press the edges firmly together to seal, smoothing the lid all the way round. Chill for 30 minutes.
12 Remove from the fridge, brush again with the beaten egg and lightly score the pastry at intervals with a knife, scoring from the centre in a curve down to the base and then cut a fluted shape around the edges of the pastry.
13 Bake in a preheated oven until puffed and dark golden (25–30 minutes).
14 Remove from the oven and allow to stand for 10 minutes then remove from the baking parchment and serve warm with the remaining prunes on the side.

Almond Tart with Honey

Serves 10

For the filling:
550g (1lb 3½oz) Frangipane
  (see page 297)
50g (1¾oz) golden syrup
4 drops almond essence

300g (10½oz) Sweet Pastry
  (see page 220)

For the topping:
100g (3½oz) runny honey
100g (3½oz) caster sugar
50ml (2fl oz) single cream
50g (1¾oz) flaked almonds

The almond flavour comes through beautifully in this tart and the honey adds a delicious sweetness. When I use frangipane I add rice flour and self-raising flour to make a lighter, more cakey frangipane – and with this honey and almond topping the result is the most delicious of tarts.

1 Grease a 25cm (10in) loose-bottomed fluted flan tin.
2 While making the frangipane, as instructed on page 297, add in the golden syrup and the almond essence just before you add the eggs. Chill the mixture in the fridge for about 1 hour.
3 On a lightly floured surface, roll the pastry out into a sheet about 3mm (⅛in) thick and big enough to cover the tin.
4 Use the rolling pin to pick the pastry up and lay it over the tin. Press down the pastry well into the tin. Return to the fridge for 1 hour.
5 Preheat the oven to 170°C/325°F/gas mark 3. Remove the frangipane mix from the fridge and allow to come to room temperature.
6 Remove the pastry from the fridge. Line the base and sides with baking parchment and fill with baking beans. Bake blind for about 15–20 minutes until lightly brown on the bottom.

Remove from the oven and leave to cool then carefully remove the parchment and beans.
7 When the tart case is cool, spoon in the frangipane filling and bake in a preheated oven for 20 minutes or until firm to the touch then trim off the edges.
8 Remove from the oven, allow to cool for 20 minutes in the tin.
9 While the tart is cooling make the topping. Place all the ingredients in a heavy-bottomed pan and bring to the boil, stirring gently for 3 minutes. Use straightaway. Preheat the grill.
10 Pour the topping on to the cooled tart while it's still in the tin, making sure the nuts are evenly distributed. Pop under the grill until a golden brown colour.
11 Delicious with a cup of your favourite coffee.

Gâteau Basque

Serves 8

For the pastry:
550g (1lb 3½oz) plain flour, sifted
1½ tbsp baking powder
1½ tsp salt
525g (1lb 2½oz) butter, softened
410g (14½oz) caster sugar
3 egg yolks
2 eggs, plus 1 egg, beaten, for brushing
4 drops lemon oil or finely grated zest of 1½ lemons
½ tsp almond oil
120g (4oz) ground almonds

For the filling:
500ml (18fl oz) Crème Pâtissière (see page 296)
100g (3½oz) griottine cherries

As the name suggests this gâteau, or tart really, originates from the Basque region of France, where there is even a museum dedicated to this classic French dessert. The first bite of this delicious and delicate gâteau will surprise you with its hidden filling of luscious cherries and crème pâtissière.

1 Grease a 21cm wide x 2.5cm deep (8in x 1in) tart ring.

2 Mix together the sifted flour, baking powder and salt.

3 Cream the butter and sugar together until light and fluffy, and add the yolks and eggs, and the lemon and almond oils.

4 Then, slowly beat in the flour mix followed by the ground almonds.

5 Scrape the pastry dough out and divide into two discs (one pat 400g (14oz), the other 200g (7oz)). Then wrap each in clingfilm and put in the fridge for 4 hours.

6 Meanwhile make the crème pâtissière as instructed on page 296 and allow it to cool to room temperature. Beat in a food mixer to soften before placing in a piping bag with a No. 8 nozzle.

7 Remove the pastry discs from the fridge and roll the larger disc out on a lightly floured surface to about 30cm (12in) round and 3mm (⅛in) thick (this will be the base) and the smaller disc to about 22cm (8½in) round and 3mm (⅛in) thick (this will be the lid)

8 Line the prepared tart ring with the pastry and chill for 30 minutes.

9 Pipe the crème pâtissière into the tart ring in spirals to fill evenly.

10 Dot the cherries evenly in the crème pâtissière.

11 Brush the edges of the pastry with beaten egg before placing the second disc on top of the crème pâtissière and crimping together the edges neatly. Allow to rest for 15 minutes and trim any excess pastry with a sharp knife.

12 Meanwhile, preheat the oven to 180°C/350°F/gas mark 4.

13 Brush the top of the tart with the beaten egg and, using a fork, create the traditional pattern of circles on the pastry as in the photo.

14 Bake for 45 minutes until the pastry is golden brown. Check the bottom is cooked properly by lifting up carefully with a palette knife and, if need be, bake a little longer.

15 Remove from the oven and leave to cool on a wire rack.

16 Serve sliced as a dessert or with coffee.

Far Breton

Serves 8

65ml (2½fl oz) Stock Syrup
  (see page 299)
65ml (2½fl oz) dark rum
65ml (2½fl oz) brandy, plus
  20ml (⅔fl oz)
175g (6¼oz) soft prunes,
  pitted
50g (1¾oz) butter, softened
120g (4oz) caster sugar
4 eggs, plus 1 egg yolk,
  beaten, for brushing
140g (5oz) plain flour, sifted
500ml (18fl oz) full-fat milk

As you can probably guess from its name, Far Breton originates from Brittany, in Western France; 'far' means 'flour' and 'Breton' 'of Brittany'. It began its culinary life as a savoury dish – Far Forn – cooked to accompany meat dishes in the 18th century. It was only when a sweet version of the Far Breton evolved in the mid-19th century – which included the highly regarded prunes – that it gained national popularity and became widely known as the French custard tart.

1 Make the stock syrup as instructed on page 229, and when cool add the rum, brandy and the prunes and leave to soak overnight (or for up to a week).

2 Preheat the oven to 180°C/350°F/gas mark 4, and grease a 21cm (8in) loose-bottomed round cake tin. Drain the prunes.

3 Cream the butter and sugar together until light and fluffy, and add the eggs one at a time.

4 Whisk in the sifted flour until fully combined.

5 Add the milk, a little at a time, whisking continuously and then the brandy.

6 Pour the mixture into the prepared tin and scatter over the drained prunes.

7 Beat the egg yolk and brush on top of the mixture before baking in a preheated oven for about 25 minutes.

8 Remove from the oven and serve warm.

VARIATION

For other boozy versions, replace the prunes with dried apricots soaked in Grand Marnier, cherries in a Kirsch syrup or raisins in a rum syrup. All equally delicious.

Linzer Torte

Serves 10

For the pastry:
160g (5¾oz) caster sugar
250g (9oz) ground almonds
300g (10½oz) plain flour, sifted,plus extra for dusting
¼ tsp ground cloves
½ tsp ground cinnamon
340g (11¾oz) butter, softened
1½ tsp finely grated lemon zest
3 hardboiled egg yolks, mashed, cooled and passed through a sieve
3 raw egg yolks, lightly beaten, plus 1 egg, beaten, for brushing
1 tsp vanilla extract
a pinch of salt

For the filling:
675g (1lb 8¾oz) good-quality blackcurrant, redcurrant or raspberry jam

We may never know who invented Linzer Torte or what its definitive recipe is but rumour has it that it is 'the oldest cake in the world', dating from 1696 and being baked in Linz in Austria. With such provenance, I wanted to ensure that I could do this cake justice so here's my recipe. My top tip, by the way, is to make sure you use a premium-quality jam.

1 Grease a 25cm x 1.5cm (10in x ¾in) tart ring and have a baking tray to hand.
2 In a bowl, mix together the sugar and almonds, sifted flour, ground cloves and cinnamon. Add the butter and rub in until the mixture resembles breadcrumbs.
3 Add the lemon zest, the cooked egg yolks, the raw egg yolks, the vanilla extract and the salt, mix until a dough forms. Cover the bowl in clingfilm and rest in the fridge for a good hour.
4 Remove the dough from the fridge and carefully roll out two-thirds on a floured surface to a thickness of 3mm (⅛in). Line the tart ring with the dough and chill for 1 hour.
5 Put the jam into a pan on a medium heat and reduce by about a quarter, stirring occasionally. Preheat the oven to 180°C/350°F/gas mark 4.
6 Roll out the last third of dough into a rectangle about 25cm x 30cm (10in x 12in), cut into 2cm (¾in) strips and then chill on a baking tray.
7 Remove the pastry from the fridge. Line the base and sides with baking parchment and fill with baking beans. Bake blind for about 15–20

minutes until lightly brown on the bottom. Take out of the oven, remove the baking parchment and beans, and leave to cool.
8 Meanwhile, on a sheet of baking parchment on a tray, draw a circle the same size as the tart. Turn the parchment over (so the pen or pencil doesn't bleed into the dough) and using the strips of dough make a criss-cross lattice. Be very careful as the strips are fragile.
9 Brush the pastry lattice with the beaten egg and then freeze for 20 minutes.
10 When the pastry case is cool, pour the warm jam into it and chill for 30 minutes to set.
11 Remove from the fridge and remove your lattice from the freezer. Brush the rim of the tart with beaten egg and then gently slide the lattice on top, and as the pastry slowly starts to defrost squeeze around the edge of the tart.
12 Bake in a preheated oven for 20 minutes until the lattice is golden.
13 Remove from the oven, allow to cool for 10 minutes in the tin and transfer to a wire rack. Serve cool with crème Chantilly (see page 296).

Where to Eat Cake...

VIENNA

The café culture in this elegant city is unique. Often housed in extraordinarily beautiful and grand buildings and dating back decades, if not centuries, the cafés are large spaces with old world décor, cosy booths and a relaxed atmosphere – perfect for taking time out at any time of day and sampling truly original pastries and cakes.

CAFÉ HAWELKA
Dorotheergasse 6, 1010 Vienna
www.hawelka.at
Bohemian rather than grand, this café sells excellent Berliners (doughnuts).

CAFÉ FRAUENHUBER
Himmelpfortgasse 6, 1010 Vienna
www.cafe-frauenhuber.at
One of the city's oldest traditional cafés, it once staged recitals by Mozart and Beethoven, back in 1788.

CAFÉ CENTRAL
Corner Herrengasse/Strauchgasse, 1010 Vienna
www.palaisevents.at
Soak up some history at this café, which opened in 1860 and became a key meeting place for intellectuals. In January 1913 alone, Tito, Freud, Hitler, Lenin and Trotsky were patrons here.

KONDITOREI HEINER
Kärntnerstraße 21–23, 1010 Vienna
(and other branches, see website)
www.heiner.co.at
Family bakery since 1840 serving amazing tortes, cute little marzipan figures, and amazing ice creams to boot.

CAFÉ LANDTMANN
Universitätsring 4, 1010 Vienna
www.landtmann.at
The place to go for apple strudel – and it has been since opening in 1873.

DEMEL
Kohlmarkt 14, 1010 Vienna
www.demel.at
Not just great cakes are found here, but also a feast for the eyes, with the ornately designed window displays; you can even watch the master bakers at work.

CAFÉ SACHER
Philharmonikerstrasse 4, 1010 Vienna
www.sacher.com
Situated in the world-famous Hotel Sacher, this cafe is still baking the ultimate Sacher Torte, to the original recipe from 1832.

FETT + ZUCHER
Hollandstrasse 16th, 1020 Vienna
www.fettundzucher.at
One of the new breed of little cake shops springing up in Vienna with the focus on home-made cakes rather than traditional Viennese pastry.

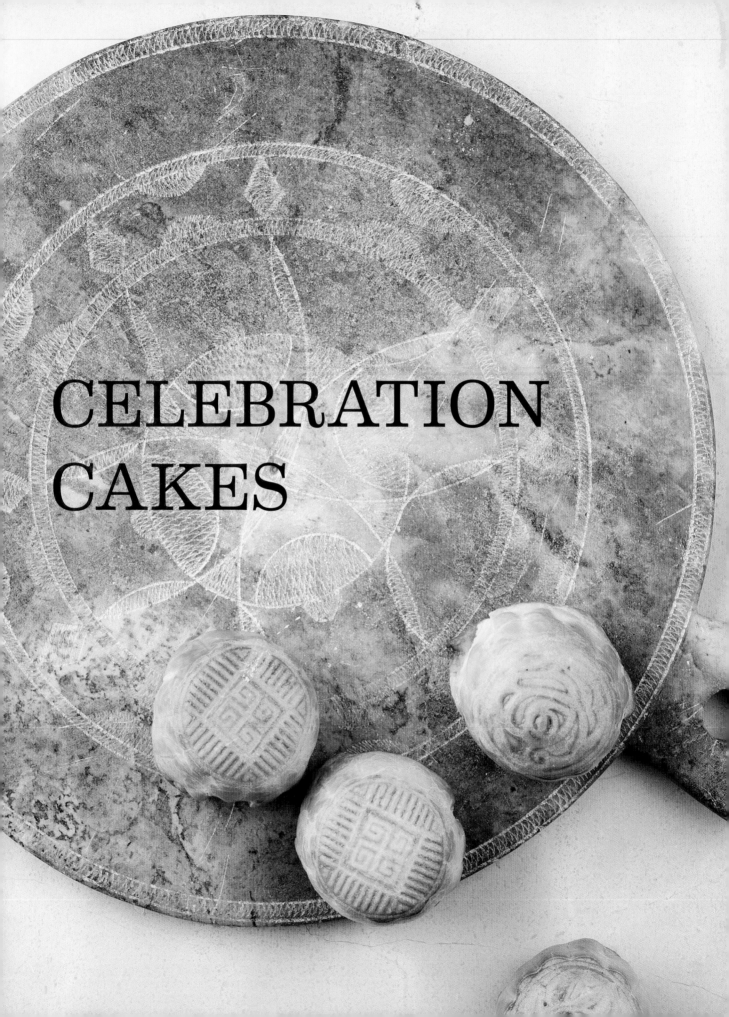

CELEBRATION CAKES

Chocolate Cinnamon Babka

Serves 12

40g (1½oz) fresh yeast
175ml (6fl oz) full-fat milk
85g (3oz) butter, softened
85g (3oz) caster sugar
4 egg yolks
1½ tsp vanilla extract
425g (15oz) plain flour, sifted
1 tsp salt
1 tsp ground cinnamon
60g (2oz) butter, softened
200g (7oz) dark chocolate
  (minimum 70% cocoa
  solids), finely chopped
icing sugar, to dust

Babka is a celebratory bread (like Kugelhopf (see page 214)) that has been sweetened and is typically baked at Easter in Poland and across Eastern Europe. The traditional shape of a Babka is a fluted tube (I used a Bundt tin) to emulate the skirts of a Polish grandmother; in fact, 'babka' is the diminutive form of 'baba', which is Polish for grandma, and traditionally Babka was only ever baked by women, never men. History has it that the cakes were left to cool on an eiderdown and no one was allowed to speak above a whisper to avoid damaging the delicate cake.

1 Grease a 25cm (10in) Bundt tin.
2 Dissolve the yeast in the milk and leave in a warm place for 15 minutes.
3 Cream the butter and the sugar together until light and fluffy and add the egg yolks one at a time. If the mixture starts to split add a little flour and scrape down.
4 Add the vanilla extract followed by the sifted flour and salt and combine well.
5 If you're using a food mixer, change the paddle attachment to a dough hook and then mix in the yeast mixture to form a soft dough. Knead slowly for 5 minutes in the machine. Otherwise, knead slowly by hand on a lightly floured work surface for 10–12 minutes. (You can prepare the dough a day in advance and leave it in the fridge overnight. Just remove from the fridge a couple of hours before proving (the next step).)
6 Leave the dough in a warm place for 1 hour.
7 Once the dough has risen, knock it back and, on a lightly floured surface, roll it out into a rectangle about 1cm (½in) thick.
8 Mix together the cinnamon and softened butter and spread over the rectangle. Then sprinkle the chocolate over the top.

9 Picking up the longest side at the edge furthest away from you, roll the Babka towards you.
10 With a rolling pin, lightly roll along the top edge until you have reached the right length to form a circle to fit inside the tin.
11 Holding one end of the Babka with one hand, cut down the middle of the rest of the Babka. Then twist the two lengths over and over each other to get a plaited look.
12 Place in the prepared tin, seam side uppermost and twist the two ends together as they meet.
13 Allow to prove for another hour or until doubled in size. Meanwhile, preheat the oven to 170°C/325°F/gas mark 3.
14 Bake in a preheated oven for 40 minutes.
15 Remove from the oven, allow to cool for 10 minutes in the tin and then turn out onto a wire rack.
16 Dust with icing sugar and serve with coffee and a crowd – no need to keep the noise down now.

Simnel Cake

Serves 10

40g (1½oz) whole almonds
360g (12½oz) currants
130g (4½oz) sultanas
225g (8oz) raisins
85g (3oz) mixed citrus peel
85g (3oz) glacé cherries
225g (8oz) plain flour, sifted
½ tsp baking powder
½ tsp salt
1½ tsp ground mixed spice
2 tsp cocoa powder
40g (1½oz) ground almonds
210g (7½oz) butter, softened
210g (7½oz) soft brown sugar
4 eggs
finely grated zest of 1 lemon
1½ tbsp brandy
1½ tsp coffee essence
600g (1lb 5oz) ready-made
    marzipan
icing sugar, for rolling out
65ml (2½fl oz) Stock Syrup
    (see page 299)
sugar paste, to decorate

The Simnel Cake is baked as an Easter tradition to signify the end of Lent and fasting in the UK and Ireland. Rich with fruit, spices and marzipan (on the top and in the middle), it is filled with all the ingredients that have been given up for Lent. All of Jesus's apostles are represented by the marzipan balls on the top except Judas, so only use 11 balls not 12.

1 Preheat the oven to 160°C/310°F/gas mark 2½, and grease and line an 18cm (7in) loose-bottomed round tin with baking parchment.
2 Place the whole almonds on a baking tray and toast them on the top shelf of the oven until golden brown, about 3–5 minutes.
3 In a bowl, mix all the fruit together with the sifted flour, baking powder, salt, mixed spice, cocoa powder and ground almonds.
4 In a large bowl, cream together the butter and sugar until light and fluffy then slowly add the eggs one at a time, scraping down after each addition to combine well.
5 Fold in the whole almonds, the fruit mixture, lemon zest, brandy and coffee essence.
6 Spoon half the mixture into your lined tin and smooth the surface.

7 On a lightly icing-sugared surface, roll out 180g (6½oz) of the marzipan to a circle the size of the cake tin and lay over the mixture in the cake tin.
8 Add the second half of the mixture and bake in a preheated oven for 1 hour or until a cocktail stick comes out clean when inserted in the centre.
9 Remove from the oven, allow to cool for 10 minutes in the tin and then turn out onto a wire rack.
10 Make the sugar syrup as instructed on page 299. Once the cake is completely cool, remove the baking parchment and dot the syrup all over the top of the cake with a pastry brush.
11 Next, roll out 270g (9½oz) of the marzipan to a circle the size of the cake and lay it on top of the cake.
12 Divide the rest of the marzipan into 11 and roll into small balls to place around the edge of the cake.
13 I browned the top of the 'apostles' with a blow torch but don't worry if you don't have one; they still look good.
14 For an Easter flourish, I added a few flowers made from sugar paste and a ribbon, but you can decorate as you wish with Easter eggs, Easter chicks or similar.

Kulich

Makes 2 loaves

20g (¾oz) fresh yeast
50ml (2fl oz) warm water
150g (5½oz) caster sugar
65ml (2½fl oz) full-fat milk
130g (4½oz) butter, softened
650g (1lb 7oz) plain flour,
   sifted
a pinch of salt
2 tsp ground cardamom
8 egg yolks
1 tsp vanilla extract
60g (2oz) raisins
25g (1oz) flaked almonds
50g (1¾oz) mixed candied
   peel
75g (2¾oz) icing sugar

Sweet breads play an important role in Russian holidays and religious ceremonies and during Easter the most popular bread is a fruited one that is baked into a tall cylindrical shape known as Kulich. Each Russian family has their own recipe and traditionally the family's matriarch brings the Kulich to church to be blessed by the priest and only then can it be eaten.

1 Mix the yeast with the water and 50g (1¾oz) of the sugar and set aside for 10 minutes. Then add the milk and mix.
2 Cream together the butter and the remaining sugar until light and fluffy.
3 Add the sifted flour, salt and cardamom followed by the yeast mixture, egg yolks and vanilla extract. Mix well to a soft dough using the dough hook of a food mixer or your hands.
4 Add in the raisins, almonds and peel, and mix well for 5 minutes.
5 Cover the bowl with oiled clingfilm and leave in a warm place until doubled in size.
6 Preheat the oven to 180°C/350°F/gas mark 4,

and grease two cake cylinders 15cm (6in) high x 13cm (5in) wide.
7 Knock back the dough and divide into two. Form into balls and place into the prepared moulds.
8 Prove in a warm place until doubled in size. Then, bake in a preheated oven for 30 minutes.
9 Remove from the oven, cool for 10 minutes in the tin and then turn out onto a wire rack.
10 Make the frosting. Sift the icing sugar into a bowl and slowly add water, stirring all the time, to make a smooth paste that is just pourable. Pour over the cake and let it set.

Runeberg Cakes

Makes 5

120g (4oz) butter, softened
120g (4oz) soft light brown
  sugar
1 tbsp finely grated orange
  zest
2 eggs, lightly beaten
120g (4oz) self-raising flour,
  sifted
60g (2oz) ground almonds
juice of 1 orange
25g (1oz) seedless raspberry
  jam, for topping
50g (1¾oz) Royal Icing (see
  page 297)

These quirky little tubular cakes were named after Johan Ludvig Runeberg (1804–1877), the national poet of Finland, who apparently ate a similar cake to this every morning with a glass of punch. They are baked all over Finland to celebrate his birthday – 5th February.

1 Preheat the oven to 180°C/350°F/gas mark 4 and grease and line (just at the bottom) five dariole moulds (6.5cm x 6.5cm (2½ x 2½in)) with baking parchment and place on a baking tray.
2 Cream together the butter and sugar until light and fluffy, and then stir in the orange zest.
3 Add in the eggs, one at a time, scraping down after each addition until well combined.
4 Add in the sifted flour and ground almonds and mix together.

5 Pour in the orange juice and mix well.
6 Spoon into the prepared dariole moulds and bake in a preheated oven for 20 minutes or until a cocktail stick inserted into the centre comes out clean. Remove the parchment.
7 Remove a cone of sponge at the top of each cake, warm the jam slightly and pipe onto the top of each cake.
8 Make the royal icing as instructed on page 297, transfer to a piping bag with No. 3 nozzle and pipe icing around each jam blob.

Mooncakes

Makes 12

3 salted eggs, for the egg yolks
85g (3oz) golden syrup
80ml (3fl oz) groundnut (peanut) oil
100ml (3½fl oz) water
475g (1lb 1oz) Italian 00 flour, sifted
500g (1lb 2oz) lotus paste (or sweet bean paste)
1 egg, beaten, for brushing

Most Mooncakes are pastry wrapped around a sweet dense filling; the pastry and the fillings vary depending on which region you're in when you're eating them. Typically, they are consumed at just one time in the year – during the Chinese mid-Autumn festival, which occurs during the full moon of the eighth month and is the second most important Chinese festival after New Year. The moon is at its brightest at this time and these cakes are eaten with friends and family during the celebrations. Deep inside the cake is salted egg yolk, which represents the full moon. Traditionally, Mooncakes have an imprint on the top – they're made in special moulds, which you may want to source – and the Chinese characters commonly seen represent harmony and longevity, as well as telling of its special filling and which bakery made it. Salted egg yolks and lotus paste can be bought online or from your local Asian supermarket.

1 Boil the eggs for 15 minutes. Cool, shell, peel off the white and quarter the yolks.
2 Mix together the syrup, oil and water in a bowl. Add in the flour and mix to a dough. Allow to rest overnight in the fridge.
3 Portion the dough into 50g (1¾oz) balls.
4 Divide the lotus paste into 40g (1½oz) portions; you'll have some left over.

5 Wrap a salted quarter egg yolk in a lotus paste portion. Repeat with the other yolks.
6 Roll out the dough balls to a 3mm (⅛in) thickness and rest for 1 hour.
7 Preheat the oven to 180°C/350°F/gas mark 4, and line a baking tray with baking parchment.
8 In the palm of your hand place a disc of pastry, add the covered egg yolk and draw up the pastry dough around it.
9 Gently squeeze the dough into your Mooncake mould, open up the edges of the pastry and trim the edge.
10 Push in the centre to ensure the mould is full and the filling isn't oozing out.
11 Brush the pastry with beaten egg and, then bring the edges into the centre to seal the cake. Turn upside down and, on a work surface, firmly push the Mooncake plunger to make an impression on the top of the cake. Then lift from the work surface and plunge again to repeat for the rest. If you don't have a mould, simply decorate using the back of a knife to create a pattern.
12 Place on the baking tray, ensure all surfaces are brushed with beaten egg and bake for 15 minutes or until golden brown.
13 Remove from the oven, take off the baking parchment and cool on a wire rack.
14 Serve with Chinese tea.

Makes about 16 slices

For the pastry:
150g (5½oz) butter, cubed
200g (7oz) plain flour, sifted
½ tsp baking powder
cold water, as required

For the filling:
300g (10½oz) raisins
400g (14oz) currants
70g (2½oz) chopped almonds
120g (4oz) plain flour
85g (3oz) soft brown sugar
1 tsp allspice
½ tsp ground ginger
½ tsp ground cinnamon
½ tsp ground black pepper
½ tsp baking powder
½ tsp cream of tartar
½ tbsp brandy
2 eggs, beaten (1 for cake and
    1 for brushing)
50ml (2fl oz) full-fat milk

Black Bun

This traditional Scottish sweetmeat is usually associated with Hogmanay or New Year in Scotland and is generally accompanied with a 'wee tot' of whisky. It is different to most fruit cakes in that the fruity mixture is baked in its own pastry case. The taste improves when left a few weeks to mature so you can appreciate it well into January.

1 Preheat the oven to Preheat the oven to 130°C/250°F/gas mark ½, and grease a 25cm x 8cm x 9cm (10in x 3¼in x 3½in) loaf tin.
2 Make the pastry. Rub the butter into the sifted flour and baking powder and add cold water a little at a time until the mixture becomes a stiff dough. Cover the bowl in clingfilm and rest in the fridge for 1 hour.
3 Remove the pastry from the fridge, dust a work surface with flour and roll out to a thickness of 5mm (¼in).
4 Wrap the pastry around the rolling pin and transfer to the tin, pushing down well inside and trim off the excess. Re-roll the pastry – you'll need enough to cover the top of the loaf.

5 To make the filling, mix the fruit and all the dry ingredients together then add in the brandy, beaten egg and enough milk to moisten the mixture.
6 Spoon the mixture into the pastry-lined loaf tin and cover with the remaining pastry. Pinch the edges of the pastry together using the thumb and forefinger of one hand and the other forefinger to create a crimped edge.
7 Brush beaten egg over the top of the pastry sealing all the sides and then prick all over with a fork.
8 Bake in a preheated oven for about 2 hours.
9 Remove from the oven, cool for 30 minutes in the tin and then turn out onto a wire rack.
10 Serve cold with a wee dram of whisky.

Bûche de Noël

Serves 10

For the chocolate sponge:
25g (1oz) plain flour, plus extra
    for dusting
1 dsp cocoa powder
a pinch of salt
3 eggs, separated
a pinch of cream of tartar
120g (4oz) caster sugar, plus
    extra for dusting
2–3 drops vanilla extract
icing sugar, to dust

For the filling:
100ml (3½fl oz) Stock Syrup
    (see page 299)
250ml (8½fl oz) Crème
    Chantilly (see page 296)

450g (1lb) Chocolate
    Buttercream (see page 298)

**For the meringue
mushrooms:**
1 egg white
60g (2oz) caster sugar
½ tsp vanilla extract
icing sugar and grated
    chocolate, to decorate

For the marzipan leaves:
50g (1¾oz) marzipan
a few drops of green food
    colouring

The Bûche de Noël or Yule Log originated in France but has become a staple of many a household around the world at Christmas time. My mother-in-law makes one every year that, after an initial reluctance to spoil the pretty Christmas scene, her grandchildren devour with wonderful enthusiasm. Here's her recipe complete with her signature meringue mushrooms.

1 Preheat the oven to 170°C/325°F/gas mark 3 and grease and flour a 30cm x 20cm (12in x 8in) Swiss roll tin.

2 Sift the flour, cocoa and salt into a bowl.

3 Whisk the egg whites with the cream of tartar until stiff. Gradually beat in half the sugar. Continue whisking until the mixture is very glossy and stands in peaks.

4 Cream the egg yolks together and beat in the remaining sugar until light and thick. Add the vanilla and stir the flour into the mixture.

5 Pour the egg whites over the mix and fold carefully together with a metal spoon until thoroughly blended.

6 Cut some baking parchment to the size of your baking tray. Blob a little of the meringue mixture onto each corner of the baking tray, then place the paper on top (this prevents the parchment from moving in the oven).

7 Pour the mixture onto the parchment and, using a palette knife, spread the mixture evenly. Bake on the middle shelf for 20 minutes. Meanwhile make the stock syrup and crème Chantilly as instructed on pages 299 and 296.

8 Remove the sponge from the oven and turn out immediately onto a clean tea towel, so it's baking parchment side up. Make a slit in the centre of the paper with a knife. Starting from the slit, carefully peel the parchment paper away from the sponge.

9 While the sponge is still warm, dip a pastry brush into the sugar syrup and dab the sponge until moist but not soaked. Then spread a layer of crème Chantilly using a palette knife. Pick up the tea towel and slowly bring it towards you to curl the sponge into a roll. Wrap the tea towel around the roll and place in the fridge to set and absorb all the flavours.

10 Make the buttercream as instructed on page 298.

11 Turn the oven down to 130°C/250°F/gas mark ½. For the mushrooms, beat the egg white until stiff and add ½ tablespoon of sugar and beat again until stiff and shiny. Gradually beat in the remaining sugar and vanilla extract. Then, using a piping bag, pipe small mushroom caps and stalks onto baking parchment. Dust the caps with icing sugar and grated chocolate and bake for 45 minutes.

12 To assemble, put the rolled up sponge on a serving plate. Cut a thick diagonal piece from one end (to make a branch on the log) and spread the diagonal end with buttercream and secure about half way down the remaining roll.

13 Put the buttercream in a piping bag with a star nozzle and pipe in circles over the three ends of the log and then pipe lines along the log, including one or two swirls to represent knots in the wood.

14 To make the marzipan leaves, first soften the marzipan with your hands and then add the food colouring a drop at a time until the desired green is achieved. Cut out leaf shapes, using a small sharp knife, and use to decorate.

15 Decorate with the meringue mushrooms and, if you like, small green marzipan ivy leaves. Finally, gently dust with icing sugar.

English Christmas Cake

Serves 12

50g (1¾oz) whole almonds
450g (1lb) currants
150g (5½oz) sultanas
275g (9¾oz) raisins
110g (3¾oz) mixed citrus peel
110g (3¾oz) glacé cherries
275g (9¾oz) plain flour, sifted
½ tsp baking powder
½ tsp salt
1½ tsp mixed spice
2½ tsp unsweetened cocoa
    powder
40g (1½oz) ground almonds
260g (9¼oz) butter, softened
260g (9¼oz) soft brown sugar
5 eggs, lightly beaten
grated zest of 1½ large
    lemons
1½ tbsp brandy
1½ tsp coffee essence

For the sugar syrup:
50g (1¾oz) caster sugar
50ml (2fl oz) water
1 tsp brandy

150g (5½oz) apricot jam,
    warmed
650g (1lb 7oz) marzipan
icing sugar, for dusting
225g (8oz) white sugar paste
green and red food colouring

With Christmas being such a busy time, it's great to know that you can bake and decorate this cake well in advance – in fact, its flavour matures and improves over time. I like to decorate my Christmas cake simply with a few flowers, leaves and berries and finish it off with a ribbon, but some people prefer to create whole winter wonderlands on top of their cakes.

1 Preheat the oven to 160°C/310°F/gas mark 2½, and grease and line a 21cm (8in) round cake tin with baking parchment. You'll also need a 25cm (10in) cake board.
2 Toast the almonds on a baking tray until golden brown, and set aside. Meanwhile, in a bowl, mix all the fruit together with the sifted flour, baking powder, salt, mixed spice, cocoa powder and ground almonds.
3 Cream the butter and sugar together and slowly add the eggs, scraping down after each addition to combine well.
4 Fold in the whole almonds, the fruit mixture, lemon zest, brandy and coffee essence.
5 Bake in the preheated oven for at least 1 hour.
6 Meanwhile, make the sugar syrup by heating the sugar and water in a pan until thick and syrupy. When cool, add the brandy.
7 Remove from the oven, cool in the tin, turn out onto a wire rack and strip off the parchment. Skewer the cake and dot all over with the syrup.

8 Transfer the cool cake to a cake board and brush the top with apricot jam. Soften the marzipan in your hands before flattening on a surface dusted lightly with icing sugar. Roll out to a circle big enough to cover the cake and lay the marzipan over the top, smoothing and flattening the top and sides with your hands.
9 Soften the sugar paste in your hands and roll out until the circle is big enough for the cake.
10 Brush the marzipan with a little cooled boiled water and then slide both hands underneath the sugar paste and carefully place over the cake. Taking your time and starting from the centre of the top, smooth the icing outwards to the edges getting rid of any air bubbles. Smooth the top and then the sides. Trim off any excess paste and wrap with clingfilm to be used for extra decorations.
11 Leave overnight to firm up before finishing off with sugar paste decorations. I like simple holly leaves and berries.

Tarta de Santiago

Serves 6–8

260g (9¼oz) ground almonds
255g (9oz) caster sugar
finely grated zest of 1 orange
finely grated zest of 1 lemon
6 eggs, separated
4 drops of almond extract
½ tsp ground cinnamon
icing sugar, to dust

Originating from Galicia in northwestern Spain during the time of medieval pilgrimage, this tart is traditionally decorated with the St James cross. In fact, this sweet delight isn't confined to Galicia and is baked and enjoyed all over Spain, most commonly to celebrate St James's Day (the patron saint of Spain) and in July and early August. With its wonderfully moist almond and citrus flavours, this torte makes a perfect dessert or partner to an afternoon café con leche (milky coffee).

1 Preheat the oven to 170°C/325°F/gas mark 3, and grease an 18cm (7in) springform cake tin.
2 Cream 180g (6½oz) of the sugar, zests and egg yolks together until light and fluffy. Next, stir in the ground almonds, almond extract and the cinnamon.
3 In a separate bowl, beat the eggs whites with the remaining sugar until stiff. Add about one-quarter of the egg whites into the thick almond mixture and beat. This is quite difficult as the mixture is stiff so needs care. Add a further quarter and repeat. Add the remaining egg whites and fold in until fully combined.
4 Turn the mixture into the prepared tin and bake in a preheated oven for 40 minutes.
5 Remove from the oven, allow to cool for 10 minutes in the tin and then turn out onto a wire rack.
6 To follow the time-honoured tradition of decoration, find the shape of the St James cross using the internet and print it out. Cut out the middle of the cross to use as a stencil.
7 Once the cake is cooled, dust the cake with icing sugar and serve straightaway.

Panettone

Serves 10

12g (⅓oz) fresh yeast
120ml (4fl oz) full-fat milk
400g (14oz) plain flour
1 tsp salt
110g (3¾oz) caster sugar
2 eggs, plus 2 egg yolks
1 tsp vanilla extract
180g (6½oz) butter, cubed
85g (3oz) glacé cherries,
    chopped
85g (3oz) raisins
85g (3oz) mixed candied peel

You almost sound Italian when you say its name out loud – Panettone (pan-eh-ton-ay) – and this most famous of the Italian Christmas breads hails from the northern Italian city of Milan. Panettone is a rich, buttery sweet bread studded with raisins and candied fruit. Many commercial varieties are available but wouldn't it be fun to try baking your own this Christmas?

1 Mix the yeast with the milk and leave in a warm place for 20 minutes.
2 Sift the flour and salt together in a bowl and mix in the sugar.
3 Next, mix in the yeast mixture, the eggs, egg yolks and vanilla extract.
4 Using the dough hook on a food mixer, mix until a soft dough forms then add the butter bit by bit and mix until well combined for at least 5 minutes. Otherwise, knead slowly by hand on a lightly floured work surface for 10 minutes.
5 Add in the fruit in 3 batches and mix to get an even spread of fruit. Then cover the bowl with greased clingfilm. Leave to prove for 1 hour until doubled in size.

6 Grease and line a 450g (1lb) Panettone tin with baking parchment.
7 Knock back the dough, form into a ball and place in the prepared tin. Rest in a warm place for 2 hours until doubled in size.
8 Preheat the oven to 180°C/350°F/gas mark 4.
9 Bake in a preheated oven for 45 minutes.
10 Remove from the oven, allow to cool for 10 minutes in the tin and then turn out onto a wire rack, and strip off the parchment.
11 Serve with a glass of sweet wine, such as vin santo.

Maple Syrup and Pecan Layer Cake

Serves 6

260g (9¼oz) plain flour, sifted
110g (3¾oz) caster sugar
120g (4oz) soft brown sugar
1 tsp bicarbonate of soda
½ tsp salt
280ml (9½fl oz) buttermilk
100g (3½oz) butter, melted
85g (3oz) maple syrup
½ tsp vanilla extract
85g (3oz) pecans, toasted and
    finely chopped

For the topping:

500g (1lb 2oz) Classic
    Buttercream (see page 298)
4 tbsp maple syrup
2 drops vanilla extract

There's no single cake that sums up Thanksgiving in America but I love this combination of pecans, which feature a lot during these festivities, with maple syrup to make this irresistible layer cake. And because you chill it you can make it a day ahead, leaving you free to tend to all the other catering for this special occasion and still turn out a fabulous finale.

1 Preheat the oven to 180°C/350°F/gas mark 4, and grease two 21cm (8in) round cake tins.
2 Mix together the sifted flour, sugars, bicarbonate of soda and salt.
3 Separately mix together the buttermilk, melted butter, syrup and vanilla extract and then stir into the dry ingredients until just combined. Fold in the chopped pecans.
4 Spoon the mixture into the prepared tin and bake in a preheated oven for 30 minutes or until a cocktail stick inserted into the centre comes out clean.

5 Remove from the oven, cool for 10 minutes in the tin and then turn out onto a wire rack.
6 Make the buttercream as instructed on page 298 and then mix in the syrup and vanilla extract to transform it into a tasty topping.
7 Place one cake layer on a serving plate or cake stand and spread with one-quarter of the topping. Top with the second layer and then spread the rest of the topping on the top and sides of cake. Using a fork, add a pattern to the buttercream, if you wish.
8 Refrigerate and serve chilled.

Stollen

**Makes a Stollen
about 35cm x 12cm
(14in x 4½in)**

Serves 12

100ml (3½fl oz) full-fat milk
30g (1¼oz) fresh yeast
1 egg
225g (8oz) plain flour, sifted
1 tsp mixed spice
a pinch of salt
1 tsp caster sugar
50g (1¾oz) butter
200g (7oz) mixed dried fruit
25g (1oz) chopped almonds
110g (3¾oz) marzipan
red food colouring

To finish:

25g (1oz) butter, melted
50g (1¾oz) icing sugar

The history of this marzipan-stuffed fruit cake dates back to the fifteenth century, when the bakers in Germany used to produce huge loaves of Stollen at Christmas. Stollen is a staple of German Christmas markets today – resplendent in wondrous gift wrapping – and makes a delicious alternative to Christmas Cake while keeping the spicy sensibilities enjoyed at this time of the year. Partner it with a glass of brandy.

1 Mix the milk and yeast together and leave to react (about 10–15 minutes).

2 Put half of this yeast 'starter' in a bowl, add the egg, sifted flour, mixed spice, salt and the sugar and mix well before adding the rest of the starter, and mix again.

3 Add in the butter, mix and then fold in the fruit and nuts by hand. Leave the dough to rise for about 45 minutes.

4 Meanwhile, preheat the oven to 170°C/325°F/gas mark 3, and line a baking tray (40cm x 15cm (16in x 6in)) with baking parchment.

5 Next, soften the marzipan in your hands and add a drop of red food colouring. Mix the colour in well – the marzipan should turn a little pink.

6 Bash the dough firmly with the heel of your hand to release any air across the whole of the dough (aim for a size about 35cm x 12 cm (14in x 4½in)).

7 Shape the marzipan into three pencil shapes the length of your dough (35cm (14in)). And with the long edge nearest you, place the first pencil in the top third of the dough. Fold the dough over the pencil pressing down firmly. Place the second pencil over the double layer and repeat. Repeat with the final pencil.

8 Put the completed Stollen on to a floured baking tray in a warm place, join side down and allow to prove for half an hour. Then bake in a preheated oven for 40 minutes.

9 Remove from the oven, take off the baking parchment and coat with melted butter. Then allow to cool for 10 minutes and transfer to a wire rack.

10 Once cooled, dust liberally with icing sugar, before serving.

Galette des Rois

Serves 6–8

400g (14oz) Puff Pastry (see page 221)
100g (3½oz) Crème Pâtissière (see page 296)

For the frangipane:
150g (5½oz) caster sugar
130g (4½oz) butter, softened
finely grated zest of 1 orange
finely grated zest of 1 lemon
1 vanilla pod, split and scraped
2 eggs, plus 1 egg, beaten, for brushing
200g (7oz) ground almonds
20ml (⅔fl oz) dark rum
30g (1¼oz) plain flour, sifted

In France, people celebrate Epiphany, or Twelfth Night, in early January by tucking into these tasty pastries. Translated as 'Kings' Cake', Galette des Rois is similar to a Pithivier (see page 252) and is baked to celebrate the day the three kings (wise men) arrived to visit baby Jesus. In France these are traditionally baked with a porcelain bean hidden inside and whoever gets the slice with the bean is 'king for the day'. French pâtisseries always sell this galette with a paper golden crown on top, so if you want to go authentic all the way then source yourself one online.

1 Make the puff pastry and crème pâtissière as instructed on pages 221 and 296 and set aside in the fridge.
2 Preheat the oven to 180°C/350°F/gas mark 4, and line a baking tray (30cm (12in)) square with baking parchment.
3 Next, make the frangipane. Beat the sugar, butter, orange and lemon zests and vanilla seeds until pale and fluffy (6–8 minutes). Add the eggs one at a time, beating well after each addition until well combined.
4 Add the ground almonds and the rum, mix to combine then stir in the flour. Set aside to chill in the fridge.

5 Remove the puff pastry from the fridge and divide into two. On a lightly floured surface, roll out one half to a thickness of 5mm (¼in). Cut a 21cm (8in) diameter circle, place on the prepared tray.
6 Take the crème pâtissière and the frangipane out of the fridge and mix together.
7 Brush the edges of the pastry circle with beaten egg and then spread the frangipane-cream mixture on top, mounding it in the centre and leaving a 2cm (¾in) border around the edge.
8 On a lightly floured surface, roll out the other half of pastry to a thickness of 5mm (¼in). Cut a 24cm (9½in) diameter circle and gently place over the top. Press the edges firmly together to seal the galette.
9 Brush the outside of the pastry with beaten egg and then scallop the outside edge with a sharp knife. You might like to create a pattern on the surface – herringbone or flowers are often seen.
10 Refrigerate for about 30 minutes to seal and then bake in a preheated oven for 50 minutes until golden brown.
11 Remove from the oven, take off the baking parchment and then transfer to a wire rack.
12 Serve with a coffee and a brandy.

Pandoro

Serves 12–24

40g (1½oz) fresh yeast
30ml (1fl oz) warm water
600g (1lb 5oz) plain flour,
    sifted
½ tsp salt
75g (2¾oz) caster sugar
4 eggs
6 egg yolks
2 tsp vanilla extract
300g (10½oz) butter, cubed
icing sugar, fresh raspberries
    and micro mint, to
    decorate

In Italian, 'pan d'oro' means 'bread of gold' and this sweet yeasty bread, traditionally baked around Christmas time, originates from Verona in the north of the country. It is a simpler-tasting cake than its cousin, the Panettone (see page 276), but makes up for it with its stunning presentation in a Christmas tree-shape. Back in medieval times, such breads were the province of the wealthy due to their expensive ingredients and were known as 'golden breads'. It is said that the top of the cake is dusted with icing sugar to represent the snow on the Italian Alps.

1 Mix the yeast with the warm water and set aside for 20 minutes.
2 Mix the flour, salt and sugar together in a large bowl.
3 Mix the eggs and egg yolks together with the vanilla extract and add in the yeast mixture. Mix lightly and pour into the bowl of dry ingredients.
4 Using the dough hook on a food mixer, mix for 5–8 minutes until the dough is elastic. Otherwise, knead slowly by hand on a lightly floured work surface for 10 minutes.
5 Cover the bowl with greased clingfilm and put in a warm place for an hour or until doubled in size.
6 On a lightly floured surface roll out the dough to a rectangle about 3cm (1¼in) thick and dot with cubes of butter (using it all).
7 Turn the dough one turn clockwise, then fold the right third over and the left third over that. Do this – fold over, chill then roll out – three times in total, chilling for 20 minutes after each rolling out.
8 Grease a 450g (1lb) Pandoro tin.
9 Using the heel of your hand, pat down the dough and shape into a ball, bringing in the corners of the rectangle. Place in your greased tin and allow to prove again for 1 hour.
10 Preheat the oven to 180°C/350°F/gas mark 4, and bake for 35–40 minutes.
11 Remove from the oven, allow to cool for 10 minutes in the tin and then turn out onto a wire rack.
12 Once cool, square-off the top and then cut into horizontal slices and place on a serving dish, rotating each slice so that it resembles the shape of a Christmas tree (see photo).
13 Sprinkle with icing sugar and decorate with fresh raspberries and micro mint or any other fruit of your choice.
14 Serve with coffee.

Passover Nut Cake

Serves 8

170g (6oz) caster sugar
4 eggs, separated
1 tbsp cocoa powder, sifted
finely grated zest of 2 oranges
175g (6¼oz) flaked hazelnuts
3 tbsp Matzo Meal
15ml (1 tbsp) orange juice
300g (10½oz) Chocolate
   Ganache (see page 297)
100g (3½oz) toasted flaked
   hazelnuts, to coat

The Jewish festival of Passover, or Pesach, celebrates the exodus of the ancient Israelites from Egypt and is one of the most important – and widely celebrated – events in the Jewish calendar. During Passover, Jewish law forbids the eating of any baked goods that contain raising agents or flour, so cakes made with nuts are very popular.

1 Preheat the oven to 180°C/350°F/gas mark 4, and grease and line an 18cm (7in) springform cake tin with baking parchment.
2 Set aside 4 tablespoons of the sugar and whisk the rest with the egg yolks and sifted cocoa powder until a ribbon forms. Then, mix in the orange zest.
3 In a separate bowl, whisk together the egg whites until soft peaks form, then add the rest of the sugar and whisk again to stiff peaks.

4 Loosen the egg yolk mixture by adding a large tablespoon of the egg whites and then fold in the hazelnuts and Matzo Meal.
5 Fold in the remaining egg white carefully, so the air doesn't come out, and then finally pour in the orange juice.
6 Spoon into a prepared tin and bake in a preheated oven for 45 minutes or until a cocktail stick inserted into the centre comes out clean.
7 Remove from the oven, allow to cool for 10 minutes in the tin and then turn out onto a wire rack and strip off the parchment.
8 Meanwhile, make the chocolate ganache as instructed on page 297 and allow to cool slightly before masking the whole cake using a palette knife to spread evenly.
9 Sprinkle the toasted flaked hazelnuts all around, including on to the sides, which you will need to press on lightly with your hands.
10 Serve with coffee.

Croquembouche

Makes 60–80 choux buns

For the filling:
1.5 litres (2⅔ pints) Crème Pâtissière (see page 296)
120ml (4fl oz) Grand Marnier

For the choux pastry:
1 litre (1¾ pints) water
400g (14oz) butter
20g (¾oz) caster sugar
a pinch of salt
600g (1lb 5oz) strong white flour
16–18 eggs, whisked, plus 3 egg yolks, beaten, for brushing

For the caramel:
750g (1lb 11¾oz) caster sugar
200ml (7fl oz) water

For the spun sugar:
250g (9oz) caster sugar
80ml (3fl oz) water

'Croque en bouche' translates as 'crunch in the mouth' and this refers to the caramel that holds together this tower of profiteroles that make this wonderfully extravagant cake. Croquembouche first appeared in the 18th century when it was served as a wedding cake. It is designed to be a magnificent centrepiece and is still the most popular celebration cake in France today. You can construct a croquembouche inside a mould or build one free hand; I would recommend using a mould, but it's up to you.

1 Make the crème pâtissière as instructed on page 296. Add the Grand Marnier.

2 Preheat the oven to 250°C/480°F/gas mark 9, and line two or three large baking trays with baking parchment or use silicon mats. You may have to make the buns in batches, depending on the size of your oven and baking trays.

3 Place the water, butter, sugar and salt in a pan and bring to the boil, making sure the butter is melted.

4 Add the flour and stir in with a wooden spoon – it is important to cook the flour fully, so don't hurry this process. The dough should come away easily from the side of the pan.

5 Place the dough in a food mixer and, while beating, slowly add enough egg to make it suitable for piping – if it's too wet you won't be able to pipe it. (If you don't have a mixer, then beat by hand, add the eggs while using a wooden spoon and then whisk to beat for 5–10 minutes.)

6 Cover the bowl with clingfilm and leave to rest in the fridge.

7 Fit a piping bag with a No. 12 nozzle and fill with the cooled choux pastry mixture.

8 Secure the paper on the tray with a little dot of mixture at each corner. Slowly pipe a bulb of choux approximately 2.5cm (1in) wide and 2cm (¾in) high, spacing the bulbs evenly. Remember to squeeze only the top of the bag as you pipe; finish the piping by pressing the nozzle firmly against the tray to break off the mixture.

9 Space the choux buns at least 3cm (1¼in) apart so they don't stick during baking.

10 Using a pastry brush dipped in beaten egg yolks, dab the tops and flatten down any spikes to create a smooth surface.

11 Place in a preheated oven and turn the oven off as soon as you put the buns in. Leave for 15 minutes.

12 Switch the oven back on to 180°C/350°F/gas mark 4 and cook for a further 30–40 minutes until the choux is nearly dry inside. I test mine by breaking one open – if it isn't cooked through continue cooking the rest for a further 10 minutes.

13 Remove from the oven, take off the baking parchment and cool on a wire rack.

14 When the choux buns are completely cooled, use a pair of scissors to push a hole into the bottom of each one. Using a piping bag with a No. 2 nozzle, pipe the flavoured Crème Pâtissière into each bun, making sure they are full.

15 Now, make the caramel. In a pan dissolve the sugar with the water and as the sugar begins to bubble, using a pastry brush, brush gently round the sides of the pan to remove any sugar to prevent crystallisation. Bring the liquid to a temperature of 170°C/338°F, being careful to wash the thermometer after taking a temperature reading.

16 Remove from the heat and leave to cool for about 3–4 minutes until the mixture thickens a little.

17 Slowly begin dipping the choux buns one by one into the caramel, very carefully, covering two-thirds of the sides and then place on your plate or board. Build up the tower, making sure each bun sticks firmly to the one next to it with the caramel. You will need to keep reheating the caramel as it will thicken as it cools. Always take great care not to get your fingers near the caramel.

If you're using a mould, line it with baking parchment and place the buns around the mould in a circle, building up each layer.

18 Now, for the spun sugar. In a small pan, boil the sugar and water together until it reaches a temperature of 170°C/338°F, being careful to wash the thermometer after taking a temperature reading. Leave to cool slightly.

19 Lay two wooden spoons on your work surface, about 60cm (24in) apart, but ensure their ends jut out from the edge. Use a heavy pan to weigh down the flat ends and secure the handles in place.

20 Ensure the area where you will work is well protected (put some newspaper on the floor, for instance), attach two forks back to back (I use sticky tape) and dip them in the sugar mixture. Quickly, whip them forwards and backwards in the air allowing the sugar to fall as strands onto the wooden handles. These quickly crystallise and you can then pick them up and carefully drape them over your croquembouche.

21 I have also added edible violet flowers but you can decorate your croquembouche with your own preference of flowers, chocolates or sweets. Now, stand back and admire.

Christopher Farrugia's Maltese Prinjolata

Serves 8

Half a Madeira Cake (see page 80), cut into 3cm (1¼in) slices (or if you prefer use a Victoria Sponge (see page 16) or Genoise Sponge (see page 26))

For the Prinjolata filling:
50g (1¾oz) pine nuts
150g (5½oz) butter, softened
320g (11¼oz) caster sugar
2 egg whites
30ml (1fl oz) water
2 tsp vanilla extract

For the decoration:
300ml (10fl oz) whipping cream
50g (1¾oz) icing sugar, sifted
½ vanilla pod, split and scraped
50g (1¾oz) pine nuts, toasted
50g (1¾oz) glacé cherries, quartered (or other candied fruit)
50g (1¾oz) dark chocolate (minimum 70% cocoa solids)

In Maltese 'prinjol' means 'pine nut' and the amazing pine nut sweet – or Prinjolata – is enjoyed every year on the Mediterranean islands of Malta and Gozo. At Carnival, at the start of Lent, beautiful displays of Prinjolata adorn the windows of all confectioneries on the islands. The cake itself is traditionally huge but I've scaled it down to a smaller size here.

The celebrated Maltese chef Christopher Farrugia runs the renowned restaurant Ambrosia in Valletta; he is a chef whose commitment to worldwide cultural cuisine I admire enormously. He says of this cake: 'Prinjolata to me is pure indulgence, not surprisingly only to be served around Carnival. It also represents the Baroque food era, and where else better for this to originate than in Valletta, a World Heritage Baroque City?'

1 Preheat the oven to 180°C/350°F/gas mark 4.
2 Spread out the pine nuts on a baking tray and bake for 4–5 minutes until lightly toasted. Remove from the oven, crush and set aside.
3 Cream the butter and 200g (7oz) of the sugar until light and creamy, and set aside.
4 Whisk the egg whites in a bain-marie (or a heatproof bowl over a pan of simmering water) until soft peaks form then add the rest of the sugar slowly while whisking.
5 Add the water and vanilla and whisk in.

6 Remove from the heat and allow to cool.
7 When cool, add in the creamed butter and sugar along with the crushed pine nuts and mix until well combined.
8 Moisten the inside of a pudding bowl (I used one 10cm (4in) high and 16cm (6¼in) across) with water and line with clingfilm and then place a layer of sponge on the bottom followed by a layer of the Prinjolata filling.
9 Continue layering in this way until the bowl is full. Refrigerate overnight to set.
10 When you're ready to decorate the cake, remove it from the fridge and turn out the cake onto a plate or board.
11 Whip the cream until thickened slightly then add in the sifted icing sugar and vanilla seeds and continue to whisk until stiff peaks form.
12 Cover the cake with the whipped cream mixture. Sprinkle with toasted pine nuts and dot with glacé cherries – or candied fruits if you have them.
13 Melt the chocolate in a bowl over a pan of simmering water and drizzle over the cake.
14 Allow to cool before serving with a glass of Amaretto.

Kransekaka

Serves 50

550g (1lb 3½oz) butter
320g (11¼oz) icing sugar, sifted
5 egg yolks
275g (9¾oz) ground almonds, sifted
750g (1lb 11¾oz) plain flour, sifted
1½ tsp almond extract
250g (9oz) Royal Icing (see page 297)

You'll need to be prepared a day ahead to make this traditional Scandinavian delicacy but all the effort will be more than rewarded when you and your guests survey the finished product. A tower of cake with icing accompanies all sorts of celebrations in Scandinavia – from weddings to birthdays to Christmas. People go to town with the decorations, too, and you'll see everything from flowers to flags to tinsel and Christmas crackers. What will you decorate yours with?

1 Preheat the oven to 200°C/400°F/gas mark 6, and grease six Kransekake tins with silicon spray and place on baking trays. (Some Kransekake aficionados prefer a free-form look to their Kransekake and simply bake the rings of dough on baking trays rather than in tins.)
2 Cream the butter and icing sugar together until light and fluffy, and add the egg yolks.
3 Add the ground almonds and flour and combine well. Drop in the almond extract and mix to a dough.
4 Place the dough in a bowl and refrigerate overnight.

5 Remove the dough from the fridge and roll out on a lightly floured surface into 18 snakes 1cm (½in) across, descending in length from about 21cm (8in) to 14cm (5½in) long.
6 Fit the snakes into the kransekake pans and pinch the ends together to complete the rings.
7 Bake in a preheated oven for 15 minutes or so or until light golden in colour.
8 Meanwhile, make the royal icing as instructed on page 297 and transfer to a piping bag with a No. 3 nozzle.
9 Remove the cakes from the oven, allow to cool for 30 minutes in the tin and then turn out onto a wire rack. The rings may join together during cooking but this is easily remedied by using a small sharp knife to separate them.
10 Tap the tins to loosen the rings. Take the largest ring first and place on a cake plate.
11 Pipe loops of icing onto each circle and build up the Kransekake as you go.
12 To serve, dismantle the layers one by one and cut into portions.

Sakotis

Serves 8

235g (8½oz) butter, softened
150g (5½oz) caster sugar
8 eggs, separated
finely grated zest of 1 lemon
2 tbsp dark rum
a pinch of salt
40g (1½oz) ground almonds
½ tsp vanilla extract
160g (5¾oz) plain flour
10g (¼oz) cornflour
3 tbsp apricot jam, warmed
icing sugar, for dusting
　　(optional)

Also known as 'tree cake', this Lithuanian specialty appears at every wedding as well as during Christmas and Easter festivities. In Polish, this cake is known as 'sekacz' or 'senkacz', and in German, it's called 'baumkuchen'. To make this spectacular cake like the one above you need a particular kind of oven, as the batter has to be dripped onto a rotating spit. So, I have altered the recipe so that you can make your own version at home in a regular cake tin, just using the grill.

1 Preheat the grill to medium, and grease liberally a 17cm (6½in) springform cake tin.
2 Cream the butter and sugar together until light and fluffy.
3 Gradually add the egg yolks, the lemon zest, rum, salt, ground almonds and vanilla extract and mix together.
4 Sift in the flour and cornflour and mix until well combined.
5 In a separate bowl, whisk the egg whites until stiff peaks form and then fold gently into the mixture.
6 Pour about 2 tablespoons of the mixture into the prepared tin and place under the grill until golden brown – only a couple of minutes.

7 Repeat with another layer of mixture and place under the grill again. Repeat until you have used all the mixture.
8 Allow to cool in the tin for about 10 minutes before turning out onto a wire rack.
9 When the cake is turned out glaze with warmed apricot jam and dust with icing sugar, if you like.
10 For an authentic Lithuanian experience, serve with a glass of herbal vodka, a beer or a strong coffee.

Prinsesstårta

Serves 8–10

4 eggs
225g (8oz) sugar
60g (2oz) plain flour
75g (2¾oz) cornflour
1 tsp baking powder

For the custard:
240ml (8fl oz) double cream
4 egg yolks
25g (1oz) caster sugar
40g (1½oz) cornflour
2 tsp vanilla extract

300g (10½oz) marzipan
green and yellow food
   colouring
150g (5½oz) seedless
   raspberry jam
240ml (8fl oz) double cream
icing sugar,
   to dust

Heralding from Sweden, the Prinsesstårta, or Princess Cake, is a wonder to behold with its unusual pistachio-green marzipan and smooth domed top. The Swedes bake and serve these for birthdays, national holidays and anniversaries; and if you want to try one first before baking your own, most good Swedish bakeries bake and sell them.

1 Preheat the oven to 180°C/350°F/gas mark 4, and grease a 21cm (8in) globe cake tin.

2 Beat the eggs and sugar until light and fluffy.

3 Sift the flour, cornflour and baking powder together and fold them into the egg mixture.

4 Pour the mixture into the prepared cake tin and bake for about 1 hour or until golden.

5 Remove from the oven, cool for 10 minutes in the tin and then turn out onto a wire rack.

6 To make the custard, place the cream, egg yolks, sugar and cornflour in a pan and whisk together over a low heat. Continue to stir until the custard thickens. Add the vanilla extract and remove from the heat. Allow to cool.

7 Soften the marzipan in your hands before adding the food colouring. Drop in as little as possible at a time and then knead it in and add more, as necessary, to achieve the desired colour.

8 Flatten the marzipan and, on a surface dusted lightly with icing sugar, roll into a circle large enough to cover your cake.

9 To assemble, slice the cake into three layers, keeping the top layer thinner than the others. Spread a thin layer of jam on the bottom layer and add half of the vanilla custard. Spread evenly and then add the next layer of cake and repeat.

10 Whip the double cream until stiff and mound in a slight dome on top of the custard layer.

11 Add the final sponge layer and then finish off the cream by spreading a thin layer over the whole cake.

12 Gently lay your marzipan over the cake and use your hands to shape over the dome. Trim off any excess marzipan, dust with icing sugar and decorate with a traditional pink rose.

13 Keep the cake in the fridge until ready to serve.

Gingerbread House

Makes 1 gingerbread house or 20 cut-out biscuits

120g (4oz) butter, softened
175g (6¼oz) caster sugar
1 egg
350g (12oz) plain flour, sifted
1 tsp bicarbonate of soda
¼ tsp ground cinnamon
2 tsp ground ginger
3 tbsp golden syrup
1 tbsp black treacle
finely grated zest of 3 lemons
1 egg white
25g (1oz) icing sugar, sifted
100g (3½oz) Royal Icing (see page 297), for decoration
various sweets, for decoration (optional)

Gingerbread – whether as cut-out shapes or as a 3D house – is an all-time hit at Christmas time, with its lovely spice and its possibilities for super-bright decorations. Lebkuchen houses in Germany are a traditional sight at Christmas as are the many types of gingerbread house in the Nordic countries of Europe. The decoration can be as simple or as lavish as you wish. I've obviously gone to town on this showstopper of a house but just simple chocolate buttons on the roof with icing outlines for doors and windows can transform the humble biscuit and transfix children, big and small.

1 Grease and line several baking trays with baking parchment.
2 Cream the butter and sugar together until light and fluffy, and add the egg.
3 Add the sifted flour, bicarbonate of soda, cinnamon and ginger and mix until well combined.
4 Warm the golden syrup and black treacle in a pan on a medium heat then pour into the mixture. Next, stir in the lemon zest.
5 Allow the mixture to rest for 1 hour and meanwhile preheat the oven to 170°C/325°F/gas mark 3.
6 Roll out the dough on a floured work surface and cut into your favourite shapes with cutters or design all the pieces of a house

(long rectangles/triangles/cut out windows/doors etc.).
7 Bake in a preheated oven for 20 minutes.
8 Remove from the oven, take off the baking parchment and turn out onto a wire rack.
9 Mix together the egg white and icing sugar to make a 'glue' to stick the pieces together.
10 When cool, assemble the pieces for the gingerbread house and stick together with the gluey mixture.
11 Make the royal icing as instructed on page 297 and use it to add your own decorations to the house or leave as plain as you like.

Baking Basics

Here you will find easy recipes for all the different creams I have mentioned in the book, as well as syrups, glazes and icing. Syrups are incredibly useful for moistening cakes and sponges and can be enhanced with endless flavours from natural zests or fruit juices to essences and alcohol. The glazes and ganaches are easy to make and can transform an ordinary cake into an extraordinary one.

A NOTE ON INGREDIENTS

It goes without saying that you should always use the best quality ingredients that you can afford. For me, butter has to be unsalted; eggs are medium size and always free range; sugar is unrefined as much as possible, I use golden caster sugar, for instance. I like to use fresh yeast but if you can't get that then use one-third of the amount as dried yeast 15g (½oz) fresh yeast = 5g (⅛oz) dried yeast. Many recipes mention minimum 70% cocoa solids when it comes to chocolate, and I always recommend buying the best chocolate you can afford as the end result is worth it.

Crème Anglaise

It literally translates as 'English Cream' from the French. This custard sauce has a nice rich and smooth texture and can be served warm or cold, as you prefer. If you prefer it a little thicker, then you can always add more egg yolks.

Makes about 345ml (11⅔fl oz)

60g (2oz) caster sugar
3 egg yolks
250ml (8½fl oz) full-fat milk
1 vanilla pod, split and scraped

1 In a bowl, whisk 40g (1½oz) of the sugar with the egg yolks until pale.
2 In a pan, bring the milk and the remaining sugar to the boil with the vanilla seeds.

3 Pour the hot mixture into the bowl, return to the pan and warm on a low heat. Stir continuously until the mixture coats the back of the spoon, or until it reaches a temperature of 81°C/178°F.
4 Remove from the heat, sieve and refrigerate straight away, covered to prevent a skin forming.
Variation: **Almond Crème Anglaise**
Add 2 drops of almond essence to the milk at the start; don't use the vanilla pod.
Variation: **Alcoholic Crème Anglaise**
Add 30ml (1fl oz) of your chosen tipple, such as Grand Marnier or Armagnac at the end and stir well.

Crème Chantilly

This sweetened whipped cream takes its name from the Château de Chantilly (or its folly known as Hameau de Chantilly) in northern France. This cream makes a lovely accompaniment to anything containing apples or red fruits.

Makes 500ml (18fl oz)

500ml (18fl oz) double cream
50g (1¾oz) icing sugar, sifted
1 tsp vanilla extract

1 Whisk the cream in a mixing bowl until ribbons just about form.
2 Slowly add the icing sugar and vanilla, and whisk till the mixture falls in ribbons.
3 This cream is best made an hour or so before you need it and kept in the fridge.

Crème Pâtissière

Also known as pastry cream, crème pâtissière is a rich, thick and creamy custard that you can use to fill all sorts of cakes, tarts and pastries, and much more. It also makes a great base for any kind of soufflés containing alcohol.

Makes about 750g (1lb 11¾oz)

120g (4oz) caster sugar
500ml (18fl oz) full-fat milk
1 vanilla pod, split and scraped
6 egg yolks
60g (2oz) plain flour, sifted
1½ tbsp cornflour, sifted

1 In a pan, put 50g (1¾oz) of the sugar with the milk and vanilla seeds.
2 In a round-bottomed bowl, whisk together the egg yolks and the rest of the sugar, followed by the sifted flour and cornflour.
3 Bring the milk in the pan to the boil and pour over the mixture in the bowl, whisking to fully combine.
4 Pour back into the pan, on a medium heat, and whisk continuously for 10 minutes (so that the flour is fully cooked out).
5 Pour into a deep baking tray and cover with clingfilm, ensuring that it touches the surface to prevent a skin forming, and set in the fridge for 1 hour.
6 Store in a bowl in the fridge and when you are ready to use it, quickly beat it again until smooth.

Variations: Chocolate Crème Pâtissière

For a chocolate version to fill some éclairs perhaps (see page 238), add the following ingredients:

20g (¾oz) cocoa powder (sift in with the flour)

50g (1¾oz) melted chocolate (add in after taking off the heat).

Crème Légère

A lighter – 'légère' means 'light' in French – version of the classic crème pâtissière. The basic recipe is half the amount of cream to the amount of crème pâtissière. You can easily add a touch of alcohol for added flavour and it's perfect for serving with poached fruit.

Makes 750g (1lb 11¾oz)

500g (1lb 2oz) Crème Pâtissière (see opposite)

250ml (8½fl oz) double cream, whipped to a ribbon

1 Remove the Crème Pâtissière from the fridge and soften in a mixer with the paddle attachment until smooth and no lumps (or in a bowl with a wooden spoon). Then fold in the whipped cream.

Frangipane

This version of frangipane is lighter and, because of the self-raising flour, more cakey than traditional frangipane (see Pithiviers page 252 for the traditional recipe). This also works well alongside stoned fruit.

Makes 800g (1lb 12¼oz)

250g (9oz) butter, softened
250g (9oz) caster sugar
120g (4oz) ground almonds
60g (2oz) rice flour, sifted
60g (2oz) self-raising flour, sifted
3 eggs

1 Cream the butter and sugar together until light and fluffy, then add the ground almonds and sifted flours.
2 Whisk together well, then slowly whisk in the eggs until fully combined.
3 Place in the fridge to rest.

Chocolate Ganache

Ganache is a smooth and velvety mixture of chocolate and cream. Some say it was invented in Paris while others cite Switzerland as its home. Wherever it was created, its basic recipe is easy to follow (and learn), and you can add flavourings easily too. This is a basic recipe useful for fillings, but if you want to have a pourable topping to a cake, for instance Boston Cream Pie (see page 36), you'll need to use a Chocolate Glaçage (see below).

Makes 300ml (10fl oz)

200g (7oz) dark (minimum 55% cocoa solids), milk or white chocolate, broken into pieces
100ml (3½fl oz) double cream

1 Melt the chocolate in a heatproof bowl over a pan of simmering water; cover the chocolate while doing this, so it melts nice and evenly.
2 When melted, pour the cream immediately onto the chocolate, whisking briskly to fully mix.
3 Use straight away.

Variation: Flavoured Chocolate Ganache

3 tsp flavouring (such as vanilla extract or Grand Marnier)

Chocolate Glaçage

Chocolate glaçage is slightly different to a ganache. The addition of the oil gives a glassy, mirrored effect to your topping and the end result is liquid enough to pour over the top of a cake.

Makes 300ml (10fl oz)

100g (3½oz) dark chocolate (minimum 70% cocoa solids)
100ml (3½fl oz) water
100ml (3½fl oz) double cream
75g (2¾oz) light brown sugar
a pinch of salt
20ml (⅔fl oz) light nut oil

1 Break the chocolate into small pieces and place in a bowl.
2 Put the water in a pan with the cream, sugar and salt. Bring to the boil and simmer for about 2 minutes.
3 Pour the hot liquid over the broken-up chocolate and mix well until smooth.
4 Leave to cool for about 30 minutes before mixing in the oil.

Royal Icing

This icing remains glossy when it's dry and so is great to use when decorating cakes. When you've made this a few times, you'll get the 'feel' of this icing – and if you want it a bit thicker then add more sugar, but remember that it only takes a very small amount of extra egg white to make it quite wet. And why not learn how to make your own little piping bag using parchment paper (there are lots of videos online), so you can write with a really fine line? Keep practising and, before you know it, you'll be signing every cake you make or decorating your gingerbread like the one on page 124.

Makes approximately 300g (10½oz)

2 egg whites
300g (10½oz) icing sugar

1 Put the egg whites in a large bowl.
2 Sift the icing sugar into the bowl and gradually beat it into the egg whites until smooth and glossy. Continue beating until a thick icing forms.
3 Transfer to a piping bag ready for use.

Cream Cheese Frosting

Whether you want a topping for Cupcakes (see page 182) or a whole cake (for instance Hummingbird Cake (see page 34) or Carrot and Walnut Cake (see page 96), this frosting is simple and quick to make. You could also add the zest of any citrus fruit to complement the flavourings in your cake.

Makes approximately 700g (1lb 10oz)

60g (2oz) butter
160g (5¾oz) full-fat cream cheese
500g (1lb 2oz) icing sugar, sifted

1 Soften the butter in a food mixer using the paddle attachment (or use a wooden spoon in a mixing bowl). Make sure the cream cheese is nice and smooth and mix in.
2 Slowly add the icing sugar on a low speed (the speed is very important because if your mixer is on a high speed you will decorate your kitchen beautifully with a lovely white layer!) and when it's fully combined, beat on a high speed for 30 seconds.
3 Use straight away, or if you can't get the smoothness you want pop it in the fridge for 10 minutes to firm up and use a wet palette knife to spread it.

Classic Buttercream

Rich, creamy and silky smooth, this simple but highly versatile combination of sugar and butter can be used as a filling or as an icing to decorate cakes.

Makes approximately 450g (1lb)

65ml (2½fl oz) water
100g (3½oz) caster sugar
225g (8oz) butter
3 eggs yolks

1 Mix the water and sugar in a pan and bring to the boil.

2 While the sugar is boiling, cut the butter up into cubes and put to one side, then add the egg yolks into the mixer.
3 Using a thermometer check the temperature of the sugar. When it reaches about 116–117°C/241–242°F, start whisking the egg yolks in the mixer until they become pale by which time your sugar should be about 120°C/248°F.
4 Remove the sugar from the heat and wait until the bubbles subside. I recommend you then quickly pour the sugar from the pan in two or three batches, depending on the quantity, into the bowl while the whisk is off, then turn it back on immediately all the sugar is in. (If whisking by hand, be extremely careful that you don't splash hot sugar on yourself while pouring. Keep whisking until the mixture becomes pale.) After you have added in the last batch, continue to whisk until the egg mix has lost most of its heat. (If you are making a big batch you may want to change to the beater attachment depending on your type of machine and the coldness of your butter.) Then slowly add the cubed

DECORATING TIP

If you're decorating any frosting or buttercream do so when it's freshly made as then any decorations will stick, so think about this before you start to frost. So, for instance, if you're doing a dozen or so cupcakes, frost three then decorate then frost another three etc. You can buy such beautiful decorations these days in practically every colour, and it would be such a shame to watch them bounce off your frosting and into the dog's mouth or onto the floor. You can cheat, by using a blow torch, but don't tell anyone.

butter until thoroughly mixed in.
5 Stop the machine to scrape down the sides and then mix for a little longer.
6 Use straight away.
Variation: Chocolate Buttercream
For a rich chocolate version, simply add in 85g (3oz) melted chocolate at the end.

Italian Meringue Frosting

Makes approximately 350g (12oz)

100g (3½oz) caster sugar
90ml (3¼fl oz) water
6 egg whites

1 Place the sugar and water in a small pan and heat until it reaches 116°C/241°F.
2 Continue to heat and begin to whisk the egg whites until in soft peaks.
3 Once the sugar reaches 120°C/248°F remove from the heat and allow the bubbles to subside before adding to the egg whites in three batches, turning the mixer off between each addition.
4 Then whisk on full power until cool and use immediately.

Honey Glaze

This versatile glaze could be used on most fruit cakes to bring out the flavour – I use it on a cake such as Greek Fig Cake (see page 98). Different honeys will give you different flavour notes.

Makes 100ml (3½fl oz)

100g (3½oz) good-quality apricot jam
juice of 1 lemon
1 tbsp honey

1 Simply place all the ingredients in a pan and bring to the boil.
2 Pass through a sieve and then brush repeatedly on the top of your cake to form a glaze.

Apricot Glaze

This super-simple glaze can be made in a matter of minutes and gives great shine and finish to most cakes.

Makes 100ml (3½fl oz)

100g (3½oz) good-quality apricot jam

1 Heat the jam in a pan with a little water until you reach the syrupy consistency you require.

2 Pass through a sieve and then brush repeatedly on the top of your cake to form a glaze.

Stock Syrup

This versatile syrup (also known as sugar wash and sugar syrup) can be used for moistening cakes and sponge layers before assembling them as well as glazing (for example on Bath Buns – brush on when hot from the oven). You can also add flavourings such as juices, alcohols or zest and spices. Follow the same recipe below but in larger quantities to make a sugar syrup suitable for poaching fruit.

Makes 65ml (2½fl oz)

65ml (2½fl oz) water
65g (2¼oz) caster sugar

1 Place the water and sugar in a pan and boil until the liquid becomes syrupy.

2 Pass through a sieve then remove from the heat and leave to cool.

Essential Equipment

You'll probably find you have the basics of what you need to create many of the recipes from this book – wooden spoons, mixing bowls, sieve, baking tray, rolling pins etc. But there are certain pieces of equipment that are essential for good home baking. Here's my must-have list.

BASIC CAKE TINS The tins I have suggested in this book are only suggestions but if you don't have a great variety I would recommend as essential one 25cm (10in) tart ring, one loaf tin and one 21cm (8in) springform tin. These will cover most types of cakes. Loaf tins are great for heavier type cakes, such as pound or fruit cakes, while springform are my preference for lighter and layered cakes. The greater the variety of tins of all types you have – tart rings, springform cake tins, loose-bottomed tins, loaf tins, tray bake tins, muffin tins, baking trays – the bigger selection of cakes you can bake. It really comes down to personal preference which ones you bake with, but for longevity it makes sense to invest in those made of good-quality stainless steel.

SPECIALIST CAKE TINS Some cakes do require specialist tins, such as petit Brioche, Madeleines, Friands, Canelles, Savarin, Bundt and Pandoro, but these can easily be bought online and if bought as non-stick and cleaned well will last a long time. I would recommend buying an Angel Cake tin with legs and in aluminium as the shape really helps keep the structure of the cake when cooling and turning out. Buying the original copper-tin-lined canelle moulds is an expensive option and they do require beeswax to grease, (which can be hard to get hold of) so, unless you are planning on making canelles regularly, I would suggest using a silicon alternative.

SILICONE MATS AND MOULDS A recent addition to the domestic kitchen has been non-stick silicone moulds and silicone mats. These are very easy to use, maintain and store, and are readily available from good kitchenware shops. Silicone mats are ideal for baking choux pastry, meringues and biscuits. If using under tart rings you will need to allow a little extra time for your tart base to cook as the heat is conducted differently through the silicon.

BAKING PARCHMENT I recommend using baking parchment for lining and cooking tarts as it is siliconised and therefore totally non-stick. Baking paper and wax paper don't remain non-stick at higher temperatures and so are useful for cooking at cooler temperatures. My preference would always be to use baking parchment if possible.

WHISKS I like to have hand whisks of various sizes: a medium one is good for whipping, while a larger balloon whisk is best for folding in ingredients. Hand blenders are very handy for blitzing fruit, making sauces and soups and, those with a whisk attachment, are great for whipping cream as long as you take care not to overwhip.

PASTRY SCRAPER I also always have a pastry scraper to hand and Matfer are the best, made from hardened pliable plastic; they are essential for scraping down as well as being useful for blocking and chopping out your dough.

PIPING BAGS AND NOZZLES I have a selection of piping bags and nozzles in various sizes. You can buy disposable bags (or make your own using parchment which I do recommend – you can go online to see how easy it is and then you can practise fine writing and decorations) or washable ones. Recipes normally give a size for a nozzle where the larger the number, the larger the nozzle. Don't worry too much if you don't have the exact size. Try to have a small, medium and large nozzle available to make the job as easy as possible. Make sure your piping bags are always comfortable in your hands and remember to always squeeze from the top while using the bottom hand for direction.

KNIVES Good knives make your life easier in the kitchen, whether chopping chocolate or nuts or slicing the fruits of your labours. I like to have a large and a small palette knife with a round end for spreading creams, icings and toppings, but prefer a step-down palette knife when covering a whole cake with something such as ganache. My preferred make is a Mac, which are expensive, but I do also have less-expensive knifes that are just as good for cutting pastry, trimming tarts and general pastry work that is done on a hard surface.

A PROBE THERMOMETER You may never have considered needing a thermometer but it is a worthwhile and fairly inexpensive purchase. You can use it when melting sugar for caramel or sugar syrups, deep frying doughnuts, making jam and even to measure the core temperature of your roast chicken on days when you're not baking.

FOOD MIXER My essential tool is my Kitchen Aid which I am lucky enough to be able to bake with and this is a true workhorse of the kitchen. With a whisk, paddle and dough attachment it has everything you need.

Index

Acknowledgements

FROM THE AUTHOR – First I must say a special thank you to my publisher, Jacqui Small, for once again giving me this fantastic opportunity to indulge my passion for baking. Thanks also to Jo Copestick for her encouragement and enthusiasm and to Lydia Halliday. A big, big thank you to my team who I feel privileged to have worked with; Sarah Rock for her fantastic design and Šárka Babická for making my cakes look beautiful, both of whom came up trumps despite a punishing schedule, as well as to my editor, Nikki Sims, who put up with my faffing, was endlessly patient and worked her magic time and again.

This book would not have happened without the invaluable help of Chelsea Football Club who have been incredibly supportive and generous throughout this process. My special thanks to Ron Gourlay and Simon Hunter, and, of course, Stephanie Bulfin, Kelly Emms and Laura Scholes.

To all the team at Marco Restaurant: Luke Patterson, Viktorija Jonikaiityte, Krzysztof Jorysz and Monir Hossain, thank you for your consistent hard work and commitment. In particular, thanks to Emeline Ancelot who was with me on every prep and shoot day and whose help, determination and positive attitude I could not have managed without. Also to Gabor Toth, Bence Godri and Eva Bote for their contributions and support.

I have called on many old friends for their help with this book, some have helped with recipes, some with opinions on cake and some with information on cafés – I am grateful to all of them – thank you – Rachel Allen, Shannon Bennett, Thierry Busset, Anne Cadle, Ian Curley, Donovan Cooke, Richard Corrigan, Simon Cosson, Christopher Farrugia, Lucas Glanville, Willie Harcourt-Cooze, Mark Hix, Takanori Ishii, Oliver Peyton, Rene Redzepi, Peter Reffell, Paul Rhodes, Barbara Skudamore Roberts, Nancy Silverton, Scott Wade, Hisako Watanabe, Robert Weston, Julie Wickenden and Paul A. Young.

Huge thanks to Marco Pierre White for his beautiful foreword and for putting up with this Manc for so many years. Special mention to my suppliers; Rhodes Bakery, Dave at Mash, Pat at Ritters Courivaurd, Raquel, Tony and Simon at Cossons Bakery, Vicky at MSK, Caroline at John Mowers and Sweet Tree Bakery – ta very much.

Finally, thank you to Penny, my wife, my love, my inspiration, my boss, my everything. Love you.

Photo credits: We would like to thank all the cafés featured in the 'Where to eat cake…' pages for supplying photos for reproduction herein. Additional credits are given for the following photos: page 225 (bottom) Keiko Oikawa; page 69 (bottom) Sugar Daddy Group; page 190 David Reiss (www. davidreiss.com.au). We would also like to acknowledge that the recipe on page 116 first appeared in Rachel Allen's *Bake*.

We would also like to thank the following for their help in the making of this book: Sara Jackson, Henry Ker and Alexandra Labbe Thompson.